T0330706

MEAT, COMMERCE AND THE CITY:
THE LONDON FOOD MARKET, 1800–1855

Perspectives in Economic and Social History

Series Editors: Andrew August
Robert E. Wright

Titles in this Series

FORTHCOMING TITLES

MEAT, COMMERCE AND THE CITY:
THE LONDON FOOD MARKET, 1800–1855

BY

Robyn S. Metcalfe

Routledge
Taylor & Francis Group

LONDON AND NEW YORK

First published 2012 by Pickering & Chatto (Publishers) Limited

Published 2016 by Routledge
2 Park Square, Milton Park, Abingdon, Oxfordshire OX14 4RN
711 Third Avenue, New York, NY 10017, USA

First issued in paperback 2015

Routledge is an imprint of the Taylor & Francis Group, an informa business

© Taylor & Francis 2012
© Robyn S. Metcalfe 2012

To the best of the Publisher's knowledge every effort has been made to contact
relevant copyright holders and to clear any relevant copyright issues.
Any omissions that come to their attention will be remedied in future editions.

All rights reserved, including those of translation into foreign languages. No part of this book
may be reprinted or reproduced or utilised in any form or by any electronic, mechanical, or
other means, now known or hereafter invented, including photocopying and recording, or in
any information storage or retrieval system, without permission in writing from the publishers

Notice:
Product or corporate names may be trademarks or registered trademarks, and
are used only for identification and explanation without intent to infringe.

BRITISH LIBRARY CATALOGUING IN PUBLICATION DATA

Metcalfe, Robyn S.
Meat, commerce and the city: the London food market, 1800–1855. –
(Perspectives in economic and social history)
1. Smithfield Market – History – 19th century. 2. Meat industry and trade –
Location – England – London – History – 19th century. 3. Environmental
health – England – London – History – 19th century.
I. Title II. Series
381.4'56649'094212–dc23

ISBN-13: 978-1-138-66191-2 (pbk)
ISBN-13: 978-1-8489-3290-6 (hbk)
Typeset by Pickering & Chatto (Publishers) Limited

CONTENTS

ACKNOWLEDGEMENTS

The guidance, support and enthusiasm of my colleagues, family and friends made this book possible. Both serendipity and relentless focus contributed to the discovery of this topic while the common tendency to lose momentum was impossible because of a few tireless and prescient advisors. The long process of the removal of the cattle market in Smithfield, London came to my attention during a class given by Diana Wylie at Boston University. Without her encouragement to take her course, *Feeding Cities,* I would not have met George Dodd. His book published in 1856 about the food of London piqued my interest about cattle market and raised the questions about why the removal process took as long as it did.

Louis Ferleger and Tom Glick provided the unrelenting goading necessary for graduate students to complete a dissertation. Brendan McConville, Harriet Ritvo, Brooke Blower, and Charles Dellheim kept me on track until the end.

In London, Diane Haigh provided me with agricultural history over oceans of hot tea and introduced me to other helpful individuals such as Andrew Saint, editor of the Survey of London and Carolyn Steel, author of *The Hungry City*. The Superintendent's Office of Smithfield Market enabled me to wander through today's wholesale meat market in Smithfield at all hours of the night and morning. The many helpful archivists and librarians at the British Library, Guildhall and London Municipal archives, the National Archives at Kew, the Institute of Civil Engineers, and the Royal Institute of Architects all contributed countless hours of assistance and advice.

Jane Glasson, my tireless researcher in London, found documents and dug deep into the many archives in London. The University of Texas at Austin Institute of Historical Studies fellowship provided generous support and an ideal environment for completing the book. And Tatjana Lichtenstein and Ruramisai Charumbira at the University of Texas at Austin, Kate Jewell at Boston University, and Susan Trausch, retired Boston Globe writer, formed a supportive and helpful reading of the manuscript. Deborah Fitzgerald and Lindy Tanton at MIT provided the encouragement to ask more questions about the market

Meat, Commerce and the City

in London. And an early comment made by Gertrude Himmelfarb opened the door to a more complicated understanding of the Victorians.

An enormous amount of gratitude goes to my family who listened to limitless descriptions of the meat market and contributed their ideas and suggestions all along the way. My parents, husband Bob, and two enthusiastic children, Julia and Max, lived through my endless accounts of London's cattle market. To them and my colleagues, I dedicate this book.

LIST OF FIGURES

INTRODUCTION

On 13 June 1855, Prince Albert looked out over the crowd gathered to com-
memorate the opening of the new Metropolitan Cattle Market in Islington,
less than three miles away.[1] Rain had begun to fall and most of the celebrants
kept dry under a large marquée as they listened to Albert's speech. 'This splendid and useful work', the Prince declared, 'could only be undertaken by public
bodies, and carried out to success by public spirit'.[2] The public bodies included
Parliament, the City, butchers, consumers of meat, urban and animal welfare
reformers, entrepreneurs who engaged their public spirit in a decades-long
struggle over the position of the world's largest cattle market. Since the Middle
Ages, the live cattle market had previously existed in Smithfield just three miles
from Islington near the City's Roman walls and was the source of meat for the
metropolis and beyond. Moving the market only a few miles from its old site had
proven a monumental task, one that collided with the arrival of the modern city.

Today, the survival of Smithfield as an urban meat market represents more
than just a Victorian struggle or a chapter in the history of urban planning. Cities are reconsidering their relationship with food markets and food markets are
becoming central to the question of how to feed the growing global population.
While Victorians wanted to make the source of their meat invisible, today's consumers seek new ways to make food origins and production visible in the city.
With the current surge of interest in moving agriculture and food markets back
into the city, might there be some relevance in understanding why they were
removed in the first place?

During the nineteenth century, Londoners saw their meat first as live animals that butchers bought from a market located in the center of London. The
butchers would kill and butcher the animals before selling the meat from their
own butcher shops located nearby. Smithfield was an urban commissariat that
supplied the world with fine British beef, mutton, and pork. Thousands of cattle, sheep, and pigs competed for space in increasingly congested and narrow
thoroughfares. Cholera epidemics placed the cattle market in Smithfield in the
crosshairs of sanitary reformers who gathered alarming evidence of the market's complicity in the deaths of thousands of Londoners. And animal welfare

reformers attacked the treatment of cattle by drovers who prodded their stock through the City streets. Indeed, the pressure to remove the cattle market from the heart of the City had been unrelenting.

Such a 'splendid' work as the Metropolitan Cattle Market was the culmination of a decades-long struggle to uproot the live cattle market from its historic grounds in the heart of London. By the nineteenth century, the old live cattle market had acquired the status of a 'nuisance' and was so described by Charles Dickens in *Oliver Twist* in 1837 as follows:

> ... covered nearly ankle deep with filth and mire; and a thick steam perpetually rising from the reeking bodies of the cattle, and mingling with the fog, which seemed to rest upon the chimney tops, hung heavily above ... Countrymen, butchers, drovers, hawkers, boys, thieves, idlers, and vagabonds of every low grade, were mingled together in a dense mass: the whistling of drovers, the barking of dogs, the bellowing and plunging of beasts, the bleating of sheep, and the grunting and squealing of pigs; the cries of hawkers, the shouts, oaths, and quarrelling on all sides, the ringing of bells, and the roar of voices that issued from every public house; the crowding, pushing, driving, beating, whooping and yelling; the hideous and discordant din that resounded from every corner of the market; and the unwashed, unshaven, squalid, and dirty figures constantly running to and fro, and bursting in and out of the throng, rendered it a stunning and bewildering scene which quite confused the senses.[3]

Understandably, Londoners in the City and surrounding parishes wanted this scene removed from their midst. But butchers and cattle salesmen resisted the uprooting of their businesses from the center of the metropolis to the suburb of Islington, and their resistance was not easily overcome. Between 1800 and 1851, over a dozen bills and petitions passed through the committee rooms in Parliament only to stall or disappear altogether. The removal of the market was slow, arduous, and sometimes erratic, but eventually innovation overcame tradition and the Smithfield 'nuisance' disappeared from the City in 1855.

The market in Islington that replaced Smithfield was a resplendent and rationalized space that embodied the latest technology. Its design incorporated new technologies in ways that signaled the arrival of the modern industrialized city. Leading other large metropolitan areas in Europe and North America, London transformed its organic provisioning system into a mechanized operation that accommodated new requirements for commerce and public health. From a reliance on human and animal networks it moved to activities powered by steam, gas, and electricity. These new mechanized networks connected London's modern meat markets in ways that improved speed and sanitation.

The relocation of London's live cattle market illustrated how cities modernized in the nineteenth century. Food markets, the heart and soul, if not stomach, of urban centers were central and visible representations of urban communities. Throughout history, cities appeared as provisioning entrepôts, often located near transportation networks such as rivers and oceans. London, first to experience an industrial revolution, was also first to reconsider how its food markets fit into a new, modern conception of urban identity. The removal of London's live cattle market heralded similar relocations of food markets in other cites, such as Paris, New York, Boston, and Chicago. These cities reacted to the industrialization and modernization of their food markets in ways consistent with their own urban culture. This book reveals how modernity, such as technology, industrialization, democratized politics, and social change reshaped urban food markets, giving new meaning to urban landscapes by responding to modern conceptions of distance, speed, and urban culture.

Public opinion increasingly influenced the outcome of the debate surrounding Smithfield, but why did it take at least fifty years for the market to move from its ancient position in the City? And why did the move occur in 1855? By the time Parliament passed the Smithfield Market Act in 1851, when the removal of the cattle market out of Smithfield was made official, arguments on both sides of the debate had become contradictory and revealed paradoxes indicative of the anxieties felt by Victorians during this period of modernization. The paradoxes and contradictions suggest that the individuals and institutions engaged in the Smithfield debate did not behave consistently and often changed loyalties. The City argued for the removal of the existing market in the early 1800s but then continued to vacillate between removal and improvement for almost fifty years. And the City spent thousands of pounds to defeat the removal bills, even though it received only about £4,000 a year from the operation of the market.[4] Although most butchers and salesmen wanted to improve the existing market, some were vocal advocates of the removal of the market to another site. Why were some of the butchers so resistant and why were others in favor of the move? Farmers and graziers were also split, as were the aldermen in the City. These shifting allegiances often confused the lines of battle and delayed the removal of the market. They also suggest that Victorians pursued their interests in varying ways relative to the shifting political and economic landscape. They also adapted their interests to London's emerging identity as a modern metropolis.

Smithfield also offers insights into the changing meanings of public and private space during the nineteenth century. Public and private interests struggled with cultural associations with meat, a national identification with trade, and an urban claim to market rights. The meat market was a private market in a public space. The provision of meat required private individuals engaged in businesses that included drovers, salesmen, graziers, slaughterers, butchers, bankers, and a network of middlemen. These private interests combined to create public anxieties. Ultimately, the removal and relocation of Smithfield represented an exceptional relationship between private individuals and public institutions, and between private and public urban space.

The transformation of urban space also reflected a change in the way city dwellers viewed food. Since the Middle Ages, Smithfield had been a fluid space with few sharp angles and corners, nestled at the terminus of a network of cattle droving roads. With the arrival of the reform era and utilitarianism, urban spaces became rationalized, straightened, covered, and controlled. When the live cattle market moved out of Smithfield, meat moved away from consumers, removing the sights, smells, and connection between production and consumption. Urban wholesale markets moved outside the metropolis, repurposing rural space and connecting the City to the countryside as railroads enabled more meat to be slaughtered outside London and transported to the City by railway. In similar ways, these new transport networks and markets enlarged London's role in a global and imperial food system. These connections situated the London meat market in a larger context of global trade.

The Smithfield live cattle market clung to its location in the middle of the City within sight of St Paul's and in the sights of urban reformers. The reluctance of London to move its ancient meat market revealed how urban myths and tradition complicated urban landscapes. Smithfield's importance in historical memory bound the market to its location in the City, to London's identity, and to the ancient traditions of trade and markets. By the mid-nineteenth century, Londoner's read their urban surroundings in new ways and began to balance their urban identity with the exigencies of modernization. By 1850, Londoners imagined themselves wealthier, civilized and refined. They rejected the rough and barbaric identities from their rural past and removed the production of meat, blood, and violence from the visible landscape. At the same, London parvenus saw meat consumption as a sign of social wellbeing.

The duration of the struggle was dictated by the inability of private individuals and institutions to grasp how a change in location would impact a highly complicated and little understood provisioning system. The provision of food to cities was both assumed by the consumers and essential to the stability of society. Consumers in cities sought a larder of comestibles complicated by seasonality and unpredictable availability, perishability and costs. London required kosher meat for Jewish consumers, mutton shanks for tavern owners, sausage for the street vendors, and beef loins for Sunday suppers. The entire apparatus of food provision to the City adapted changes in transport, sanitation, and the price of grain to satisfy this variegated, finicky and fickle marketplace.

George Dodd, a nineteenth century statistician and journalist in London, attempted a description of London food markets in 1856. Who, exactly, he queried, provided London with its food? Dodd declared, 'Nobody does it'.[5] No single entity planned, controlled, or distributed food to London, unlike Paris where a centralized administration established by Napoleon dictated the provisioning of the capitol. Instead, Dodd believed that the provision of food to

London was accomplished by Adam Smith's invisible hand, 'through the agency of men who think each of nothing beyond his own immediate interest'.[6] He marveled at the network of individuals in a complex and ancient provisioning system that balanced a complicated resistance to centralized governance with an entrepreneurial and individualistic spirit that saw the need for new urban spaces, public health, and safety. Dodd's observation was shared by British politicians who, while uncomprehending exactly why the meat market continued to function with remarkable efficiency, dared not tinker with a system that might have been inherently volatile. Robust and predictable markets were and are requisite for social and political stability. History had already illustrated how food shortages could ignite violence and social unrest. Parisian food riots in the eighteenth century provided examples of the consequences of food shortages.

Thomas Malthus had informed politicians and urban reformers of the bleak outcome that would result from population increases that outran Britain's capacity to feed itself. As Londoners rethought their relationship to food in their city, they were pondering the message delivered by Thomas Malthus at the turn of the eighteenth century. In *An Essay on the Principle of Population* (1798), he warned the inhabitants of London that their food supply would not keep pace with population growth. His message caused the members of Parliament to equivocate and to resist any changes to the markets as long as Londoners continued to be amply fed.

London needed to accommodate rural laborers who sought industrial jobs in the City, a daunting task for politicians who wondered how long food supplies would last. The 'Hungry Forties' only reinforced the predictions of Malthus. During the 1840s, harvests were poor, trade declined, bread prices increased, and the Irish potato famine disrupted the British food supply. The Corn Laws and trade tariffs had revealed a national anxiety about food supplies. By the late 1840s, the British provisioning system appeared to be more robust than the government had earlier imagined. With new foreign supplies and a lull in cholera epidemics, the climate for change had arrived. By 1850, politicians, reformers, and innovative individuals eventually amassed enough political power and public support to overcome these tensions. They brought together the interests of free trade, the state, the champions of classical liberalism and managed capitalism. The new market allowed the intricacies of the market to function while the state addressed public health, transportation, and safety.

Also by mid-nineteenth century, London had experienced industrialization, doubled in size, increased economic prosperity, and sensed its new identity. The city survived two cholera epidemics and gained a new appreciation for the fragility of public health and the fatal consequences of filth upon a crowded urban population. The public was more informed with increasing literacy and number of publications that described urban problems and potential solutions. The reform era (1820s–1840s) compelled the inhabitants to address urban blight, corruption, sanitation, and environment. Utilitarianism sent improvers into the streets to find rational means for reorganizing streets and urban space. Railroads sliced into London's corpus, connecting the metropolis in new ways to the countryside and other continents. Individuals with a new sentimentality and sensitivity towards nature joined groups such as the Society for the Prevention of Cruelty to Animals. Restrictions on the British economy were loosened, bringing foreign livestock into the market, drawing upon concerns about government regulation. London's markets were becoming free of the old system governed by guilds and entrepreneurs found business opportunities within an expanding consumer market. Retail specialists appeared on London's streets as covered modern market spaces took the place of the old market fields. During the nineteenth century, industrialization provoked new technologies, increased demand by an expanding middle class and upturned the landscape with the arrival of new streets and railroads. By 1850, London had come of age, a modern age ready for a more rational and mechanized provisioning system.

On a broader level, the removal of the market represented a Victorian approach to modernity. The Smithfield live cattle market was swept away by the anxieties caused by modernization. The story of the market illustrates how people reacted in the face of these anxieties in ways that maintained social stability throughout change. The Victorian approach brought the sentimentality of some reformers along with the desire for rationalized solutions from the utilitarians. Urban reformers referenced the effects of Evangicalism and the desire for order within a rapidly changing scene. This Victorian sense of duty, morality, and rationalism allowed the market to smolder, not combust.

By most accounts, public and private interests gathered undercover in the shade of the marquée seemed reconciled and relieved that day at the opening of the new market in Islington. In his speech, Prince Albert acknowledged that, 'a certain dislocation of habits and interests must inevitably attend the removal of the great City market'. A 'comparative security' provided in the new market would subdue the cyclical contention that had characterized the existence of the market in Smithfield for at least five centuries.[7]

During these contentious times three individuals and institutions transformed and shaped the events that led to the speech given by Prince Albert that day in Islington: John Perkins, Charles Pearson, and Robert Peel. All three played important roles in the determination of Smithfield's fate by innovating and pressuring the varied interests engaged in the debate about the market. During the 1830s, John Perkins, an enterprising resident of Islington, built and opened a competing market near the future Metropolitan Cattle Market, replete with technical innovations and modern improvements. London butchers and salesmen refused to switch their trade and within a few years Perkins' market failed. But Perkins contributed an important model of a modern cattle market and proved that a site north of London would likely be the optimal location for a new market. Charles Pearson, the City's solicitor, was a social improver who founded a railroad company that would later slice through and service a new dead meat market in Smithfield. He and his team of engineers invented and explored new ways to build railroads in urban environments. By selecting the space around Smithfield for the first underground railway, dug through and around Smithfield, Pearson prepared the public imagination and the space itself for new uses. Robert Peel, Britain's Prime Minister during the 1830s and 40s, swept away the regulations that inhibited the provisioning system, repealed the Corn Laws and lifted the tariffs on foreign livestock. These actions enabled Britain to provide enough food to its growing population. Smithfield, and later Islington and Deptford, were markets for these foreign cattle, continually filling the meat supply chain with fresh meat.

Three institutions joined these individuals in the effort to relocate the cattle market. Most obvious was the City, a corporation that owned and administered the heart of the metropolis, the area in and surrounding the old Roman walls of *Londinium*. The City took a pragmatic position relative to the market, initially supporting its removal but eventually digging in with its efforts to improve the market in its historical position. Parliament took on the bills and petitions that sought a solution to the market's location, convening and adjourning multiple committees and one royal commission that sought information for all interests, inhabitants, butchers, drovers, and whip makers. Voluntary associations increased in popularity and became institutions that advocated for reform in the areas of sanitation and animal welfare. These small but no less powerful groups did much to influence public opinion and, ultimately, Parliament as it moved towards the removal bill of 1851.

The story of the struggle to relocate the cattle market ended when the market closed in 1855. Although the opening of the modern cattle market in Islington was festive by all accounts and provided an impressive display of new technologies, it did not significantly remove the 'nuisances' that drove the market out of the City. Drovers continued to move cattle through the streets of London, animals still suffered from the cattle prod, and private slaughterhouses continued business as usual for the next fifty years. After Prince Albert opened the modern live cattle market in Islington, London's meat provisioning system would take another five decades to fulfill the vision of the early nineteenth century urban reformers. But the short-term success of the market removal was undisputed. The market continued to flourish, meat continued to arrive on the tables of increasingly carnivorous Londoners. And the fears engendered by Malthus became of no consequence.

A walk through the Smithfield Central Markets today offers visual reminders of Smithfield's history as the site of Britain's largest live cattle market during the

Victorian period. Located in West Smithfield, in the City of London, the Central Markets contain the wholesale meat trade for London. The markets, opened in 1868, settled into the space previously occupied by the live cattle market in 1855. Today the Central Markets teem with wholesale customers, porters, and meat salesmen from ten at night until late morning the following day. The meat business still permeates the area around the Smithfield Central Markets. Street names telegraph Smithfield's past: Skinner's Lane, Giltspur (from its history as a venue for knights and their tournaments), and Cow Cross Lane.

The struggle for a meat market in Smithfield continues. In 2004, SAVE, a London-based building conservation organization announced a campaign called, 'Don't Butcher Smithfield' to resist development by the City of the Smithfield General Market Buildings. The City had an elaborate plan for an office block that would replace the Victorian buildings designed by Horace Jones. In a video produced for the campaign against the effort of the City to develop buildings in the market space, Londoners observed that Smithfield is 'imbued with history' and represents a 'tradition of markets, the identity of London'. Some felt that Smithfield represented London's identity and character. One historian argued that Smithfield was 'evocative, moving, and represents ancient history in old buildings, bringing the past and present together. An architect and past president of the Royal Institute of Architects noted that Smithfield possessed a 'natural sense of regeneration, of being a survivor, and had a scale that the gives a story of the market'. He opined, 'If you start eating away at it, you'd lose that story'.[8]

The campaigns of SAVE and English Heritage were successful and in August, 2008, the Secretary of State for Local Government and Communities denied the City the right to redevelop the General Market Building.[9] Smithfield again survived to face the next assault. As this recent development illustrates, the story of urban markets is still in the making for modern urban historians.

Cattle, Commerce and the City: The Smithfield Market

This book examines the private and public interests that shaped debate about the Smithfield meat market system. The Smithfield meat provisioning system included individuals and institutions both outside and inside the marketplace. The protracted public and private debate about Smithfield fell within two periods. The first included the years 1800 to 1840 when the key issues were articulated and efforts to both remove and improve the market began to take shape. The second period began in 1840 and ended with the passage of the Act to Remove Smithfield Market in 1851. I discuss the first period and follow with an examination of three key issues, space, public health, and morality. Finally, these issues lead to a narrative of the second period of Smithfield debates when the public and private interests came together to remove the market from the City.

The first chapter introduces the reader to the meat provisioning system with its network of producers, distributors, buyers, and sellers at the beginning of the nineteenth century. Centered in London, the 'Smithfield System' was a complex machine that included interdependencies, relationships, and regulations. Reforms in one area of the Smithfield system affected the entire meat-provisioning network. Starting in the countryside, meat travelled by hoof on drovers' roads to graziers, attended by salesmen, sometimes handled by middlemen such as forestallers and engrossers, and entered the market where wholesale butchers sought the fattest and finest beef for their select customers.

Chapter two focuses on the buyers in Smithfield. The demand of the market, the consumer culture, and British identification with meat animated the debate. Butchers, cookshops, tavern owners and ordinary Londoners exerted their influence both inside and outside the market, consuming increasing quantities of meat while contesting the presence of the livestock cattle market in Smithfield.

Chapter three describes the series of petitions and bills that reached both Parliament and the City between 1800 and 1840. The testimonies of hundreds of witnesses that appeared before the committees of Parliament in response to proposed legislation supply insights to the issues that became entangled with the market removal. The confrontation of private and public interests encountered the slow evolution of metropolitan governance, an evolution that remained incomplete by the time that the market left Smithfield. The reform years saw major advances in technology, and London experienced a surge in urban renewal and redesign. Select committees repeatedly convened to consider the testimonies of individuals in this period of increasing democratization. This chapter discusses the main issues that enjoined this protracted debate: space, sanitation, and morality.

Chapters four, five, and six provide evidence from the debates about these three key areas of concern. Chapter four examines Smithfield as a space, including its topography, size, and location. Much of the debate surrounding the removal or improvement of the market in Smithfield centered upon the limitations of London's urban landscape to accommodate growth and modernization. New railway technologies appeared as the market in Smithfield and the producers in the countryside demanded more speed and capacity. This chapter addresses the impact of railways on the Smithfield network as urban reformers reconstructed the landscape.

Chapter five explores the issue of sanitation. Cholera epidemics brought Smithfield into the center of efforts to understand the relationship between the environment and disease. Smithfield was suspected of causing disease through contaminated air, water, the refuse from animal slaughter, and contact with diseased animals. Several individuals, including Edwin Chadwick and John Farr, carried out statistical surveys that led to gradual improvements in the drainage system that carried the refuse from butchers' shops into the Thames River. But the resistance of the butchers to calls for public abattoirs under government inspection created obstacles to sanitation reform.

Chapter six includes two areas of moral concern. Witnesses before the select committees maintained that the market, particularly the butchers and drovers, encouraged animal cruelty and threatened the moral characters of the men and women who passed through Smithfield. Reformers accused the market of depriving drovers of their Sabbath and women of their enjoyment of shopping in the City.

Chapter seven describes the final phases of the debate, beginning with the 1840s and ending when the Metropolitan Cattle Market opened in Islington and the market in Smithfield closed in 1855. This chapter conveys the increasing momentum of the debate, fueled by developments in the political landscape. The relentless efforts of the select committees during this period to gather evidence to support the removal of the Smithfield market occurred in parallel with the mounting efforts of the Markets Improvements Committee of the City to focus on improvement rather than removal. The press followed the proceedings, providing the public with a impression of a reformist Parliament and a increasingly irrelevant City government. These images and the realities of a modernizing urban landscape converged with the concerted effort of Parliament to pass the Act in 1851.[10]

1 THE SMITHFIELD SYSTEM IN THE NINETEENTH CENTURY: A GRAND COMPLEXUS

The Smithfield system was one united whole, complete in itself. The paved area, the bars and pens, the mud and filth, the drovers, the dogs, the salesmen, the butchers, the bankers, the publicans, the oaths, the blows, the noise, the confusion – all formed part and parcel of one complexus.[1]

Smithfield: The Early Years

In 1847, as Parliament debated the future of the live cattle market in Smithfield, Angus Reach, a London journalist who revealed the contempt of those who were weary of the years of parliamentary commissions and select committees, blamed the controversy on the City's reluctance to relinquish its ancient monopoly of the Smithfield trade. 'Oh! The force – the destiny-like power – in this civilized land, of the words "old use and wont". We reverence much the dust of gold, but still more the dust of time'.[2] By the time Reach penned these words, the cattle market in Smithfield had been gathering the 'dust of time' since the departure of the Romans in the fifth century.

The history of the live cattle market, where Londoners purchased meat that arrived on the hoof, began earlier than other London markets. The area called Smithfield eventually contained four markets: the live cattle market, a hay market, a horse market and a cloth market. But its use as a market started with the Roman occupation (43–c. 400). London had been a trading centre, moving its produce, salt and fish throughout the Roman Empire. By the late Saxon and into the Middle Ages, London markets grew to feed an every-expanding population (in spite of the Black Death). The live cattle market existed within a constellation of other markets in London.

From the early Middle Ages, London's food markets and trades occupied specific areas in the City, often giving their names to the thoroughfares near their activities. Street markets combined with shops along Cornhill, Gracechurch Street and Eastcheap provisioned Londoners with food provided by fishmongers, poulterers and butchers, all powerful social groups within the City. In the twelfth century, cheap, meaning 'trade' and 'buying and selling', was the name of the main street where the food markets established their businesses. Cheapside was the central market for Medieval England. Food markets eventually spread throughout the metropolis and by the nineteenth century became a network of specialized purveyors to wholesales, retailers and the general public.

The name 'Smithfield' appears to come from 'Smoothfield' (from Saxon 'Smeeth Felde'). Some sources suggest that the construction of St Bartholomew's Priory during the twelfth century in Smithfield included a leveling of the field, lending the name 'smoothfield' to the space.[3] The Roman wall divided legal and sanctioned trade from illegal and foreign trade. Livestock sold outside the regulations of the walled City joined other illicit and unorganized trade. Foreigners, non-freemen, joined informal and often illegal markets. Smithfield eventually became the site of several markets and one religious institution, the priory of St Bartholomew the Great and its hospital.

Founded by Rahere, a former court jester for Henry I and ecclesiastical, the priory was established by royal charter in 1133. St Bartholomew, named after the patron saint of tanners and butchers, remains the iconic figure of the butchers guild in London today. The priory and hospital operated the cloth market and a fair; the livestock market shared the space and the horse and hay market became ancillary markets to the livestock market in later years. At first, the cloth fair and livestock market operated for only two days in August, but eventually the cattle market did most of its business on Mondays, the hay market on Wednesday and the horse market on Fridays. Shakespeare refers to the horse market in *Henry IV* when Falstaff's page buys a horse in Smithfield.

The cloth market, also called a fair, became the St Bartholomew's fair and grew to become a well-attended 'nuisance' by the eighteenth century. London clothiers and drapers operated the cloth market and the City of London had the rights to the livestock market. Next to the cattle market, the fair became more of a carnival than a market. Known then as a site of 'amusing vagabondism' and 'riotings and debaucheries', the fair (formerly the cloth market) was managed by the City of London. The fair provided such entertainment as prize fighting, puppet shows and displays of wild animals. The City saw the fair as a much-needed source of revenue and was pressured to regulate the fair by limiting the number of days and its activities. By 1700, St Bartholomew's fair had become more and more disassociated from Smithfield's market and its exotic activities appeared only to interfere with the activities of the livestock market that occupied the adjacent space. The cockfights at the fair, later depicted by Hogarth, juxtaposed animals for both entertainment and consumption.[4]

In 1546 a wealthy London merchant, Sir John Rich, bought the market rights during the dissolution of the monasteries in the sixteenth century.But even before the fair gave Smithfield the reputation of a orgiastic display of rib-aldry, other activities cast Smithfield as a place where uncontrolled and chaotic, sometimes violent activities took place. Beginning in the Middle Ages, extravagant tournaments took place in Smithfield, filling the space with tilting yards and knights in armor. Early chroniclers, such as William FitzStephen, John Stow and John Strype, provided a general historical narrative of the cattle market in Smithfield in 1200. During this period, Smithfield was noted as a space that teemed with both legal and illegal commerce, pageantry and crime.[5]

The association of Smithfield with spectacle, combat and violence continued into the decades of dissent and religious upheaval.[6] William Wallace, a Scottish patriot, met an inglorious death by being drawn, quartered and eviscerated in 1305.[7] Punishment for illegal activities was part of the spectacle in Smithfield. Witches were burned or boiled, apostates were hanged, drawn, quartered and eviscerated. In the fifteenth and sixteenth centuries, religious persecutions joined the spectacles in Smithfield. In April 1551, a Dutch surgeon, George Von Paris, was burnt in Smithfield for his Arian beliefs, viewed as a heresy against the church. Smithfield was the site for executions of dissident Protestants, as Queen Mary dispensed with the religious reforms of King Henry VIII.[8]

The City paved the field in Smithfield in 1615 to improve drainage, after deciding that the muddy fields were an impediment to the health and sanitation of the market. References to this event suggest that the paving of the market signaled the City's recognition that the field was London's livestock market. Around the same time, Ben Jonson's *Bartholomew Fair* offered a view of the public spectacle in Smithfield when the affairs of the Bartholomew's Fair mingled with cattle.[9] The topsy-turvy, carnival-like space captured by Jonson in his play emanated throughout the market space, causing 'confused senses' later described by Dickens in his novels. The market stalls, licensed by the City, became part of the stage as Ursula, the pig-woman, portrayed the degradation, prostitution and immorality of the fair, all unlicensed behaviour. Jonson's play opened in London in 1614; he drew upon the cattle market for his characters: Bristle, Cutting, Knockem, Leatherhead and Mooncalf. This amusing satire of society and commerce appropriated the images of Smithfield, meat, carnival, sensual pleasure and temptation in sumptuous subversion of authority and order.

The general confusion of the senses in Smithfield also included public riots. In 1647, butchers, protesting an excise tax on meat, led a crowd to the excise office where they burned down the building. (City officers rushed to quell the riot and Parliament withdrew the tax.) In 1662, Samuel Pepys related in his diary how his coach passed through Newgate, knocking several pieces of meat onto the ground and evoking angry remonstrations from the nearby butchers.[10] In 1674, a sixty-year-old widow, Ann Petty, met her death in Smithfield for 'clipping of money', the illegal practice of cutting or mutilating coins as a way of obtaining silver. The archives of the Old Bailey contain frequent accounts of cattle and horse thievery, a crime often punished by death.[11]

All this mayhem in the market space in Smithfield existed within a market culture that included regulation. Market regulations, particularly within the City walls, played an increasingly important role by the Middle Ages. Even before Jonson's depiction of the fair in Smithfield, the King passed regulations in attempt to create order within the market. The legal armature for regulation rested upon royal charters given to individuals, or in the case of the City, to a corporation. In the charter of 1327, King Edward III outlined liberties and regulations for trade in London.[12] Merchants who came from outside the City had to sell their wares within a certain time and were required to board with freemen in the City while they were engaged in selling.[13] The King's charter for Smithfield gave the City a monopoly on the live meat market by outlawing any other meat markets within seven miles, 'for the bettering of our city of London, and for protecting the trade of the City'. The royal charter stated, 'no market from henceforth shall be granted by us or our heirs, to any within seven miles in circuit of said city'. These 'ancient rights' provided the foundation for the subsequent royal charters and acts that gave the City a sense of independence that, in later years, inhibited its ability to reform its own governance and integrate metropolitan needs with those of the City. This medieval law was the sticking point that derailed one attempt to remove Smithfield in the 1830s.[14]

Throughout the seventeenth century, the Crown, Parliament and the City continued their attempts to regulate the legal and illegal commercial activities, sanitation and morality of markets, including Smithfield. The regulation of markets addressed the intersection of public and private interests. *Lawes of the Market*, published by the City in 1620, forbade market stalls in the streets, sales of unwholesome or stale meat and the disposal of butcher's refuse into the ditches or sewers of the City.[15] Later, the regulation of animal welfare, meat inspection, oversight of adulteration and weights, restrictions on traffic and the eventual licensing of slaughterhouses became embroiled in a public concern about markets and other issues relative to commerce, sanitation and morality.[16]

On October 18, 1638, Charles I issued a charter that confirmed the City's market rights and its right to collect market tolls. This charter reaffirmed the right of the City to gather tolls not only in Smithfield, but also in Cheapside and Billingsgate. It went further to describe the rights of the City to determine and administer weights, to prohibit garbling (the process of picking or selecting commodities or of removing the refuse or the inferior specimens from merchandize) and to enlarge or improve the space, to receive tolls and rents from the market.[17] This charter was confirmed by Charles II but nullified later under a *quo warranto* (a royal letter providing evidence based upon English law to support a grant of powers or rights). Charles II was unhappy about the City's petitions against the trial of several nobles accused of participating in 'popish plots'. Charles revoked the City's market rights, attacking a vital source of revenue for the City. More than just denying the City the right to collect tolls, Charles rejected the City's right to be its own governing body with all its privileges. After the Glorious Revolution, during the reign of William and Mary, the ancient rights were re-granted in 1689 when the Crown restored all the rights and privileges of the City. Throughout this period, the comings and goings of market rights were more examples of political maneuvering with little impact upon market operations. When the debate about the presence of the cattle market in Smithfield began in the late eighteenth century, the City was in control of Smithfield's markets with little outside interference.

By the nineteenth century, the Smithfield complex had evolved out of the 'shambles'[18] of the Middle Ages to become entrenched in London's historical memory. And even though the cattle market in Smithfield had a long history, Angus Reach admitted that although Londoners followed in the footsteps of their ancestors, they did so only 'to the letter, but not in the spirit of the law'.[19] He described a modern Londoner who nominally professed to follow their forefathers' example but exhibited an ability to negotiate new meanings for their ancient laws, meanings that accommodated the arrival of new technologies, new identities, a rising spirit of improvement and reform.

The modern, industrializing spirit of London had gained momentum by the early nineteenth century. In 1856, George Dodd, a journalist who documented London's manufacturing industries, described Smithfield's live cattle market:

> ... imbedded in the midst of a busy city, surrounded on every side by miles of streets and thousands of houses, associated by its burnings with the intolerant zeal of past ages, by its fairs with the amusements of thirty generations, and by its markets with the daily wants of two or three millions of people ... [20]

Some saw the market as a 'provoking, broad, impertinent' space.[21] It incorporated a web of private commercial interests into an economy recently kindled by the Industrial Revolution.[22] Individual entrepreneurs, merchants, farmers and inhabitants of the City engaged in the business of providing London with meat. They represented the private interests that profited from the movement of live animals from farms to the butchers' stalls in London. This supply chain, the physical layout of the marketplace, and labour practices shaped and supported an organic, carne-centric culture.

The cattle market in the City was the nexus that gathered the web of private interests into and through the urban space in Smithfield. Smithfield, a meat-provisioning network that consisted of humans and non-humans, connected the countryside and the urban environment. Before new technologies arrived, the Smithfield system operated according to a long tradition of human and non-human relationships. Transactions of buying and selling throughout the network relied upon trusted conversations and practices developed over time. Popular periodicals reminded their readers of the ingrained attitudes and habits embedded in these established relationships within the Smithfield system. Angus Reach, the London journalist, alleged that the system of provisioning was 'guarded as jealously as though it had been Eden. As on the banks of the Ganges, so on the banks of the Thames, the cow (including the male members of the family) appears to be a sacred animal'.[23]

The Smithfield meat system included relationships involving the butchers' guild, city planners and architects, animal welfare and sanitation reformers, technology, the international food market and the environment. Representatives of these interests in London's meat provisioning network clamoured for participation in the debate about the market during the first half of the nineteenth century. The guilds and liveries, such as the butchers, woolmen (winders and packers of wool), curriers (dressers of tanned leather), skinners and tallow chandlers, all well-established members of the Smithfield system, articulated their concerns.

The Smithfield system also included stock delivery, stock bundling, market transactions and wholesale and retail markets' locations.[24] The meat markets were integral members of the network. Each retail butcher had complex relationships with wholesale butchers and the salesmen in Smithfield. The activities of these individuals suggested Adam Smith's 'invisible hand', an economic equilibrium based upon the self-interests in the market. These private interests in Smithfield had for centuries evolved towards equilibrium of the supply and demand of meat. As the nineteenth century arrived, this market system became the target of reformers and public institutions that challenged this market with concerns about public health and safety. The private interests, represented by the City of London, turned to Parliament, who enacted laws and provided funding in an effort to balance the public interests with the need to protect the operation of the Smithfield market system.

London's position in the provisioning network of Britain conjoined the towns, regions and other countries into a national market.[25] The nationalization of the meat trade had already begun to occur by the early sixteenth century, when livestock came to London from as far away as Scotland and Wales.[26] Essex and Norfolk were also important suppliers of the London markets, and both areas provided cattle to Smithfield. One description of Essex farmers, written in 1594, mentions that they had 'often use Smythfelde and other lyke places with fatt cattle, wher also they store themselves with leane [*sic*]'.[27]

By the nineteenth century, a network of drovers and salesmen transmitted information about prices, supply and demand to and from Smithfield market. Improvements in transportation (steam vessels, carriages, postal service) expedited the transmission of market intelligence throughout the Smithfield system. The system also communicated aspects of British identity within a national and international context. The market was 'a national exposition of our greatness', as one observer exulted, including 'slaughterhouses, triperies, bone-boiling houses, gut scraperies and the mutton-chops, scrags, saddles, legs, sirloins and rounds, which grace the smiling boards of our noble imperial capital ... ' Smithfield was a vast 'commissariat to the world' by the nineteenth century and was entangled in multiple representations of British identity situated in an imperial context. The cattle sold in Smithfield came from Belgium, Denmark, France, Germany, Holland, Norway, Portugal, Russian, Spain, Sweden, the U.S. and South America.[28] And by the nineteenth century, Smithfield was under pressure to accommodate an increasing number of larger animals brought to market by an increasing number of middlemen who complained about the congestion and competition. An overview of these competing interests in the marketplace will reveal aspects of the 'nuisance' known as Smithfield.

Farmers, Graziers and Their Livestock: 'Breeders and Feeders'

The flow of meat to London began on the pastures of small and large farms throughout England and Scotland. Many of agricultural practices in the nineteenth century had emerged from the preceding two centuries when agricultural land ownership and practices experienced a long 'agricultural revolution'. As Parliament enclosed farmland previously held in common, individual farmers controlled their fields and sought ways to utilize their land in more productive ways.[29] Crop production increased with the introduction of labour-saving practices and animal husbandry benefited from new techniques of breeding and feeding livestock for the market. These changes brought England into the meat-producing business on a large scale as farming shifted from arable crops to mixed, pastoral farming. In part, farmers were responding to the increasing demand for food and wool that resulted from the rise in urban populations throughout Britain. Individuals such as Jethro Tull, who provided the seed drill, and Charles Townsend, who introduced turnips as forage, transformed agriculture in ways that impacted Smithfield. Before the use of turnips as forage, farmers were unable to feed their stock during the winter; their stock would lose weight and required additional grazing throughout the following summer, which lengthened the time it took to raise animals for the market. The arrival of turnip forage enabled farmers in the north of England, where forage growing seasons were short, to continue to feed animals throughout the year.[30] It was standard practice to kill livestock in the fall since most cattle were unlikely to survive a winter with little forage. These new forage technologies shortened the time it took for animals to reach market weight and increased their overall size. Individual breeders such as Robert Bakewell did much to improve breeding technology and contributed to the increase in the size and weight of livestock by the nineteenth century.[31] Individuals travelled to his farm to learn how to improve their own stock and to see Bakewell's renowned Dishley ram.

By the beginning of the nineteenth century, growing foreign competition and the rise in consumer demand placed pressure on English farmers to increase production.[32] The idea that agriculture was indeed a science had entered the discourse among agriculturalists, and contemporary agricultural literature contained lectures, exhortations and advice on ways to utilize the latest implement, cultivation technique, or breed type to increase productivity.[33] Farmers learned from general publications such as *Chamber's Information for the People* about new ways to fatten animals for the market.[34]

The Smithfield Cattle Club became a forum for livestock breeders to learn of new agricultural practices and to promote the improvement of cattle bred for the market in Smithfield. Founded in 1798 by a group of gentlemen farmers, including Arthur Young, the club sought ways to breed animals 'in a manner more economic and expeditious ... for cattle intended to furnish the tables of the inhabitants', of London. Its shows and prizes, awarded by a panel of gentlemen farmers and butchers, emphasized weight gain and innovative forage practices.[35] (The club met near Smithfield until the market moved to Islington.)[36]

As a result of a more systematic and technological approach to farming, 'scientific agriculture', productivity rose and was temporarily in balance with increases in population. An analysis of agricultural productivity for livestock is complicated by ambiguous statistics; official livestock censuses did not occur until later in the nineteenth century. In addition, statistics alone do not adequately reflect productivity increases because of the increases in the size and the quality of the stock.[37]

Although called a cattle market, Smithfield market also sold sheep and pigs. The archives contain very little about the history of the movement, sales, prices and practices associated with sheep and pigs compared to cattle. But then the word 'cattle' derives from chattel, which implied all sorts of living capital, such as cattle, sheep and pigs. Families kept small numbers of pigs for their own pork supply. Since pigs were scavengers and known for eating just about anything, Londoners were wary of pork. But by the 1850s, pig breeders had taken on pig breeding with serious intentions. As Charles Dickens stated, 'Pig-breeders have become philosophers, knowing that the quality of pork depends on the food of the animal'. Statistics for Smithfield sales include pigs in some years and not others, and there was a separate area in Smithfield for pigs. Butchers bought pigs as sucklings for fresh pork and for bacon. The Irish pigs went to London salted for use as bacon. Dickens surmised that over 700,000 pigs travelled to London for this purpose by 1850. He also estimated that 40,000 pigs entered the Smithfield market; Newgate and Leadenhall sold pork as 'dead' meat. Numerous products came from pigs: bristles for brushes of all types, leather for saddles and pocket books and oils, ointments and creams from the lard. He noted that English diets regularly included pork, especially for the poorer families who kept pigs.[38] Farmers and graziers produced livestock according to rhythms of breeding and gestation and raised them on pastures dependent upon variable climatic and environmental conditions. Farmers were often graziers; the role of a grazier was to fatten lean stock for market, either on his own property or on another landowner's estate. The graziers who fattened livestock before they reached the market were the first link between the farmer and the marketplace.[39]

William Youatt, a nineteenth century English veterinarian and prolific agricultural journalist, described the activities of a grazier in his classic book about raising sheep. He explained how the methods used by graziers for fattening sheep depended upon variations in geography, climate, soil, breed, feed and the timing of the birth of offspring, not to mention the 'caprice' of farmers. Farmers bought pregnant ewes in the fall and fattened them until lambing time in the spring when both the ewe and lambs are sufficiently robust and the lambs are good prospects as for the spring market. Some purchased 'store' (young, unfattened stock) lambs in the spring and fatten them for the market. The goal of all the fattening systems was to make the most of the natural traits of the animal (size, ability to convert forage to fat) in the shortest possible timeframe.[40]

By 1800, farmers and graziers had become increasingly more productive than their rural ancestors as a result of land policies and new agricultural technologies that shaped the countryside in different ways.[41] Farmers and graziers experimented with a range of grasses, hay and legumes, such as clover, not to mention turnips. Soil amendments such as zinc, Epsom salts, ginger, iodine, arsenic, myrrh and turpentine were all used at some time by farmers as they fattened their livestock for market. Grain and oil cakes were popular and believed to add the right kind of fat, the marbled fat praised in agricultural publications. In some cases, farmers in England sent their pedigreed stock, such as Devons, to Scotland and Ireland for breed improvement. Scottish farmers began selling lean stock that would fatten outside London and eventually learned how to fatten their own stock using turnips.[42]

Cattle left a farm either as fatstock, ready for purchase by a butcher, or as lean stock, ready for purchase by a grazier. It was usual for animals to leave a farm relatively thin and to be fattened on the way to Smithfield. For example, Scottish and Welsh cattle arrived in England for fattening. Prime livestock fattening areas were south of London, the south midlands, and areas of East Anglia. 'Store cattle', lean and ranging in age from six months to three years, were sold to graziers for fattening. Otherwise, farmers slaughtered their cattle either for their own consumption or for local markets.[43] A farmer not fortunate enough to occupy land with good turnip or grass producing soil or not wealthy enough to purchase other fattening agents such as the new oil-cake would almost always sell stock to a grazier.[44]

By fattening the animals, graziers added value to the cattle before moving the animals to Smithfield when the market opened each week.[45] Graziers were sometimes criticized for unfairly lowering the income received by the farmers for cattle, while increasing the income of graziers. Some farmers were concerned about the growing number of graziers, a situation that led to the diversion of an increasing amount of revenue away from some rural areas. At the same time, graziers protested the congestion of the market and on the roads leading to Smithfield because they felt the increasing human and vehicular traffic discouraged them from entering the market in order to sell stock without the interference of middlemen (even though they themselves acted as middlemen.) Graziers were compelled to hire drovers who could navigate the narrow streets and avoid damaging the animals on the way to market. They petitioned Parliament for any changes to the Smithfield system that would improve their position in the provisioning network, and permit them to have direct access to the market.

Both the farmers and graziers benefited by decreasing the amount of time it took for animals to reach market weight. The faster an animal passed from birth weight to market weight, the greater the profit. In one case, a pair of Welsh oxen fattened on pastures for a year, increased in value from £33 to £60 by the time the animals reached Smithfield.[46] The age of an animal making its way towards Smithfield varied according to the season and geographic origin. In northern regions where growing seasons were limited, animals were not ready for market until perhaps age three or six, depending on the breed.[47] In regions where forage was plentiful for a longer time, animals were sent to market at a younger age, since they reached market weight in a shorter period.

Distances and breeding cycles extended the time it took for farmers to respond to consumer demand in Smithfield. Although farmers made adjustments to their practices in response to the market in order to increase their profits, their response was slow and lagged the market by at least five years. It would take at least two years to see the results of cross breeding in any consistent sense and even longer to develop a herd that bred consistently according to a new set of desired traits. Most often, farmers concentrated on increasing an animal's rate of gain and the quality and quantity of fat on its carcass.[48]

Observers of Smithfield market in the early 1800s confirm that cattle entering the City were larger and yielded more meat for the consumer. Some meat consumers were critical of the emphasis on 'improving' animals by breeding for weight gain.[49] An observer at one of the Smithfield Christmas cattle shows remarked on the improved cattle on display:

> The Christmas show of fat cattle in Baker Street is the result of an entirely new order of things. The only fair way of regarding meat is to consider it – as it is really – a man-ufactured article ... And, as in manufactured goods – so also in beef – it is produced in various farms, differing in quality.[50]

This observation suggests that the emphasis upon fattening animals was becom-ing more methodical and rationalized, replacing the centuries-old system of animal husbandry with scientific principles either on a conscious or unconscious basis. As a result, by the early nineteenth century more meat arrived in butch-ers' stalls near Smithfield to meet the growing demand. All these improvements in meat production, in addition to the increase in the number of middlemen, placed increasing pressure on the streets surrounding the market in Smithfield. The graziers were only the class of middlemen.

Middlemen: Forestallers, Regrators, Engrossers

As the demand for meat increased in London, entrepreneurs, willing to take risks, became middlemen and took advantage of the opportunity to bring ani-mals from further away and to consolidate transactions in order to maximize profit.[51] Drovers, salesmen, jobbers, forestallers and engrossers (or regrators) lev-eraged their access to livestock and the market in ways that affected prices and availability. Gordon Mingay and Joan Thirsk estimate that by 1750, 'most of the trade beyond the farm gates was already in the hands of middlemen'.[52]

Middlemen proliferated and had names that became part of our modern day vocabulary, such as 'forestalling'. A forestaller would purchase stock before it reached Smithfield and hold it until prices rose to a certain level. Sometimes a grazier would also forestall livestock, keeping cattle in his pasture while he per-suaded those in the market that the price of cattle should be higher. By restricting trade in the market, forestallers manipulated the market, interfering with normal price-setting mechanisms. Engrossers, also known as regrators, would buy small groups of animals and combine them into larger groups. Hoping to monopo-lize the market, engrossers purchased animals wholesale and then sold them in Smithfield at a higher price, which disrupted the pricing system established by the market. Butchers complained that stock had sometimes been sold more than once on the same day in Smithfield.

Forestalling, regrating and engrossing were unpopular and considered an infringement on trading rights as early as the twelfth century. These middlemen were active during periods of food shortages and generated an enduring resent-ment because the public believed that they restricted access to and raised the

price of food. Penalties for acting as a middleman were often dire: forfeiture of
the goods, humiliation in a pillory or stocks, imprisonment and fines, and ban-
ishment from the City or town.[53]

In the twelfth and thirteenth centuries, forestallers were punished through
royal statutes for 'oppressing the poor' and 'deceiving the rich' by using 'craft
and subtlety'. William Petty, a writer of 'political arithmetic' in the seventeenth
century, described forestallers in the seventeenth century as 'Gamesters', as 'veins
and arteries, to distribute back and forth ... the product of Husbandry and Manufacture'.[54] In the early seventeenth century, regulations attempted to curb the
activities of London butchers who acted as graziers:

> ... concerning the combination of the Butchers of London, in the putting downe of
> Barnett Market, and theire practize in becomeing Graiziers, as well as Butchers, and
> hyreing to that purpose most of the Marshes and feeding Grounds neere London,
> both which tend to the greate damage and Prejudice of all Landlords and Graiziers
> dwelling northward from thence, and the later of them tending to the Greate Preju-
> dice of Noblemen, Gent., and other his Majestie's Servants and Subjects, liveing neere
> or resorting to London, by converting all those Grounds which formerly furnished
> the City with hay into Graizeing [*sic*].[55]

However, the early negative attitudes towards middlemen indicated by the regulations of the Middle Ages through the seventeenth century gradually shifted
by the nineteenth century.[56] Middlemen became accepted as part of the labour
required to fuel economic growth, rather than impediments to trade. Still, the
general feeling was that middlemen added unnecessary activities to the provisioning of meat and made the system more adamantine as they resisted any
change that would threaten their existence.[57]

Some market middlemen acted in multiple capacities, combining forestalling, regrating, and engrossing. Jobbers (a dealer who bought in one market and
sold in another, or who sold the same animal multiple times in the same market)
who owned grazing land around London would buy stock from graziers and from
drovers on their way to Smithfield. They accumulated stock on their land, waiting until prices were favourable for sales in Smithfield.[58] Some middlemen would
tell farmers that Smithfield prices were higher than they actually were in order
to encourage the farmer to sell stock to the jobber. This practice would drive the
farmers into the arms of the jobber when the farmers failed to obtain these high
prices on their own.[59] As J. S. Girdler noted in the early nineteenth century, jobbers, 'a very numerous class of men ... made it their business to go about into the
grazing counties, and to buy up large quantities of live cattle ... they jobbed them
again, and sold them three or four times ... enormous sums were obtained by these
men. One instance had been stated of a Jobber getting 2000 l. *in a minute* [*sic*],
by buying up cattle ... '[60]

Drovers

In *Far from the Madding Crowd*, Thomas Hardy described the sights and sounds of drovers driving herds and flocks to the market:

> ... in a slow procession they [the sheep] entered the opening to which the roads tended, multitude after multitude, horned and hornless – blue flocks and red flocks, buff flocks and brown flocks, even green and salmon-tinted flocks, according to the fancy of the colourist and custom of the farm. Men were shouting, dogs were barking, with greatest animation, but the thronging travellers in so long a journey had grown nearly indifferent to such terrors, though they still bleated piteously at the unwontedness of their experiences, a tall shepherd rising here and there in the midst of them, like a gigantic idol amid a crowd of prostrate devotees.[61]

Throughout the eighteenth century and until the 1830s, canals and drovers brought livestock to London. By 1840, railroads began to replace canals, but the main conduits for livestock on its way to Smithfield were networks of dirt roads. Drove roads or 'ox roads', some ten feet deep, provided the links between towns and cities. Drovers, who were responsible for transporting livestock to the market, became key figures in the debate about Smithfield's location since they were responsible for bringing the cattle to market, adding to the congestion building in the streets and displaying behaviour that would become increasingly repugnant to workers in London, newly arrived from the countryside, who embraced a new, urbanized identity.

Drovers brought 'fine, fat bullocks' to London from as far away as Scotland and Ireland throughout the nineteenth century.[62] Along the way, drovers contributed to the economic landscape of the countryside – frequenting inns, paying for grazing rights, employing blacksmiths and buying additional cattle.[63] As a result of this linkage of agricultural and urban geographies, Smithfield increased land prices as far away as Scotland and raised meat prices in many local markets. As bonded transporters of assets to market, drovers were sometimes accused of possessing too much power, as farmers and graziers came to depend upon them and cattle salesmen to get the best prices and to dispose of all their cattle in a drove.[64]

A grazier would pay a drover to take his livestock to a salesman at Smithfield to whom the grazier had consigned the animals.[65] The drover issued a bill of exchange, backed by letters of credit, which the drover would accumulate throughout his travels while he assembled his drove.[66] The size of a single drove could range from one to two hundred animals to about a thousand animals, all gathered from different farms.

Three classes of drovers brought cattle into Smithfield. A country drover delivered livestock from a farm to either another regional market or all the way to London; a salesman's drover took the cattle from outside London in Islington, where the animals assembled before entering the market, into Smithfield itself; and a butcher's drover brought animals purchased from the salesman to the butcher's shop.[67]

Drovers brought cattle into London from all directions, but most of the traffic came from the north of England. In 1810, those investigating the enlargement of the Smithfield estimated that half the animals intended for the market arrived from the North, with one-fourth coming from the West and the rest from the East and South. At the end of each week, large numbers of cattle entered Islington via the Great North Road, a turnpike road, in preparation for the Smithfield market on Monday morning. They continually complained about poor road surfaces, especially roads that were hard or rutted, which caused physical harm to their charges. Drovers were also resentful of the delay and lost revenue caused by the unrelenting tolls required from users of the roads and bridges that connected the countryside to the London market.[68] The extent of their discontent concerning the tolls was evident when a group of drovers in women's clothing, calling themselves the 'Daughters of Rebecca', swarmed tollgates during the 1840s, attacking the gatekeepers and demanding freer access to the roads.[69]

Master drovers, sometimes called topsmen, employed assistants to help maintain the drove speed and to protect the moving enterprise from marauders, highway robbers and hecklers who might throw rocks or poke animals in transit. The master drover's role was often similar to that of a salesman or jobber – purchasing cattle from farmers for sale to the market. Other than the topsmen, drovers were not that well paid, even by the standards of all agricultural labourers.[70] Some estimates suggest that around two thousand drovers participated in the Smithfield cattle market in some capacity.[71]

Before telegraphy was ubiquitous in the nineteenth century, drovers and middlemen were the main source of market intelligence with regard to prices, livestock supply and livestock quality. Newspapers were slow to arrive in many rural areas, often delaying the reports of Smithfield market activity. Without market intelligence 'the breeder cannot avail himself of that range of experience which commences with copulation and terminates in the shambles'.[72] George Culley, an agricultural innovator from northern England, advised farmers on ways to fatten livestock destined for Smithfield, noting that fatstock sold for higher prices in Smithfield than at any other market in England. He also advised farmers to establish relationships with jobbers who interacted with drovers so that the jobbers might share market information.[73]

Because the drovers carried both market intelligence and the assets of farmers to Smithfield, their personal integrity was under scrutiny by their employers and those in the market. Moral character was an important consideration not only in the selection of a drover but also in the general discourse. Drovers in

Smithfield became the target of social reformers in London who criticized them for their alleged violent behaviour.

Drover scams were not unheard of: some would claim that they were robbed en route and pocket the funds.[74] The City issued tin licences intended to indicate a drover's moral and trustworthy character; drovers wore these on their arms, prominently displaying their numbers for the market superintendent and toll takers. Early statutes required that drovers must be thirty years old and married, both seen as assuring a drover's integrity.[75]

Edward VI first introduced licences to protect consumers against abuses by drovers. In *Much Ado About Nothing*, William Shakespeare employed the image of honest drovers when Benedick said that Claudio had just 'spoken like an honest Drouier' [*sic*] (*Act II, Scene I*). During the reign of Charles II, 'An Act to prevent Fraudes in the buying and selling of Cattell in Smithfield and elsewhere', outlined the requirements for drover licences. No graziers or butchers could receive a drover's licence unless those individuals refrained from selling cattle within sixty miles of from the place they purchased cattle. Also, any drover's licence prepared by a Justice of the Peace within eighty miles of London was considered void.

As the long cattle drives neared London, most of the drovers brought their animals to lairs, open fields where livestock rested before entering the market on Monday mornings. Without lairage, livestock would arrive in the market emaciated or too thin, even if fattened by a grazier, especially after a long passage from Scotland. Animals transported by drovers from shipping ports were exhausted from both sea and land journeys.[76] Often a grazier owned a lairage and would hold and fatten the stock delivered by a drover.

Salesmen, ink bottles attached to their waistcoats, ready to take orders, sometimes bought cattle as they rested in the lairs, a practice that gave the lair the appearance of a secondary market. Critics called the lairs 'little better than open spaces of waste ground, without shelter or accommodation ... '[77] Samuel Rhodes and Richard Laycock, a dairyman, both operated lairs near Islington.[78] By 1820, Laycock had several hundred acres in use as lairs, including some with covered sheds for cattle and sheep. Some salesmen purchased *milch* cows directly from Laycock's lair before the cows ever reached Smithfield.[79] Almost fifteen hundred cattle could be accommodated in his lairs, but cattle arriving from the south of Smithfield were not afforded such amenities.[80] Lairs in Mile End and the fields belonging to Laycock became the most popular lairs because cattle were known to be stall-fed and were well rested when they entered the market. But Laycock had his own critics: In 1828, the House of Commons select committee thought that Laycock's lairs might have been a response to the limited size of Smithfield and a reason for high prices of cattle in the market.[81]

Market Day, To Buy a Fat Pig, Oxen, Sheep

In Smithfield, Monday and Friday were the two livestock market days, with Monday being the larger of the two markets. On Saturday, the working classes came to Smithfield to purchase the poorer cuts of meat at low prices. Livestock included cattle, sheep, pigs and, on Friday, horses and donkeys. On Tuesday, Wednesday and Thursday, the straw and hay market took place. (The largest cattle and sheep market occurred during December when the Christmas season increased demand for meat for holiday tables.)

On Sunday, country drovers gathered in Islington with their stock. Drovers sorted their animals according to owners, and the Smithfield salesmen selected the animals they wanted to take to the market. In the early hours of Monday, thousands of animals crowded through the London streets on the way to market, accompanied by drovers carrying torches, filling the streets with the sights and sounds vividly captured by journalists of the day.[82] The salesmen's drovers brought livestock to Smithfield through St John, Turnmill, Clerkenwell and Aldersgate streets from the north and over London Bridge through Cheap Street from the south. Animals arriving from the west travelled through Holborn and from the east they came from Norfolk and travelled through Mile End. Some cattle travelled down Great Russell Street through Bloomsbury Square, and Theobald's Road. Other stopping areas included Paddington, Bayswater, Holloway, Knightsbridge and Newington for cattle coming from the north, west and south.[83] Cattle also arrived from the west into Paddington fields over the Fleet River before it was covered up in between 1769 and 1870, and through Gray's Inn Lane through Turnmill and Cow Cross. Some went down Oxford Street through Holborn and Snow Hill to Smithfield. From the south the drovers travelled over the London Bridge, but mostly over Blackfriars Bridge. This livestock transit network overlapped other traffic, such as foot, wagon, horse, omnibus and, eventually, rail.

Some drovers held off cattle between Smithfield and Finsbury, clogging the streets with cattle until the market opened or until space was available. These 'off-droves' alarmed those concerned about animal welfare and re-enforced arguments that Smithfield was unable to accommodate all the animals that came to market. Some cattle stood for several hours in St John Street awaiting the opening of the market on Monday morning. Sheep arriving though Holborn on Sunday night rested in Hatton Gardens, contributing noise to the surrounding area. Cow Lane, Hosier Lane and King Street also filled with animals.[84] William Hickson, a shoe warehouseman, observed cattle backed into Giltspur Street, Skinner Street, Long Lane up to Barbican and into the Smithfield Bars area.

Inhabitants near the droving thoroughfares provided colorful descriptions of the passage of animals. The movement of cattle was 'accompanied by sounds not a little bewildering to unaccustomed ears. The cracking of whips, the heavy thumping of stocks, the barking of dogs, the bawling of angry voices, and the ever-surging monotonous ba-a-ing, making up a babble of such strange utterances as you would find it difficult to match elsewhere'.[85] Many observers were in awe of the drover's ability to keep their livestock separated from that of other droves and to retrieve strays that escaped down narrow, darkened streets. Criticisms of drovers related more to their treatment of animals and their violent behaviour than to concerns about pricing and unfair market practices.

Salesmen

Farmers and graziers often employed a salesman, also called a broker or factor, to buy and sell animals at Smithfield or other markets on the way to London. Salesmen communicated in writing with their employers about the market, and the farmers informed their salesmen about livestock availability. Salesmen sold an average of fifty to sixty animals per week for a commission calculated by the head and were often the target of regulations that attempted to control the activities of middlemen.[86]

Cattle salesman William Collins said that he sold almost 300 cattle per week. Salesmen sold either to butchers or to victuallers who occupied shops near the market. The salesman was responsible for reporting the number of animals in his drove to the Clerk of the Market who collected information about the number of animals in the market as well as tools and rental fees. Salesmen paid a toll to the City for each animal that entered the market – two pence per head, tied up in the market, and one pence for animals situated in off-droves, often untied. Clerks and salesmen marked the beasts as they were sold, and town drovers moved the cattle to the buyers' sites, which could either be a carcass or retail butcher's premises.[87]

Smithfield operated with its own system of weights that included the term 'sinking the offal', a phrase used to describe a price that included a discount for the amount of offal, roughly one-third to one-fourth of the live weight. For example, if the live animal weighed 100 pounds and sold for £10, the price per pound was for approximately two-thirds of the animal's live weight, or roughly £6 per pound. The butcher sold the offal and so benefited from this pricing system.[88]

More animals came to the market than were sold; at the end of the market day, between late morning and late afternoon, the unsold animals were either removed to nearby lairs or driven back to graziers outside London where they might be held for the next Smithfield market day or another market. Most animals were sold by ten o'clock in the morning on Monday morning. When the sale of cattle in Smithfield did not meet the price agreed upon between the drover or salesman and the farmer, it was the farmer who had to take the loss upon payment by the drover. Sometimes, salesmen would hold their animals in pastures outside the market until prices rose, in effect acting as a forestaller, or enter into contracts with a grazier who would keep the animals until the market in Smithfield improved.[89]

About six hundred salesmen operated in Smithfield and they were there to mitigate risk and organize transactions between buyers and sellers.[90] Salesmen were vocal in the Smithfield debate regarding the removal of the cattle market since they lived and worked near the market. They were powerful figures in the system because they provided farmers and graziers with banking services while leveraging their relationships in the wholesale meat market.[91] Salesmen worked with the drovers to gather stock that would command the best prices. This required monitoring the prices of dead meat in the Newgate and Leadenhall meat markets, the prices of other salesmen and the general supply of stock in the country.

Inside the Market

When animals entered Smithfield in the early morning hours, they filled the market space to capacity.[92] At the beginning of the nineteenth century, Smithfield occupied three acres and by mid-century grew to encompass six and one half acres. As time passed, the City improved the layout of the market. By 1850, about 4,000 cattle and 25,000 sheep, 1,000 pigs and 500 calves could squeeze into the market.[93] Cattle and sheep were in one area, separated by Long Lane and King Street. Pigs and calves occupied another area on the end of the market nearest West Street. [94] When the market opened in the morning, animals filled the hundreds of small wooden pens and rails in the large open market space. One observer, critical of the market, described the size of the pens as 'large enough to accommodate a moderate sized statue'. He suggested that 'if all these wretched animals were converted into marble or bronze, surely after thousands of years, the nations of the earth would journey to Smithfield to study the character of this our time in that vast field of monuments'.[95] The sights and sounds of Smithfield became metaphors for other Londoners who saw Smithfield as a representation of their city and their time in history.

Cattle were tied onto rails located around edge of the market. Some salesmen, like Charles Merritt, preferred to let their animals stand loose, unless an officer of the market reprimanded them. When there was no longer any room on the rails, drovers arranged the animals in rings, tying them in groups of up to twenty cattle head to head, called 'ring droves'. These efforts to accommodate additional livestock were the object of criticism by those who felt this practice was a source of potential injury to the animals. Some observers commented on the poor condition of the animals tied up in the market. Land agent Henry Jem-

Figure 1.1: Smithfield Market, from the Bear and Ragged Staff Inn, Augustus Charles Pugin, 1811

mett described them as being 'so exhausted as to drop, from complete fatigue
and debility, and to have expired upon the spot'. William Hickson, a shoe warehouseman in Smithfield, stated, 'the cruelty practiced upon them [cattle], in
beating them into rings, no person can believe, unless they had seen it ... '[96]

The sounds of the market included 'the barking of dogs, the bellowing of
cattle, the cursing of men, and the dull blows of sticks – a charivari of sound that
must be heard to be appreciated'. Some thought the scene more a 'hideous nightmare than a weekly exhibition in a civilized country'.[97] This 'hubbub', described
by Emily Cockayne in her study of London's filth and noise, seemed to be more
noticeable to Londoners by the turn of the nineteenth century.[98]

Around the Periphery: Bankers and Byproduct 'Manufactories'

Transactions involving farmers, graziers, drovers, salesmen and butchers culmi-
nated in remittances turned in to the Bank of England every Monday night. This
system of credits and promissory notes played an important role in the Smithfield system, connecting these farmers, graziers, drovers and salesmen in the
country to the City, as assets travelled to London in return for payment to the
farmer. This network connected regional economies with local credit networks,
known for their 'fickleness' and fragility dependent upon trusted relationships
between buyers and sellers.[99] Most transactions were accomplished through the
use of notes, but sometimes 'ready' cash changed hands when salesmen doubted
a buyer's credit. The movement of cash, notes and other financial equivalents
throughout the Smithfield system led to the establishment of early banking
institutions and shaped financial transactions within the market in Smithfield.[100]
Cattle banks, organized around the periphery of the marketplace, were part of
the Smithfield system and provided the financing mechanism for these transactions. Dodd estimates that there were about six hundred bankers and seven
'banking houses'.[101]

Salesmen acquired animals from farmers and graziers for sale in Smithfield based upon negotiated prices. When a butcher purchased animals from a
salesman, he received a bill from the salesman for the purchase price minus the
salesman's commission. The butcher then took the bill to a cattle bank or money-
taker who carried the bill to a bank. The money-taker subtracted his fee from the
amount conveyed to the farmer's bank. This process enabled farmers and grazers
to receive payment the day after a transaction, at the latest. Some farmers, anxious to be paid, were concerned with the safety of those carrying the bills.

Other members of the Smithfield market system were businesses that utilized the butchers' byproducts, including horse knackers, bladder blowers, catgut
factories and tallow renderers as well as hide and fur dressers, boot makers, shoemakers, saddlers and blacksmiths. These activities were the object of criticism as

they created smells and sights that offended those who saw London as an emerging representation of civility and modernity.

The City: The Corporation of London, Regulations and Rights

The City not only had the ancient rights for the cattle market but also owned much of the land in and around the market. The private commercial and entrepreneurial interests of the City influenced most of its decisions relative to Smithfield. Before 1835, the City Lands Committee administered Smithfield, including its finances as approved by the Court of Common Council. From 1835 onward, the City's Markets Improvement Committee managed Smithfield and communicated with both Parliament and the Court of Common Council concerning petitions, bills and other issues related to Smithfield administration. The City paid the Commissioners of Sewers to keep the market clean and to provide lighting, maintenance and improvements out of tolls and fees for services.[102]

Estimates for the profit obtained by the City for Smithfield ranged from £3,700 to £4,000 per year. Critics of the City's resistance to the market's removal accused the City of obstinacy, since the relatively small financial gain would hardly justify keeping the market in its current position. These skeptics pointed to the considerably larger sums the City paid to protect its interests in the market and for improving Smithfield (between 1828 and 1846, the City had spent almost £40,000 on improvements).[103] The legal ambiguities surrounding the ability of the City to collect tolls and other revenues if the market were relocated to Islington contributed to the reluctance on the part of the City and Parliament to support moving the market. These legal issues were contested at several points throughout the long debate.

The City's position relative to the operation and administration of the market impacted all those in the Smithfield system. And the system was under assault as a result of social, cultural and technological changes. One observer wrote, 'The very changes in our social conditions which new invention and new states of existence produce, also produce new groupings of character, new classes of individuals'.[104] Meat consumers increased, purchases reflecting social class and a new identity shaped by modernity. The emerging consumer culture that had its beginnings in the seventeenth and eighteen centuries, now gathered momentum and became entangled in the debate about the location of food markets. Who were these consumers and how did they perceive meat in their diets and as part of their urban identity? The next chapter will explore the complicated layers of the consumer culture, providing evidence that Britain's meat culture and urban identity combined to complicate the moving of its meat markets.

2 THE SMITHFIELD SYSTEM IN THE NINETEENTH CENTURY: THE CONSUMERS

A sacré Dieu! Vat do I see yonder?
Dat looks so tempting, red and white?
Begar I see it is de roast Beef from Londre.
Oh grant me one letel Bit.[1]

Integral to the Smithfield market system, the buyers and consumers of animals and meat were at the terminus of the supply chain. They directly influenced both the quantity and quality of animals available for purchase. Farmers, graziers, salesmen and butchers were also keenly aware of changes in consumer buying habits. As fashion turned, so did the public taste for mutton, pork and beef. The more labourers from the countryside saw themselves as modern urban dwellers, Londoners, the more meat sold in Smithfield. The same individuals that shaped the debate in the various select committees in Parliament also ate the barons of beef and tucked into saddles of mutton. Of these consumers, the butchers were on the front line of London's meat provisioning system and had practiced their profession for at least 800 years before their presence in Smithfield became a public concern. This fiercely independent group had the most to lose by the removal of the cattle market and their protests continued up to and after the removal of the market to Islington.

The Smithfield Butchers

Butchers were the buyers of live animals in Smithfield and of dead carcasses in the meat markets around Smithfield. Over the centuries, butchers were often reviled because their trade was associated with noise, congestion, refuse, unsightly practices and animal cruelty and because of the perception that they possessed low moral character. Various ordinances regulated their activities and moved them from one location to another as their so-called antisocial practices offended religious interests and reformers. Some observers, however, had some positive things to say about this trade. A writer in the *Farmer's Magazine* said, 'the beauty and cleanliness of the meat as exhibited in London, excites the admiration of every spectator ... [the butchers] display great science in their trade'.[2] The London butchers were both reviled and tolerated; they were necessary to the production of meat, the heart of British cuisine so deeply enmeshed with national identity. The butchers belonged to a working class of tradesmen but a class that held little political power when it came to determining the fate of the meat market.

The butchers obtained their skills through the butchers' guild established in England in the Middle Ages that also enabled its members to obtain trade privileges and protections. However, by the early nineteenth century, the City had relaxed its restrictions on the operations of non-guild butchers in order to keep meat prices low and the guild's major activity was related to the transmission of the required technical skills. Apprenticeship was important to the trade as butchers transmitted slaughter, retail and preservation skills from one generation to another. The art of assessing an animal's health and weight were additional skills that enhanced the perceived value of the butcher's craft. Independent and protective of their trade, butchers often came from generations of family members in the trade.

The Experienced Butcher, written in 1816, and various trade publications described the skills and practices of the butcher's craft. Butchers knew how to 'kill, cut up, and dress their Meat to Advantage, but [also] how to buy a Bullock, Sheep, or Calf, standing; They must judge of this Weight and Fatness by the Eye; and without long Experience are often liable to be deceived in both'.[3] This real and perceived skill possessed by butchers contributed to their recalcitrant character and their general resistance to change that threatened these entrenched and time-honoured professional practices.

The butcher's trade in Smithfield included both carcass (wholesale) and cutting (retail) butchers.[4] The wholesale butchers and some retail butchers purchased live animals and slaughtered them for sale in their own or another retail butcher's meat shop. (Some butchers also went to country markets such as those in Barnet and Southall, northwest of London, to buy stock from country drovers.) After purchasing animals from salesmen in the live cattle market, the wholesale butchers used drovers to bring them to either their own slaughterhouse or, in rare cases, a public slaughterhouse.[5] The private slaughterhouses, some located in cellars, others with their own lairs, operated in Smithfield, Newgate, Whitechapel and other areas around the metropolis, usually within one mile of Smithfield.

The professional boundaries between these trades were fluid, and as a result butchers sometimes acted both as wholesale and retail butchers. By 1836, Pigot's trade classification survey noted that there were about 1,650 butchers in London, not including 'porkmen' who formed a separate trade and numbered 295 at the time. Surveys of the butcher's trade did not consistently distinguish between wholesale and retail businesses.[6]

Each Monday, the largest market day in Smithfield, the wholesale butcher would purchase 40 to 60 cattle in the live cattle market. Not all were sold and those who remained in the market were often returned to a grazier outside Smithfield until the next market day. In general, butchers killed their stock on the same days as they purchased it. Thus, the meat would be available for sale to consumers on Tuesdays when the public needed fresh stores.[7] However, this was not always the case as some butchers held live animals in their own lairs, slaughtering them throughout the week as demand required.[8] William Giblett, a wholesale butcher, said he always had ten days' stock on hand. This enabled him to rest the cattle before slaughter, a practice much approved of but not enjoyed by those butchers who could not afford the luxury of owning land near the market.[9] Edward Bartram of Walworth, a wholesale butcher, slaughtered animals and stored the carcasses in his own backyard. He sold meat to the retail butchers almost two miles away. Sometimes the wholesale butchers killed for their own inventory, from 40 to 50 'beasts' to 200 to 300 sheep a week, and often complained about rough stone pavements in the City that caused meat to become damaged and spoiled as they transported meat from their premises to retail markets.[10]

Dickens described a retail butcher shop 'only a step' from Smithfield, frequented by housekeepers, professional cooks, and 'thrifty wives of clerks and working men'. Butchers had 'red book' customers, their best customers who had regular orders for meat and paid for the best cuts.[13] Retail butchers also sold to families as far away as six miles from the centre of the City. Dickens was right to describe a nimble meat provisioning system that was accommodated different locations, classes, tastes and budgets. Dickens describes 'all orders of people' that bought meat on Saturdays for their Sunday suppers; different consumers had their own buying preferences. Places like 'Spitalfields and workhouses wanted inferior meats' while other customers wanted veal from the country. Butchers frequently purchased large sheep that produced the shoulder of mutton for the working class who 'otherwise would go without any meat at all'.[11] Saturday was the day when the middle class came to the market, mostly to linger and peruse the meat, while the lower classes took the opportunity to purchase cheap meat that had been held by the butchers all week. It would appear that the meat available in London declined in quality as the week progressed. And while meat was a staple of British consumers in most social classes, often those in the poorer class ate little if any meat until the second half of the century when wages improved and meat supply increased.[12]

'Beasts' or cattle, rather than sheep or pigs, were the most profitable animals in Smithfield. They 'dressed' well (were easily killed and prepared for consumption) and provided ample offal at the highest price. The retail butchers hung meat in their shops until it began to spoil and then they sold discarded meat to the poor, or to sausage makers, and sometimes marketed it as good meat after engaging in some subterfuge to mask its inedible status. Butchers also sold blood to sugar refiners: John Cramp, a Smithfield butcher, received £100 a year for blood he sold for refining sugar.[14] These relationships between professions evolved over time, further complicating the removal of the market.

In the time of Dickens, retail butchers were regarded as skilled tradesmen who used their keen appreciation of a good carcass to purchase an assortment of animals for his customers. Dickens described the 'model' butcher as able to select animals that would 'die well', meaning that the animal's carcass would produce ample, healthy and profitable meat. His description favours the butcher who does his own slaughtering while acknowledging that the public slaughterhouse 'is an indispensable adjunct of every great cattle market'. In his description, the private slaughterhouse is 'a much more economical arrangement'. It allowed for the butcher to kill when he needed meat, to guard against the 'pilfering of loose fate that goes on when a number of strange men are collected together', and to take care with the offal so that he can get a good price.[15] The London butchers would remain advocates of private slaughterhouses until the early twentieth century.

Conflicts between the two types of butchers were common. Accusing salesmen and wholesale butchers of greed, the retail butchers thought the two groups too eager to move from 'obscurity and indigence into opulence and pride'. Benjamin Stubbing, a Smithfield wholesale butcher, described a retail butcher's business as precarious: they 'begin with little and end with little'. Retail butchers also accused wholesale butchers of forestalling: 'The cattle so bought up never came to market, but were sent to private repositories. Hence the markets were *made* to *appear thin*, and a *high price* was demanded of the Retail Butchers [sic]'.[16] A petition of retail butchers in 1795 described how the wholesalers brought cattle to small markets miles from the City, forestalling the cattle until higher prices appeared in Smithfield. The retail butchers often accused the wholesale butchers of creating a monopoly that collectively set prices. The retail butchers accused the wholesale butchers of 'early and unfeelingly squeez[ing] great fortunes out of the bowels of the poor'. They also made unsuccessful attempts to eliminate the wholesale butcher, the 'nefarious ... blood-suckers' in order to sell meat to Londoners at wholesale prices, thereby providing meat to the poor at lower prices.[17]

Over fifty years later, the wholesale and retail butchers continued their objections over the practices of middlemen. In 1854, the retail butchers weighed in again against the persistence of forestallers and jobbers. They held a meeting in the George Tavern to organize a petition to the City to quash these monopolizing middlemen. Shouting 'extortion!' in response to the practices of middlemen, the butchers described the 'exorbitant' prices charged for wholesale meat. Jobbers would purchase cattle right off the train in the countryside, paying about 30 per cent more than Smithfield prices. (This particular practice diminished City revenue since the purchase of cattle before they reached the market precluded the City from collecting tolls for each beast entering the market.) Concern about the poor was commonly embedded in the objections to middlemen, aligning 'pernicious' forestalling with exploitation of the poor classes. A cattle salesman who was the purveyor to the Royal Family, William Collins, described how the jobbers got to the market at five in the morning, buying up all the best cattle before the butchers.[18]

The butchers entered the market in Smithfield having acquired some knowledge about the prices of meat for that day by attending other markets, talking to salesmen and drovers, and consulting their own records. Butchers became accustomed to dealing with a particular salesman and would seek him out in his usual place in the market. They assessed the weight and health of an animal and proposed a price to the salesman.[19] Other factors might also influence pricing, such as seasonality of livestock production and the weather. They might haggle a bit over price but usually quickly settled; most butchers and salesmen operated in Smithfield over a long period of time and had created trust through established relationships. Salesmen would visit the meat market to ascertain market prices before they set the live weight prices. They also observed the 'tone' of the trade, the general level of trading activity that helped them ascertain market demand.[20] Some retail butchers preferred to purchase live animals because they could be certain they could acquire the quantity and quality they sought rather than depending upon the selection offered by a wholesale butcher. This price-setting practice relied upon a single market in London where butchers and salesmen could exchange information about supply, demand and prices. When reformers later proposed dividing up the market into several locations, butchers and salesmen protested, claiming the markets would compete in such a way as to lower prices and remove their ability to set prices.

After the butcher and salesman agreed on a price, they marked the animal as sold by making a small cut on the tail, flank or fleece of an animal.[21] If a butcher noticed that these marks were missing, he suspected that the animal had been sold in Smithfield with the intent of being sold again, a sign of regrating.

But even with the possibility that butchers and salesmen were controlling prices, others claimed that the market operated according to the dynamics of a free market. James Mills, a nineteenth-century civil engineer, studied the capacity of Smithfield and the butchers to feed London and beyond. He concluded, 'the mouths, fix the price, and not the butchers; that Adam Smith has settled'. His statement would appear to negate the observations and practices of the butchers who recognized that in addition to demand, other factors dictated price. For example, transport difficulties affected prices in Smithfield if roads were in poor condition because of rain or wear. The markets on the periphery of London also influenced the prices in Smithfield. In addition, complications arose when calculating the price of an animal in different seasons of the year. During the summer, the price of offal would decline since it would decay rapidly and be of little use. Hides were also thinner in the summer since animals tend to grow thicker skins during the winter. (Sheep grew more wool during the winter when the demand for wool was at its peak, reducing the cost of the meat to the butcher.) Tallow was worth less in the summer, since candles are in higher demand during the winter. In the same manner, holidays influenced prices. The Christmas roast was more expensive because of the increased demand for premium cuts of beef. Some festivals entailed the consumption of calf's heads and so raised the price of that delicacy. Wholesale butchers argued that long winters, droughts and cattle and sheep diseases contributed to increases in meat prices.[22] These seasonal and geographical factors were all part of the price calculation process.

Since refrigeration did not exist until after Smithfield relocated to Islington, sales in Smithfield were complicated by representations of the meat's freshness or wholesomeness. Particularly in the warm months of the year, butchers were faced with rudimentary technologies for maintaining the freshness of meat.[23] In the winter, animals could be killed and the meat kept longer before selling. In the summer, slaughtered animals had to be sold sooner to avoid spoilage. This meant that on a hot summer's day, butchers had to slaughter and sell their animals in a short time period, creating a frenzy of activity and congestion. The relationship of time, distance and temperature and the threat of spoilage continually plagued the butchers in Smithfield and was a critical concern to the trade as Parliament proposed increasing the distance between the meat market and the butchers' slaughterhouses.

Since there was not a generous profit margin for dead meat, butchers concentrated on ways to mitigate the inevitable spoilage. The City inspectors fined butchers who sold 'unwholesome' meat and confiscated the offending product, some more ambitious butchers concocted ways to portray meat as fresh. Visual subterfuge often trumped the olfactory facts. While salt was the traditional way of preserving meat, Smithfield butchers sought other ways to present meat to the consumer to satisfy London tastes. In lieu of salting, butchers found that by wrapping meat in linen cloth and placing it in a sand-filled box, they could keep meat sweet for several weeks, stored in an 'airy, dry, and cool chamber'.[24] Boxes of wrapped meat rattled around as the carts moved across cobblestone pavements, further damaging the meat. Butchers found that the exposure of these boxes to the sun along with the agitation of the uneven pavement during transport degraded the meat and invited even lower profits. *The Experienced Butcher* thus suggested ways to redeem the quality of meat that had suffered from heat or rough handling. One recommendation was to boil the meat with a burning piece of coal that would absorb its impurities, including any off-putting smell.[25] A still more deceptive practice was that of meat polishing; the butcher would layer fat around an offending piece of meat and then rub the fat and meat with hot cloths, thus producing an even, smooth appearance.[26] Despite the vigilance of City inspectors, techniques such as polishing allowed butchers to sell diseased or damaged meat to unsuspecting customers.

The specter of government control of the slaughtering business made butchers anxious about their role in the meat provisioning business. These practices and their cultural, social and commercial implications played no small part in shaping the debate about the location of the cattle market. Most of the butchers resisted the removal of the market that would uproot their long established practices, threaten their private property rights and challenge their claim for privileged skills and information gathered over the centuries. The author of one trade publication declared 'Butchers are necessary; yet it is almost the last Trade I should chuse [*sic*] to bind a Lad to. It requires great Strength, and a Disposition no ways inclinable to the Coward; ... The Wages of a Journeyman are not much more considerable than that of a common Labourer'.[27] While public concerns about animal welfare and public health urged the government to regulate and relocate the butchers, the public hesitated to attack the butchers for fear that the 'practical men' would cease to prepare the meat that had become embedded in British identity.

The Consuming Public

The centrality of meat to a Londoner's identity shaped public attitudes about their markets, particularly their meat markets. The connection between Londoners of all social classes and their meat was one of the reasons why the cattle market was allowed to remain in the heart of the metropolis so long. Peter Lund Simmonds, a prolific nineteenth-century British author, described Britain's passion for beef: 'Next to the Habeas Corpus and the Freedom of the Press, there are few things that the English people have a greater respect for and a livelier faith in than beef ... they are never tired of crowding to the Smithfield Club cattle-show; and I am inclined to think that it is their honest reverence for beef that has induced them to support so long the obstruction and endangerment of the thoroughfares of the metropolis by oxen driven to slaughter'.[28] The bond between Britons and beef existed at least as early as the sixteenth century, when writers penned such statements as 'Beef is a good meate for an Englyssheman'. Shakespeare mentioned the importance of beef in his play *Henry V.* Meat, particularly beef, was increasingly associated with Britishness in the eighteenth century when it became the emblem of aristocratic cuisine sought by the middle classes.[29]

The association of England's strength and vitality with its beef infused British identity throughout the eighteen and nineteenth centuries. Henry Fielding's *Grub-Street Opera* (1728) included the ballad, 'The Roast Beef of Old England', which became a popular song at many a tavern and pub. As a rousing tribute to roast beef as 'the Englishman's food', the ballad became a song of patriotism, connecting beef with the English character and identity, as the ennobled meat that 'enriched' the Englishman's blood. The ballad also laments the loss of England's character, as Englishmen learned to eat from 'all-vaporing France' while they 'dwindled' to a 'half-begotten and tame ... race'.[30] William Hogarth, born in 1697 in Bartholomew Close near Smithfield, painted a scene in 1748 depicting the struggle between France and England for the port of Calais. The painting, *O the Roast Beef of Old England (The Gate of Calais)*, which hangs in London's Tate Gallery, shows a French monk and a British tradesman vying for possession of a side of beef. Although both Fielding and Hogarth present complex meanings in both of these works, they reinforce a cultural linkage that embedded the Smithfield market in urban myth and memory.

In addition to cultural connections, beef obtained social meaning though the establishment of men's social clubs. The Sublime Society of Beefsteaks, founded in 1736, gathered in London's theater district to dine exclusively on British beef. A gridiron, essentially a meat grill, became the club's symbol, and members met to debate social and political topics, but mostly to eat and drink together. An aristocratic gentlemen's club, with the motto 'Beef and Liberty', it had as their song *The Roast Beef of Old England*.[31] While the members of this social club and other Victorian improvers looked admiringly at France's 'enlightened' politics and cuisine, they refused to forfeit British character or identity.[32]

Britons were immensely proud of their beef and believed, along with many others, that British beef was the best in the world.[33] British beef had an international reputation for flavor enhanced by the method of fattening and increased maturity, both results of the British 'agricultural revolution' and 'scientific' agriculture introduced in the eighteenth century. An observer of the 1854 Smithfield Christmas cattle show remarked on the improved cattle on display:

> The Christmas show of fat cattle in Baker Street is the result of an entirely new order of things. The only fair way of regarding meat is to consider it – as it is really – a manufactured article ... And, as in manufactured goods – so also in beef – it is produced in various farms, differing in quality.[34]

In 1846, the *Illustrated London News* published an account of the Smithfield Cattle Club Show with a poem satirically lauding the meat produced by the cattle bought in Smithfield. The cattle so admired at the show were described thus:

> ... 'to be spoiled in the eating', But such is the fate of all things upon earth;
> Our foes, like our beefsteaks 'grow better by beating',
> And the land of best beef is the land of true worth.
> A rumpsteak and ale as Elizabeth's *dejeuner*,
> *A la fourchette:* and who glorious as she'
> She valued by half even Essex's calf

More than toro of Spain and its proud chivalrie.
Mat his diner, as I am a sinner'
'L'etat c'est moi' said Louis Quatorze.
Cassius was there, and may cynics be thinner
Who carp against fat ... the diaphanous bores
A stake and a chop a la Mary, we give them
Who sneer down improvement in any degree
Let us laugh and grow fat; the best method to grieve them,
For a baron of beef is *the* baron for me.[35]

Peter Lund Simmonds, in his *The Curiosities of Food*, amplified the link between Londoners and their beef:

> Beef is a great connecting link and bond of better feeling between the great classes of the commonwealth. Beef makes boys into men. Beef nerves our navies ... A baron of beef at the same time is enthroned in St. Georges's Hall in Windsor's ancient castle, and is borne in by lacqueys in scarlet and gold ... When the weary pilgrim reaches the beloved shores of England after a long absence, what first does he remark ... but the great tankard of stout and the noble round of cold beef in the coffee-room of the hotel? ... He looks at the beef, and his eyes filling with tears, a corresponding humidity takes place in his mouth; he kisses the beef; he is so fond of it that he could eat it all up; and he does ordinarily devour so much of it to his breakfast that the thoughtful waiter gazes at him, and murmurs to his napkin, 'This man is either a cannibal or a pilgrim grey who has not seen Albion for many years'.[36]

This identification of British identity with meat and especially beef, saw Smithfield as a national market centre with imagined power as an engine of national and international commerce.[37]

Beginning in the late eighteenth century, the consumption of food and entertainment occupied the newly arrived middle classes.[38] Increasing demands for variety and choice shaped a new consumer behaviour, one that pushed British markets, such as Smithfield, to change in ways that would accommodate the consumer who adopted the practices of the upper classes in appearance if not in reality.[39] Whether or not London consumers had the means to buy the best cuts of meat, they wanted to be seen as finicky customers, desirous of beef, not bacon, or a proper Sunday roast, not blood sausage.[40] The spectacle of fashionable dining, heightened by the possibility of acquiring meat from European farms in countries such as Germany and Holland, led the market to expand to meet the desires of insatiable consumer society.

The butchers were delighted with this burgeoning consumer society. Benjamin Stubbing, the wholesale butcher in Smithfield, exulted, 'There are sorts of buyers, that is the beauty of the thing; there are buyers of all descriptions to take away every thing'.[41] The Sunday supper was the weekly ritual that drew upon the supply of cattle in Smithfield:

The Sunday dinner! Just as the streets are crowded with people returning from church or chapel, and the servants of the licensed victuallers sally out to supply each customer with porters, the bakers open their doors. Then issue a stream of persons, male and female, the father or the son, but more generally the other or the daughter, bearing home the family dinner, which, for the charge of 2d has been baked in the baker's oven. Out of some bakers' shops there will be brought, in a few minutes, sixty, eighty, or a hundred dinners, joints of meat or huge pies. Let a stranger walk about on o'clock on a Sunday, through any part of London densely inhabited by the working-classes, and his olfactory nerves will soon testify to him how universally enjoyed in the 'Sunday's dinner'.[42]

It was inconceivable for the nineteenth-century middle or upper class midday meal not to include meat, most likely a 'hot shoulder of mutton ... a good pie baked of a leg of mutton, and a cold chine of beef'.[43]

Meat – a 'rich treat' – brought Londoners to Smithfield, Newgate, Leadenhall and other retail meat markets, 'feasting their admiring eyes on the glorious 'barons of beef' hung up around'.[44] Those consumers who purchased meat from the butcher possessed a rich repertoire of meat recipes. Recipe (or receipt) books from nineteenth century London helped textualize nineteenth-century meat consumption. Often anonymously written by women, these early cookbooks illustrated how consumers viewed meat in their diet, what they knew about meat, and the relationship of meat to the consumer. Cookbooks expressed British national identity with its emphasis on meat as central to its national cuisine. The associated practice of meat carving became ritualized and systematized, as it was viewed as an essential practice for any competent cook. Cookbooks included diagrams of animals, cuts of meat and explanations for the cook preparing household meals.

Recipe books had several structural commonalities: the meat 'receipts' at the front of the book and a chart representing the seasonality of meat, a description of all the wholesale and retail cuts, and instructions on how to buy meat. The entire animal provided sustenance: recipes for tripe, trotters, cow's heels, calf's feet, heads, tongues, udders, palates and stomachs filled the pages of London recipe books. *New London Cookery* includes a Fricassee of Lambstones (testicles). A recipe for 'Stuffed Calves Ears' mentions the necessity of scalding the hair off the ears.[45]

These books indicate that cooks frequented Smithfield and saw animals before and after slaughter. Purchasing instructions note the importance of choosing animals that 'attain full growth' and that are 'well fed, improved by being older'. In *Domestic Cookery*, the author reminds the reader of the importance of 'observation that will supersede rules of necessity' as the means of selecting quality meat at the market. One recipe warns the buyer to be wary of 'hairy feet' that are weighed with the legs, 'enhancing the cost'.[46] Cooks should look for 'short thick animals' instead of 'tall and skinny' ones, cows instead of bulls and sows instead of boars. They should be sure that 'the veins of the neck and shoulders are bright and blueish'. Recipe books also instructed readers on cooking times according to the time elapsed after slaughter. 'If just killed, let it roast an hour, if killed the day before an hour and a quarter'. After purchase, meat hung for a period of time in order for the meat to achieve a desired tenderness and flavor. One cookbook states that the meat should hang for up to ten days, with 'the knuckles downwards ' to preserve the juices.[47] These practices illustrate how Smithfield defined the rhetoric of recipe books.

Consumers were also becoming more informed about the 'science' of food and nutrition. Justus von Liebig's ideas about organic chemistry and its relationship to food nutrition had begun to circulate in popular scientific publications during the 1840s, bringing a new awareness of the relationship between food and health.[48] He theorized that meat's organic properties fueled the movement of human muscles. In addition, the theory of humors, developed by the Greeks and Romans, still influenced culinary practices. The concept that the balance of four substances called humors contained in the human body ensured a healthy state. Meat consumption could affect these substances and so the view that the body's health was contingent upon eating healthy meat influenced purchasing decisions. Consumers continued to believe that if an animal became frightened or was cruelly or violently treated, the animal's blood would be adversely affected and subsequently harmful to humans.

The emerging consumer culture animated social relationships, fashion and the Smithfield market. As Londoners' wages increased, their tastes changed, as did their meat buying habits.[49] One writer for *Penny Magazine* said, 'the heaviest purses carry off a large portion of the best [food] ... but the 'million' have a very considerable choice according to their means, of the 'good things' with which the markets are provided, and they do not neglect to avail themselves of it, especially for that favourite meal the 'supper'.[50] When the officials of the City of London gathered in 1840 with Sir Robert Peel and other MPs to honor Peel, they tucked into familiar fare. In between toasts they ate 'fifty-four tongues, two barons of beef, two quarters of house lamb, three rounds of beef, three stewed rumps of beef, thirteen sirloin rumps and ribs of beef'.[51]

The population of consumers multiplied during the nineteenth century. As Neil McKendrick and John Brewer point out, the move away from agricultural occupations to manufacturing occupations in London increased wage payments in cash instead of in kind.[52] Scholarship about the Industrial Revolution and its effects on wages and the cost of living in Britain includes both optimistic and pessimistic arguments. But the optimists win out if Smithfield is evidence of increasing wages and the growth of consumer culture.

But here's the paradox. With such an elaborate system for buying and selling in Smithfield and the expanding carnivorous culture, the flow of animals into Smithfield should have been increasing, placing expected pressure on the capacity of the market to provide ample stocks to the trade. While meat consumption increased, Smithfield, while still congested and guilty of having inadequate sanitation and outdated facilities, never failed to function. Somehow, the meat travelled to London through other channels.

The increasing productivity of British farms was evident, but meat consumption rates are complicated by the lack of comprehensive livestock censuses, differing carcass weights, dressing characteristics, seasonal considerations and the lack of a tracking system other than tolls paid at the market. Nonetheless, we do have Mulhall and others to rely on for their statistics for farm production and meat consumption.[53] These statistics, together with the historical data from this period, indicate that domestic meat production, combined with imports and increasing supplies of meat delivered by rail from the countryside satisfied demand, even as it grew.

While the sales of animals sold in Smithfield did not keep pace with the population, animal carcass sizes did increase. Between 1750 and 1831 London's population increased 218 per cent while the number of cattle sold in Smithfield increased 110 per cent (117 per cent for sheep). This dislocation continued throughout the nineteenth century, causing speculation about the space required to accommodate the future growth in the demand for meat to feed the growing population.[54] The increases in the supply of cattle per capita in London were satisfied by increases in deliveries of country-killed mutton by rail. In addition, butchers made use of cheaper and less desirable parts of a carcass to satisfy demand at the lower end of the market.

Aware of increasing demand for food and the need for increased supply, Prime Minister Robert Peel sponsored a bill to increase the supply of cattle by lowering and eventually removing the tariffs on live foreign cattle during the 1840s. The eventual repeal of the Corn Law also enabled Smithfield to respond to the increasing demand for meat. Corn laws not only created tensions between farmers, landowners and politicians, but also caused shifts in agriculture, moving some farmers to put their land into pasture rather than into grain. Peel considered the cattle question in light of the potato crisis, making the connection between social stability and the economic health of Britain as farmers began to move from arable to pasture or mixed farming. This concession to free trade belied Peel's pragmatic conservatism as a means of maintaining social and political stability within a gradual and loosening of trade restrictions and protectionism.[55] This change brought a new trade to Smithfield as animals arrived at English ports from Europe and Baltic countries, but the increase may have been relatively insignificant. Some reports indicate that only 12 per cent of the cattle and 5 per cent of the sheep that were slaughtered in United Kingdom by 1862 were of foreign origin. But other sources point to a higher percentage by midcentury, indicating that up to 50 per cent of the cattle were foreign.[56] Without accurate statistics on the foreign cattle trade, an accurate understanding of the impact of foreign supply are problematic. But, the meat supply was adequate to meet demand and the increase in foreign cattle after Peel's tariff reform surely figured in the total supply of meat to the capital. The Deptford Foreign Cattle Market opened in 1872 to accommodate the arrival of foreign livestock, particularly in the interest of curtailing the effects of livestock diseases upon British livestock populations. This redirected cattle away from the new Metropolitan Cattle Market in Islington, easing pressure to make full use of the new space.

Demand statistics for meat in London during the period between 1800 and 1850 are illusive and require critical assessments and cautious conclusions. Accounts of the amount of meat (not cattle) shipped by rail to London suggest how much meat Londoners consumed that did not come from Smithfield, but the statistics are unavailable about meat that arrived by boat, on canals and by horse-drawn carts and wagons. Many Londoners slaughtered and ate animals, especially pigs, that they grew themselves. The statistics for meat consumption and sales in Smithfield give a general but not complete picture of live cattle supply and demand in London. The number of animals sold in Smithfield was recorded in contemporary publications, in City records, and in newspapers. Scholars rely on the documentation of contemporary observers combined with extrapolations from related data, such as market tolls, taxes, imports and surveys. Some animals went through the turnpikes and tolls several times as they returned from Smithfield to the lairs or went to markets outside London. As animals gained more weight, the amount of meat produced from their carcasses increased, distorting any comparisons from year to year as to actual meat production based upon the number of animals. Generally speaking, the number of animals sold in Smithfield gradually increased, with the increase in the late 1840s because of changes in tariffs.

According to Dodd, Londoners consumed about 70 pounds of meat per capita in 1750; by 1840 they tucked into about 153 pounds per capita, based on a wildly generous calculation of animal weights.[57] Other sources claim that annual meat consumption from 1831 to 1840 was 86.8 pounds per capita and remained unchanged until the 1870s.[58] Still another estimate of meat consumption comes from a calculation from the *London Saturday Journal* in 1841. Using the capacity at Smithfield for 1,500 cattle, 400 calves, 12,000 sheep and 1,200 pigs and the sales numbers from the City, combined with estimates on live and finished weights of each carcass type, the publication concluded that weekly consumption of meat in London was almost five million pounds.[59] Mulhall illustrates this gradual increase in consumption and the rise in supply based on a combination of home production and imports.

Consumption of retail butcher's meat also responded to the rise and fall in the economic condition of poor Londoners. As once observer stated, 'an advance of price causes little abatement of the customary demand among the wealthy, but when the mechanics and labourers are generally depressed, it almost instantly sinks to very much less than it had previously been'.[60] Simply put, demand for butcher's meat rose in relation to the incomes of the working population in London, and prices for meat remained relatively steady.

Scholars offer differing views of consumption rates. According to Hobsbawm, meat consumption declined in the first four decades leading to the 1840s.[61] R. M. Hartwell's analysis presents a rosier assessment of meat consumption during the first half of the nineteenth century. Acknowledging the same flaws in the data, he argues that the British living standard rose during that period and included an increase in meat consumption. Despite some reports of lower rates of slaughter at Smithfield per capita, he accounted for his conclusion by noting the increased carcass weights and the dead meat brought into London from the countryside as a result of railway transport.[62] How do these numbers square with the arguments for more space in Smithfield? The pressure to remove the market came partly from the perception that the demand was growing at such a rate as to threaten Smithfield's capacity as a market space in the future. Whether the animals brought to Smithfield were bigger or cattle numbers were displaced by killed meat, the market, while congested, managed to adapt to an increase in meat consumption.

Those that maintain the view, like Hobsbawm, that meat consumption declined, may have focused on data that described the poorer classes of London society. They suggest that there was a decline in food demand elasticity in relation to income growth. Gregory Clark, Michael Huberman and Peter H. Lindert describe some of these contradictions in what they call the 'British Food Puzzle' – the decline in food demand between 1770 and 1850 at the same time as British income grew and domestic farm production and net imports remained almost constant, data that is contradicted by other reports, but useful for their argument. They propose that statistics ignore the differences between agricultural raw inputs and 'value-added' food consumed.[63] The Puzzle offers an insight to the complexities food systems, both in historical and contemporary terms. Food travels through multiple channels and processes before reaching consumers, complicating data and the categorization of foodstuffs. For example, meat consumed in soups may not be counted in the statistics for meat consumption or in the data about the value of meat sales.

These debates about meat consumption demonstrate the complexities involved in determining whether the amount of space occupied by the cattle market in Smithfield inhibited the market from satisfying growing consumer demand. All the available statistics seem to support a relatively steady rate of meat consumption per capita and sales of livestock in Smithfield, increasing amounts of meat brought to London to supplement livestock sales in Smithfield beginning in the 1840s, the arrival of foreign livestock and the continuing popularity of meat in the British diet.

The accounts of grand banquets where meat is the dominant fare confirms the increasing consumption of meat throughout the nineteenth century. When the Smithfield removal act passed in 1851, the 42,000 hungry visitors to the Great Exhibition each day consumed 80,000 meat patties, 70,000 pounds of ham and 260,000 pounds of beef tongue and other cuts. And in 1853, Smithfield salesmen sold 277,000 cattle and 1.6 million sheep to the wholesale trade.[64]

While the Smithfield system filled the meat-provisioning network to capacity, the market attracted the attention of reformers, politicians and the public. Chapter 3, describes the initial barrage of petitions and bills challenging the market in Smithfield as the Napoleonic War ended and Britain began to stabilize its economy and political system. Representatives from the 'complexus' of farmers, drovers, butchers, salesmen, graziers, began to insist on a hearing in Parliament. Thus the Smithfield debate began in earnest before the Duke of Ellington ended the ambitions of Napoleon at Waterloo.

3 THE SMITHFIELD BATTLE BEGINS

Round One: Rules of Engagement

> Smithfield is going a begging: there is, as it were, a great nuisance in the market, and
> we are not surprised that nobody is willing to have it at any price.[1]

By the early nineteenth century, Smithfield, the former site for royal jousts,
became the battleground for a protracted contest over the location of the cattle
market. The years between 1800 and 1840 saw parliamentary consideration of
petitions submitted to either improve or remove the market. The testimonies of
witnesses called by the parliamentary committees revealed the issues that persisted until passage of the bill in 1851. Smithfield's cattle market was,

> ... viewed with distrust by sanitary reformers and street improvers, attacked in the
> committee-rooms of parliament and in the columns of the daily journals for number-
> less shortcomings, defended with a pertinacity worthy of better cause by those who
> insist on the sacredness of vested interests ... [2]

This chapter will set the stage for the battle by explaining the social, political and
economic context. Against this background, the issues at the centre of the struggle will emerge. Subsequent chapters will explore some of the most intractable
issues that illustrate the forces of modernity and how they played a role in shaping attitudes about the Victorian urban landscape.

As the nineteenth century arrived and the Napoleonic Wars ended, Britain
began a decades long period of adaptation to the effects of the industrial revolution. Between 1800 and 1840, political and social crises contributed to unrest
both in and outside of the government as Parliament evolved from an institution governed by the aristocracy to one gradually engaged with an enlarged
electorate. During this period, Robert Peel emerged as an example of how the
government negotiated a new political era while still clinging to tradition and
conservative values. Peel began as a Tory and gradually became a Conservative,
taking unpopular and often contradictory positions as he realized that change
and modernization required new accommodations. The memory of bread riots

in France moved Peel to engage with social and political activists in ways that would avoid a food crisis in Britain. Reform and laissez faire economic policy became Peel's means of avoiding a revolution.

A growing sense that the nation's political systems were bereft of the mettle required to adapt to a rapidly industrializing society became a concern of political economists and reformers. Anxieties about monopolies that could interfere with food markets deepened those divisions. Londoners were divided and often inconsistent in their attitudes towards government intervention in the economy.

Disparate interests mingled in a contentious discourse that crossed boundaries of private and public interests. Traffic and congestion, public health and safety and morality were the issues that defined the debate and continued with varying degrees of priority until the passage of the relocation bill in 1851. Throughout this period, urban reformers argued for a rationalized use of urban spaces that would incorporate emerging technologies such as railroads, steam power and telegraphy. Sanitation reformers were outraged that the City would allow the continued flow of blood and entrails, which posed a threat to public health. Animal welfare reformers pleaded for the safety of animals that were so visibly jostled and mistreated in the public streets. Greater representation of these voices in the political process concerned the merchants located around Smithfield who feared the potential loss of valuable trade, private property and custom from the shoppers and workers in the market. The City, the owners of Smithfield, resisted any change that would threaten the existing system of tolls and rental income.

The years of reform raised questions of the impact of change upon social, political and economic order as Londoners observed Europe's preparations for revolution. When the debate about Smithfield unfolded, butchers and other consumers of animal products wondered if proposed changes to the market would affect the timing of food purchases, the capacity of the market, the ability to compete and to obtain market intelligence, meat quality and prices. Londoners worried that government intervention in the market might interrupt the process that kept meat on their tables. The concerned public still felt it desirable to consult those individuals who participated in the Smithfield market system to ensure that their experience as 'practical men' be considered 'before any attempt is made to enforce measures for the public interest in connection with any of the arts which may not have the sanction of experience'.[3] The attitude that politics, religion and society *should* and *could* adapt kept society from plunging into political and economic chaos and instead led them to explore the contentious issues related to Smithfield's presence in the City. Concepts of how to reform, what to reform and if reform was necessary all were examined in the many debates about the market leading up to 1851. And by 1840, the question of who should do the reforming was still unresolved. During this period, reform was sought at the level of economic policy, sanitation practices, food regulations, urban design, the treatment of animals, public safety and of the trades associated with the market. Targets for reformers seemed to be everywhere.

Important events leading up to the reform years included the growth of manufacturing as the economy adjusted to the post-Napoleonic era, declines in agricultural profitability, the conflict over the Corn Laws, a drive to unionize trades and social unrest as banks failed in 1825. The reform years followed this period, influenced by the ideas of the English Enlightenment, Benthamites, John Stuart Mill and Evangelicalism. The number of local improvement acts passed by Parliament surged and included changes, not only in politics and governance, but also in urban infrastructure. This enthusiasm for the political process coincided with the resurgence of the Whigs in the 1830s. The increasing influence of the Whigs in Parliament and the arrival of Earl Grey as Prime Minister signaled the end of a period of political ambivalence about the arrival of greater inclusion in politics (with Catholic emancipation) along with intense resistance by both parties for political reform. The Reform Act of 1832 marked the arrival of a new political class, one that included the merchant class of London and one that fed the growing population of London. Although the increase in Parliamentary representation was not of a magnitude to revolutionize government, the expansion of representation and reforms in the boroughs presented more opportunities for public opinion to influence Parliament. The increasing number of petitions seeking the removal or improvement of the meat market fell within this changing political scene and the coffeehouse patrons responded with public debates.

While private individuals drinking coffee and eating meat appeared to be the dominant stakeholders, their private interests were mingled with such public issues as sanitation, health and transportation. Was the Smithfield 'nuisance' a public or a private problem? As London's municipal governance evolved, public and private institutions questioned their legal right to make changes to Smithfield. Was the City of London, as a private corporation with its rights of private property and trade, the best steward of the live cattle market? Or was the food of the metropolis a public concern best controlled by public institutions such as Parliament? Private entities like the City, farmers, salesmen, money-takers and drovers generally considered their commercial interests. Protection of private property rights motivated the arguments of private individuals and institutions that saw ancient rights as a defining characteristic of British political philosophy.

At the time, the public interest, also called the 'mutual interest', was 'the practice which will return the greatest weight and best quality of butcher-meat, while creating at the same time the least obstruction to the traffic in the streets.'[4] The public was keenly interested in public health and the unimpeded flow of goods and people throughout the metropolis. Many supported the removal of Smithfield based upon their perception that Smithfield system had malfunctioned, leading to high meat prices, unfair profits, immoral behaviour, disease and a distortion of the market system. Some critics saw the possession of market rights by the City as tantamount to a monopoly for food. Individuals owned some markets – for example, the Duke of Bedford owned Covent Garden – so the argument about monopolies was unclear. The lines between public and private interests were becoming fluid as the size of London's urban problems grew in magnitude. The battle over Smithfield was hardly a brief contest but rather a slow, laboured process. As one observer noted: 'The 'wisely-and-slow' principle, which in matters of legislation suits the genius of our people, operated to defer the final sentence'.[5]

These permeable boundaries between public and private interests created complications and mistrust. Public officials and private individuals attacked each other for seeking their own interests at the expense of the health and safety of the inhabitants of London. During the debates surrounding the removal bill of 1809, MPs expressed concern about the City as it proposed the bill 'without the parties interested having notice of their intentions' and requested 'indifferent' individuals to testify in the House of Commons instead of those representing the Guildhall.[6] Since some cattle salesmen had become members of the City's Court of Common Council, the interests of the City and the Smithfield salesmen were mingled, adding to suspicions that the City would not act in the public interest. The 'class of tradesmen', allegedly acting in the interest of the publicans (owners of public inns and taverns) in Smithfield, would lose a substantial amount of business if the market departed.[7]

Much as historians enjoy arguments that suggest that one social class preyed on another, in the case of Smithfield historians would be hard pressed to find a single group who consistently argued throughout the decades before the bill passed. Because of overlapping identities in all interest groups no one single interest group held a unified position concerning the market. Aldermen in the City were MPs, butchers were salesmen and salesmen were bankers. City officers complained that City bills to remove or improve the market were rejected because some of the members of the House of Lords also served as governors of the Charterhouse Seminary. While most butchers and the City were against the removal, some butchers and City Aldermen supported the relocation. Testimonies from the witnesses called by Parliament to its several select committees demonstrated the formation of *ad hoc* collaborations of public and private institutions motivated by technological and social circumstances.

Political and Economic Landscapes

At the beginning of the nineteenth century, important political and economic changes created a context for discussions about the future of Smithfield. By the end of this period, John Stuart Mill's utilitarian philosophy had begun to shape the view that markets needed discipline or some type of intervention by the government in order to ensure the delivery of adequate food supplies to the greatest number at a reasonable price. Mill suggested that monopolies could cause the market to fail and so the market required that the state intervene to create the type of equilibrium articulated by Adam Smith.[8] Londoners distrusted monopolies that prevented the establishment of a competing market. Putting the provisioning of London in the hands of a single individual or institution seemed risky and likely to distort prices. In the case of Smithfield, while the City held a monopoly for the trading of live cattle within seven miles of St. Paul's, Parliament argued that it had the right to remove the market for the public good. But Parliament's ability to act was limited by political ideologies that did not support its right to regulate the market. Both the City and Parliament attempted to prevent a potential disruption of the market by the middlemen whose activities lowered prices for farmers and raised prices for consumers.

Provisioning became a greater concern to the metropolis as rural labourers moved from the countryside to London. Robert Malthus's latest edition of his *Essay on the Principle of Population* came out in 1826, and his ideas were evident in the debate about Smithfield. The government called attention to the growth of London's population, the influx of rural labourers into the metropolis, and the decline in agricultural productivity. Robert Gordon, reformer of lunacy laws, reminded his peers that, 'It was the business of all good governments to economize food; if, therefore it could be shown that the present system caused a diminution of food, the government ought to entertain [a] petition.'[9]

Both those for and against Smithfield's location utilized petitions as a means to get their opinions heard and to affect the legislation of both the City and Parliament. Concerned Londoners expressed either support for the *status quo*, improvement of the existing market, or the removal of the market. Placards in windows of businesses near Smithfield invited customers to sign petitions against the removal of the market. Butchers, graziers and salesmen also sent petitions throughout the debate, beginning with a burst of activity at the turn of the nineteenth century. The use of petitions as a means of political expression confirmed individual engagement in the debate but also raised questions about the legitimacy of signatures and evidence included in the petitions; forged signatures and misrepresentation were common. Sometimes petitioners signed blank sheets. Some signers could not read and did not understand what they were signing. James Mills, a civil engineer who presented evidence in a Smithfield Parliamentary commission, revealed the weaknesses of the process. When asked if any of the signatures on his petition were acquired under false pretenses, he responded, 'I cannot say what I did not see ... '[10] His response suggested some specious use of petitions purported to communicate to Londoners 'facts' about Smithfield, which were often amplified and repeated in newspapers and journals.

Some of these petitioners were merchants who had gained new economic power through the wealth generated by industrialization. Harold Perkins points out that the entrepreneurial class that emerged from the eighteenth century found its political voice with the liberalizing of the franchise in 1832. And Peter Earle suggests that the new middle class of the eighteenth century was already expressing its tastes and economic power by consuming greater quantities of meat.[11]

Political Developments

From 1812 to 1827, when Lord Liverpool was Prime Minister, efforts to reform politics were impeded by the unstable atmosphere of radical activities, leading Liverpool to support the *status quo* in an effort to maintain order. By 1830, the select committee hearings to review a bill to remove Smithfield that began in 1828 lost momentum. No one possessed the political courage or power to overrule the City's interests. Robert Peel and Lord Russell's influence grew and the political climate warmed to the idea of an increasing role of government to act in the marketplace, and important political and economic reforms facilitated changes in urban institutions such as Smithfield market.[12]

During this period, London's governance underwent a transformation from local, parish-based control to metropolitan-centred control whereby different aspects of governance were shared among local parishes, private enterprises and municipal and national bodies. Francis Sheppard described a 'correlative tension between the drive for centralization, the desire to limit the power of government and the maintenance of a 'collection of private contractual relationships freely entered into by each individual'.[13] The Smithfield contest could have been a site where a range of British anxieties surfaced during this period of urban modernization, anxieties that not only included those of governance but also of identity and power.

The unsettled spaces of public and private interests were sites for a negotiated redesign of London's urban spaces during this period. London lacked a Haussmann-like approach to urban design or a centralized authority that had power to govern the metropolis. Some observers bemoaned that London's public markets were not rationally planned but rather reflected the hybrid local and public administration of the City.[14] Local administrative bodies and individuals offered London the opportunity to respond to the pressures of sanitary and social reforms but also delayed the possibility of looking at urban development in a systemic sense.

Since the boundaries of municipal administration were so fluid, they allowed both the City and Parliament to exert their power whenever their interests demanded attention.[15] The question of who would ultimately determine the cattle's market's fate was far from clear. Parliament and its various commissions administered the metropolis, including the sewers, rail system and lighting companies, but municipal governance was the responsibility of local parishes, wards and the City of London. The Crown and Parliament enacted laws to protect the public from high prices and unwholesome meat. The City created its own systems and practices to protect the business interests of those in the market. Robert Peel offered a compromise that included both the City and the government, stating that the appointment of Parliamentary select committees was important to all the interests in the market. He was cautious about the food markets, stating that 'Government, in this country, could not take charge of such institutions; they must be left to individuals as a great many others were ...'[16]

The regulation of the cattle market raised many issues of jurisdiction and clashed with the changing boundaries of the metropolis. As a result, enforcement was particularly problematic. J. S. Girdler, a solicitor who was concerned about the ability of England to feed its inhabitants in 1800, indicated that enforcement of laws regulating food and markets was inconsistent, hampered by the difficulties of understanding exactly how an alleged perpetrator operated and of obtaining sufficient evidence of wrongdoing. Girdler described the intent of the laws as that of preserving private interests, the 'mutual advantage of the farmer and the consumer, and under the shadow of which, God neither lost the praise, nor man the benefit of his bounty'. The statutes were intended to preserve virtue, to prevent avarice and to avoid 'artificial scarcity of any duration'.[17]

Both the City and Parliament acted to ensure an ample supply of meat for Londoners at a fair price, a collaboration of private interests and public institutions.

Even the determination of what constituted London made the establishment of a central metropolitan administration problematic. The definition of 'London' was complicated by shifting boundaries. Some representations of London included including districts such as Chelsea and Kensington or concentric circles that defined London in relation to the Post Office. Joseph Fletcher, writing for the *Statistical Society of London* in 1844, commiserated with his fellow statisticians that London's boundaries were still unclear. He declared that by then, the term 'London' meant 'the whole of the vast town and wide-spread suburbs inhabited by the metropolitan population ...'[18]

Dodd referred to the problem of the City's jurisdiction when he asked this:

> Where does London end? Shall we adopt, as our representative of the metropolis, the city of London, which ... comprises only one square mile of surface? Or the 'Bills of Mortality', which under the old system included the cities of London and Westminster, and about forty out-parishes?[19]

Defining London's urban space was only part of problem facing those who wanted to regulate Smithfield. Urban planners, architects and engineers were just beginning to professionalize in ways that would allow them to define a city space as a combination of services, geography, technology, commerce and transport. A citywide authority empowered to remove the market was absent until the appearance of the Metropolitan Board of Works (MBW) in 1855, which shared some of the administration with Parliament but did not achieve effective power until the Thames Embankment project, which began after Smithfield's removal. The evolution of this new municipal entity represented a compromise between individual private interests and a growing civic interest that supported centralized political power. This gradual change in government administration was an important factor in the effort to remove Smithfield from the centre of the metropolis. Richard Perren's analysis of the debate underlying the removal of Smithfield fairly describes the situation.

> The one body that could have cut through the web of vested interests and inertia which stood in the way of reform was itself the prisoner of these forces. Financial interests both overt and covert, prevented the Corporation of the City of London pursuing any radical policy of reform. That body did have a committee to consider the question of improving the meat markets but it merely represented the school of thought who still considered it perfectly reasonable to send droves of cattle though Oxford Street ... [20]

The relationship between the City and Parliament appeared to be amicable, since interests in both institutions were often conjoined. The City's Committee of City Lands indicated its willingness to support Parliamentary recommendations by maintaining 'every facility would be given by the City to any measure which Parliament might think fit to adopt for the accommodation of the Public'.[21] But it was impossible to ignore the slow response of the City to the bills and petitions entering Parliament, especially after 1830.

According to Joseph Fletcher, by the 1840s, the City's political power existed only 'through historical associations, the accident of position, and the continued exercise of great local trust'. He viewed the City as 'a shell of a metropolitan life which no longer inhabits it'.[22] But in spite of the growing opinion that the City was losing its political power, the city played an important role as a regulator and police force for the market. The Metropolitan police force enforced London's municipal laws after the creation of the force in 1829; up to that time, City officers or volunteers enforced regulations and laws.

Witnesses called by the select committees to consider the fate of Smithfield offered inconsistent observations about the City's effectiveness as an administrator and regulator of the market. Some accused the City of a failure to enforce existing regulations designed to control the treatment of animals, traffic, congestion and sanitation. Others felt that enforcement was difficult because the public did little to call infractions to the attention of City officials. Some merchants offered that in order to file a complaint, they had to travel to Guildhall, which was often impractical because they needed to remain at their shops. Some merchants argued that they were unable to locate a City officer when problems arose. Cattle salesman William Collins revealed that there was a 'password' used by those in the market to indicate when an officer was present, alerting the drovers to proceed carefully.[23] John Ludd Fenner, a member of the Royal College of Surgeons, said that accidents in Smithfield occurred from the 'very inefficient and irregular manner in which the regulations of Smithfield market are acted upon'. He criticized drovers who lacked badges and constables who exercised 'the least check or hindrance' upon drovers who failed to conform to the regulations governing their behaviour toward the animals. Drovers sometimes sold their badges for a drink, then fabricated fake badges to continue to operate. Rather than removing Smithfield, Fenner felt that if the regulations were enforced, 'the cruelty in the streets might be prevented'.[24] The lack of a central regulatory administration created these inconsistencies and lapses. And many felt that regulations might interfere with the operation of the market.

Some salesmen and butchers felt that the City officers were performing adequately and that practices had improved since they began supervising the market. William Clay, a woolen draper who attended the Court of Aldermen at Guildhall, was sympathetic with City efforts to enforce its regulations; he noted that the rough treatment of animals by drovers was greatly reduced after the City began putting officers in the market. Cattle salesman Charles Merritt reported that he had seen only three officers until the City increased its efforts to supervise the market. (Although the officers were directed to wear a blue coat and buff waistcoats, they were commonly accused of not wearing their distinctive attire.) Salesman John Warmington said that he 'never looked for them without finding them'. He noted that the blue coats worn by the officers were recognized by most of the men who operated in the market.[25]

When City authorities failed to act, voluntary associations sometimes helped to enforce regulations, but without much success. Butcher William Giblett, like others working in the market, felt that it was in their interest to prevent acts of cruelty so that the market would function without harm to buyers and sellers.[26] He suggested that something like the Pie Poudre Court at Bartholomew's Fair might work for Smithfield, where there would be a court nearby where immediate action could take place. Pie Poudre Courts were tribunals usually set up for markets and fairs for the purpose of resolving disputes between buyers, sellers and others who were accused of interfering with the market. Called Pie Powder courts from the French, *pied poudreux*, the name of these courts referred to the dusty feet of travelling traders. These ad-hoc means of enforcing order and civility in the cattle market existed within the context of a disorganized and decentralized metropolitan administration.

Economic Developments

Economic philosophy also played an important role in shaping the debate about Smithfield. The 'invisible hand' of Adam Smith's eighteenth century world had been increasingly visible as the nineteenth century unfolded. Evident from the repeal of the Corn Laws and Peel's easing of the trade tariffs, England's laissez-faire economic philosophy avoided interference with food markets. Any changes that had the potential of restricting a fair price, the delivery of 'wholesome' meat, or the provision of adequate supply to the growing population were eschewed whenever possible. Even a change in market days or market location could upset the intricate machinery of trade and create imbalances to supply and demand.

Business interests were often ambivalent about a possible relocation or removal of Smithfield. While an improvement of the existing market might increase trade, the removal of the market might also expand market space and encourage more buyers to attend the market. The City representative of business interets received financial benefit from the rent of pens used to contain animals in the market and tolls that the salesmen paid tolls 'dues' for animals that entered the market. These dues provided a source of income for the City, but an insignificant source since it was offset by the expense of ongoing improvements of the space. Since the meat market had stabilized, the City resisted any change that would threaten revenue and require additional investments. This rang particularly true in light of forecasts for a flat meat market.[27]

Greater benefit to the City resulted from the rents received from the businesses located in and around the market. William Savage, a cheesemonger, said, 'I would rather Smithfield remained a market as it is, liking bustle myself, than see it an open square for pleasure'.[28] Savage may have been referring to sites such as Cremorne Gardens near the Thames River where greenhouses, menageries, rides and concerts provided public entertainment. This complicated the appeals for the removal of the market, since the City possessed the market rights and revenue sources, both inimical to the relocation of the market.

Some business owners in Smithfield openly supported the removal of the market. Suggesting the origin of the phrase 'bull in a china shop', Robert Padmore, a shop owner, noted how a 'beast put his head through the window' of his shop, requiring him to post an employee by the door to prevent animals from frightening his customers. Robert Barron, a druggist in the Smithfield area, complained that people in the streets took 'refuge in our counting-house, which is a very considerable interruption to our business ... and six weeks ago, an ox came into the counting-house'. William Ascot Wilkinson, an upholsterer in Smithfield, described how female shoppers frequently sought refuge in his shop when cattle frightened them. And he and others complained about the difficulties in getting carts and wagons to and from their places of business, especially on Mondays, the main market day.[29] For these businessmen, the removal of the market from Smithfield would improve their trades and placate their female customers.

Other business interests were concerned about the negative impacts of moving the market to another location. Joseph Pocklington, a banker, felt that a market site outside the City would impede communications between salesmen and graziers and delay bank transactions moving funds from buyers to sellers. Innkeepers and pub owners who stood to lose business if the market left, were continuous objectors to removing the market. John Bumpas, a bookseller who lived on Skinner Street, pointed out that numerous innkeepers who provided accommodation to those who came to the market would be among the biggest losers if the market were relocated.[30]

Businesses such as blacksmith shops and saddlers where drovers and others associated with the market purchased supplies and purchased services also would be affected. William Hickson, a shoe warehouse owner in Smithfield, felt that if a 'large and commodious building, under proper regulations, was built for the meat trade, 'the opposition would immediately cease'.[31] Hickson, like many other merchants, thought that the removal of Smithfield was unlikely. Many entrepreneurial individuals felt investing in improvements in Smithfield rather than relocating would enhance its commercial value to themselves and others.

Some merchants in Smithfield were willing to support the relocation of the market as long as their property rights were respected.[32] The retail butchers viewed their shops as their personal property and felt that a removal of the market would interfere with their rights of property ownership. These merchants made clear that their approval of the market's removal was dependent upon some just level of compensation for lost business and resulting inconveniences. The issue of property rights would resurface throughout the subsequent decades.

Social and Cultural Considerations

Social and economic change expanded the range of individual interests heard in Parliament. As both Dror Wahrman and John Brewer argue, the growth of the middle class and an increase in participation in the political process during the eighteenth century contributed to changes in political power during the early nineteenth century. The public became increasingly engaged with the social and political changes occurring in London.

The voices of London consumers were influential in the political process. The growing number of publications available to Londoners during this period, such as newspapers, had become a thriving conduit of information to a society newly aware of the empirical process, 'scientific knowledge', and the ambiguous nature of 'facts'. The press reported the deliberations about the future of the Smithfield market that took place in taverns and coffee houses throughout London. Publications associated with animal welfare described the gruesome details of Smithfield slaughterhouses and advocated the market's removal. With the liberalizing of the franchise as a result of political reforms in 1832, members of Parliament realized that public opinion would be a significant factor in their re-elections. The press and public opinion pushed and prodded the MPs and the City into action, either to improve the market or to remove it. The press played to the middle class interests and the general distrust of Parliament and of government officials in the vestries.

The popular press appeared sympathetic to the removal bill, although some publications, including the *Edinburgh Review* and the publications of Charles Knight, such as the *Penny Magazine*, did not support it. Thomas Challis, a meat salesman, accused *The Times* of quashing the 'public voice, closing its columns continually against any views that differed from its own'.[33] *The Times* was in favour of the removal of Smithfield, as was the *Morning Chronicle*. *The Times,* hostile to the City's interests, fanned this distrust in its columns, railing against the City's reluctance to remove the market as the decades passed. William Alexander McKinnon, a liberal conservative and advocate of free trade, called *The Times* 'The great leader of public opinion in this country ... the Bude-light of the press, and which was remarkable for either following or leading public opinion on all occasions ...'[34] Literature appropriated the Smithfield scene to provide depth to other political narratives set in the City. Political cartoons found Smithfield rich in metaphors for commentary about Parliament or about the market removal itself.

The House of Commons select committees on Smithfield were undoubtedly swayed by public opinion. Mackinnon wrote a treatise about public opinion, stating that the 'The House of Commons was the organ of public opinion'.[35] While Mackinnon's view was probably hyperbole, some observers thought that the testimony of witnesses in Parliamentary committees inquiring into the Smithfield market was 'the shortest answer to any of the attempts to swell out the attacks of two or three of the members of the press into an expression of public opinion'.[36]

Early Actions and Reactions

As the dissenters raised their voices and social and political reformers gathered both courage and momentum, public pressure to move Smithfield led the City to undertake a more structured and focused effort in the form of market improvements. While Parliament and the City regulated the activities of Smithfield, the City of London began its extended and protracted efforts to enlarge and improve Smithfield. The private interests of the City and those who worked and owned property in Smithfield pushed against the rising tide of public opinion that argued that Smithfield had outgrown not only its space but also its position at the centre of the metropolis. The City looked for ways to increase the size of Smithfield while also providing licences, inspections and oversight of the activities of middlemen.

Figure 3.1: 'Miseries of Human Life, ...', describing dance steps required to avoid injury by the bulls in Smithfield. George Moutard Woodward, *c.* 1800.

During the first decade of the nineteenth century, the City repeatedly approached Parliament with proposals for improvements to Smithfield.[37] The City presented a petition to enlarge the market in 1802, but Parliament tabled it – more pressing issues were demanding attention including the wars in Europe and the agitation to abolish the slave trade. Subsequent petitions for enlargement of the market were submitted in 1803 and 1805. In 1805, St. Bartholomew's Hospital offered the City twelve acres near Goswell Street near the Charterhouse as a new site for the market in order to move the market farther away from the hospital. In 1806, Sir Charles Price, a successful banker and former Lord Mayor who represented Smithfield in Parliament, proposed additional regulations for the market.[38] In 1807, Parliament discussed a similar petition, and in 1808 the City proposed to purchase property along Long Lane, the street that bordered the market, in order to increase the size of the market.[39] Those in favour of the City's plan applauded the 'pulling down of old sheds, and ruinous buildings ... a great part of which are already the property of the Corporation of London'.[40]

The cattle salesmen were against the idea of expanding the market, maintaining that its size was adequate. Protecting their interests as the sole representatives of farmers in the market, they argued that graziers were unreasonable in demanding more room. They thought that a better arrangement of cattle and the elimination of traffic at certain times would placate the butchers' concerns about congestion in the market. They also berated those who complained about the necessity of tearing down buildings in order to enlarge the market by pointing out that the buildings in question were sheds, vacant, and a 'Harbour for Thieves'. Conversely, the salesmen were skeptical of the City's estimate for enlarging and improving the market, suggesting that the actual expense would increase the price of meat and would actually be 'a tax on Agriculture'.[41]

In February 1809, Sir Charles Price submitted a bill to the House of Commons to remove the market, stating that the market 'was too confined to answer the purposes for which it had been originally intended'.[42] Although the City initially wanted to expand the four-acre and one-half acre market to twelve acres, it acknowledged that it was only likely to be able to procure an additional two acres. The government's Board of Trade felt that enlarging the market in this way was futile; it agreed that the market needed at least twelve acres to meet the needs of the growing meat market.[43] Alderman Combs represented the rather confused view that 'all those who live where the present market was held wished it to continue there, and all who lived where it was intended to remove it to, objected to such removal'.[44]

Lord Bathurst, Master of the Mint and President of the Board of Trade, convened a subcommittee to explore the contending proposals for Smithfield. He reported to the City 'another consequence of the removal will be the increase in value of the estates of foreigners, while those of the citizens will be reduced in the same proportion. Should we not call that nation improvident which parted with several branches of its commerce'. Foreigners were inhabitants of London that were not 'freemen' of the City of London. He lamented that the removal of the meat trade to a site outside the City would expand trade to non-citizens and threaten the trading rights of London citizens.[45] It was also unlikely, the Board thought, that the rise in tolls would offset the expenses incurred by the City for the acquisition of additional lands and the tearing down and rebuilding of the slum dwellings.[46] The Board concluded that although an enlargement of the existing market would 'provide for such progressive increase of the business of the market as might reasonably be expected', it would be unlikely that an enlargement of the market would 'meet the convenience of the public in any manner what ever'.[47]

St. Bartholomew's Hospital was against the removal because it feared that its property would decline in value without the market, but this position was not supported by all hospital representatives. The hospital administration was divided. One governor of the hospital believed that the removal would improve property values. The House of Commons agreed with the governor that removal of the market would lead to a general increase in property values. Others worried that a market expansion would allow St. Bartholomew's Fair, a raucous annual event, to expand into the larger Smithfield space, increasing 'the Quantum of Riot, Confusion, Vice, and Immorality' in the City. MPs pressured the City to upgrade the Smithfield neighbourhood by rebuilding around the market where slums and dilapidated housing contributed to Smithfield's deleterious reputation.

Although it may seem that the butchers were united in their opposition to the relocation of the cattle market, some of butchers were also against enlarging the market and were instead in favour of a new site. These divides in opinions may have evolved from the different interests of wholesale and retail butchers. Some wholesale butchers argued for moving the market to an area north of Smithfield where cattle could pass to and from the market without impeding traffic. Graziers and salesmen joined the butchers, exasperated by the City's apparent inertia and its conviction that the only solution was the enlargement of the existing space.[48]

The Board of Trade attempted to intercede in the debate and began to take action. Concluding that the only way to increase the size of the market was to move it to another site where it would be less onerous to acquire space, the Board of Trade recommended that Parliament go about using its power 'to compel the owners and occupiers of ground eligibly situated to sell the same at such prices as should be estimated by a Jury'. The members of the Board were confident that Parliament would extend the necessary market rights for the City to the new site.

The City eventually proposed two sites for a new market, one near Gray's Inn Lane and one near Sadler's Wells, although some expressed concern that a site near the Gray's Inn Society might impinge on the activities of the barristers who studied there.[49] Other possible sites included fields and tracts of land ranging from six to almost twenty four acres in surrounding areas, including Spa Field, owned by the Skinner's Company, and several areas around Bagnigge Wells Road.[50] Some of the land was owned by the New River Company, a company that was constructing a system of pipes to deliver water from the area around Islington to the City.[51] A 14–acre site in Islington, almost three miles north of Smithfield was also considered.

The parties seemed unable to agree on an alternative site. The graziers thought that they might not be able to find space for their stock in Smithfield if the market continued in the current site. George Ponsonby, leader of the Opposition in the House of Commons, expressed his concern that the City would usurp the private property rights of those in Smithfield if the market moved elsewhere. Some conservative MPs could not understand why change was necessary at all. Henry Martin, a Whig MP from Ireland, who described himself as 'one of those old-fashioned persons who continued to labor under that inveterate prejudice of former times ... ', supported the deferment of the bill and declared that it was 'absolutely impossible for them to find out any better spot than the present site'.[52] Any change in the market worried Smithfield landowners who felt that they could not rent their buildings because they might need to relinquish their land to make way for market improvements.[53] An optimistic City suggested that an expansion of Smithfield would cost half a million pounds, which would be paid back by raising the tolls on animals, thus eliminating the need to add to public debt.

However, no agreement was reached on how to proceed. Most engaged in the debate about the market's future felt that the problems associated with Smithfield might continue wherever the market was placed. Some critics of the market hesitated to inflict Smithfield's problems on another location. With no consensus on a new site, the MPs felt obliged to defer serious consideration of the bill.[54] Not without a sense of humor, the Attorney General, Spencer Perceval, soon to become the only assassinated Prime Minister of England, suggested that the only way to alleviate the noise and confusion of the cattle in the market would be to ask the City officers to accompany the beasts on the way to the market.[55]

The bill also proposed to change the market days from Monday to Tuesday and from Friday to Thursday.[56] The intent of this move was to reduce the number of animals in the market at any one time. If Friday's market could be moved to Thursday, then animals slaughtered on Thursday could hang in butchers' shops on Friday for sales on Saturday, a popular retail market day. However, cattle salesmen were against any change in the market days, maintaining instead that the market should continue 'without the Interference of any legal Order or Regulation whatever upon the subject, but effected by a System that has grown out of the Wisdom and Experience of Ages, and so completely organized in all its Parts. The Petitioners cannot but feel that any Alteration which would tend to disturb the smallest Portion of the Arrangement, may prove a most dangerous Experiment'. The City was also against changing the market days.[57]

Concurrent with the discussion about Smithfield's market days, the nineteenth century also brought a general increase in the number of market days in London. Throughout the debates about Smithfield's location, the select committees in Parliament and participating witnesses continued a consideration of a change in the frequency and placement of market days in Smithfield. While Parliament's grant for a market typically included limited specific market days, Parliament increasingly allowed for daily markets as consumer demand increased during the early nineteenth century. Changes were complex and far-reaching since markets existed within a timed and often sequential relationship to other markets. This was particularly the case in the relationship between the wholesale and retail markets. The market days of Smithfield, Newgate and Leadenhall were dependent upon one another. As the discussions about changing Smithfield's market days escalated, butchers and salesmen became concerned about the impact upon the activities of other Smithfield market activities, such as the hay and straw market and the horse market. These concerns were never really addressed before the market bill passed.

While some urged changes in market days, others were more skeptical. Samuel Gurney, a member of the Common Council and a bill broker, spoke out against a removal of the market, representing the interests of the 'purchasers of cattle' in Smithfield. He cautioned that concerns about the increase in the number of cattle brought to Smithfield were based on an exceptional few years when short-term demand from the Royal Navy increased. An increase in demand, he argued, would be met by country-killed meat that would 'operate as a check upon the business of Smithfield Market'. He felt that his critics were 'meddling with a trade which they are wholly unacquainted with', and 'out of their depth'.[58]

The concern about the proximity of other markets also bothered the salesmen who pointed out that butchers often moved between livestock markets in order to find the best price and best livestock. They argued that if there were more than one livestock market in London, butchers would have difficulty establishing their prices, suggesting unwanted competition. And, the rearranging of the drovers' routes would upset the existing established routes that had served the market well for centuries, delivering the animals in the quiet of the night when the streets were empty.[59] With these debates still ongoing, the bill proposed in 1810 languished in Parliament and the future of Smithfield remained unresolved.

In 1813, the House of Commons proposed another bill for enlarging, improving and regulating the market.[60] The recommended enlargement was only an additional three-quarters acres, with the improvements consisting of restrictions on cattle driving on selected thoroughfares. Opposition came this time from Charterhouse, a nearby hospital on the grounds of the old Carthusian monastery. Those supporting the improvements argued that the market existed in its current location before the hospital. The City acknowledged that 'the *Bleating* [sic] of the Sheep, during Market Hours, may be rather more plainly heard at the Charter House' after the improvements, but felt that the enlargement of the streets near the hospital would increase property values.[61] The City succeeded in limiting the number of booths at the St. Bartholomew's Fair but failed to limit traffic through the market from six o'clock in the morning until noon because the streets were out of the City's jurisdiction.[62] The City considered other improvements, but no further bills appeared in Parliament until 1828.

Meanwhile, salesmen, butchers and merchants in the Smithfield area decided to join the City's efforts as members of the Court of Common Council. Armed with the support of local publicans (pub owners) and influential ties with the butchers' guild, these individuals formed the resistance within the City to the removal of the market.[63] The publicans, in particular, were impressive constituents in the Smithfield neighbourhood; their interests became synonymous with the public good, which the publicans understood as access to public houses ('pubs').

Despite this opposition, the House of Commons continued to receive petitions for the removal of Smithfield. Agitation for political reform mounted. Sir Yorke suggested that the 'nauseous details' of the activities in Smithfield sent a 'general vomit through the House'.[64] Change was imminent, but the elements for change in Smithfield had not yet materialized.

Some MPs, like Colonel Trench, an avid improver of buildings in the metropolis and a follower of utilitarianism, thought that London should follow the example of the Parisian slaughterhouses. 'Nothing could be more perfect ... ' and 'worthy of imitation', agreed Henry Parnell, agricultural protectionist and supporter of the Corn Law of 1815.[65] In 1818, public abattoirs (originally conceived by Napoleon) opened in Paris. The Parisian system intended to eliminate the need to drive animals across Paris since several public abattoir on the outside of the City took in animals from the different regions of France.[66] There were two markets and five public slaughter facilities. Even though English observers promoted the Parisian system, they were careful not to embrace the French. They navigated the thin edge of bi-culturalism by prefering the French system over the English while embracing English meat and rejecting French culture. Engineer Mills admired the Parisian system of abattoirs and Gurney, who visited Paris to observe the system 'not thinking it would ever be the subject of inquiry in this country', found his observations entirely useful for purpose of his testimony to the committee. Mills said, 'to borrow and take an example of them' was entirely acceptable. But Gurney was not impressed. He said, 'Every thing in London is superior to what you see in Paris, whether it relates to meat or any thing else'.[67]

Detailed descriptions of the French system appeared in London periodicals and the Paris slaughterhouse system became a model for reforms.

Alderman Matthew Wood, son of a serge maker and a hop merchant, pointed out that the City had already proposed several bills for removal and enlargement, impressive evidence of its commitment to alleviate the problems. Alderman Robert Waithman, was also critical of the 'great odium' directed at the City in spite of the fact that the City had done much to improve Smithfield. In contrast to others' admiration of the Paris model, Waithman denounced the Paris slaughterhouses as poor substitutes for the markets in Newgate and Leadenhall.[68]

On June 12, 1828, the House of Commons referred the various petitions to remove Smithfield market to a select committee, which convened on June 28 to consider 'the Slaughtering of Cattle in the Metropolis'. Almost seventy butchers, salesmen, London inhabitants, doctors, graziers, clergymen and business owners testified during the hot, humid days of the summer of 1828. The witnesses included several butchers, livestock salesmen, merchants in Smithfield and the surrounding areas, several ministers and a vicar, members of the Corporation of the London (the City), and a soldier. These witnesses revealed how the public perceived Smithfield, their perceptions of political power, and the details of market operation.

The debate within the City, in Parliament, and in the press centred on congestion, commerce, animal welfare and civility. After all that the City had done to improve the market, the butchers, graziers and salesmen were sceptical that much would come of yet another effort and were concerned that further improvements would only further increase tolls and therefore their own costs. (The City had restricted carriage traffic through the market during market hours.)[69] The select committee considered three proposals: The removal of the market, the enlargement of the existing market along with the regulation of traffic on market days, and the continuance of the existing market with the addition of several outlying secondary markets.[70] Witnesses called by Parliament contributed to testimonies from a wide range of social classes and occupations.

While diverse interests were represented, the list of witnesses all confronted what it meant to provide credible information to the select committee. The complicated meanings of fact and evidence do not detract from the effects of witness testimonies or the use of petitions but point to the necessity for cautious consideration of their importance to the removal of the market.

During this period, witnesses described how they gathered information to inform their opinions about Smithfield. Similar to those who went to Paris, reform-minded individuals conducted their own surveys by visiting the businesses of the butchers and salesmen who worked in the market. One witness visited several slaughterhouses in London for the purpose of gathering information to support his testimony. Land agent Henry Jemmet took his friends with him to investigate the slaughterhouses in Whitechapel, to 'learn the state of the case ... ' and to make themselves 'masters of the subject'.[71] In some cases, the committee criticized a witness for not being aware of information presented by other witnesses that would contradict their own. The groups of men who toured butchers' shops reinforced their opinions by associating their 'facts' with their own empirical investigative process.[72] Salesman Warmington, who offered detailed descriptions of the market, explained that he 'knew the practice of the market' and the 'confusion' through the eyes of his men 'as if I was there'. Butcher Cramp asserted that his estimate of losses because of overdriving animals was confirmed by others: 'We are sure, not only myself but many persons in the trade, that the damage must be at lest that; many persons are of opinion it is considerably more'.[73]

Witnesses often reinforced the authenticity of their facts by arguing for the integrity and reputation of the individuals who provided them with information. Engineer Mills declared that his sources were a 'deputation [of butchers] of a most respectable class': that 'all agreed in the correctness' of his facts. Mills defended his statistics, stating that, 'I cannot judge any more than any other gentlemen'. When Mills was asked about the veracity of his claim that 'exrementitious matter' made animal food unhealthy, Mills retorted, 'It is a matter of fact'.[74] Reverend Daniel Wilson had 'every reason to believe [it] from what is constantly told me by my churchwardens ... and a multitude of persons'.[75] The observations of the physical realities of Smithfield, acquired by others, often replaced direct observation and relied on the impressions of realities, not 'facts' gathered by first hand accounts.

Some witnesses employed suspect methods for gathering information. Fenner testified that he bought a slaughterman a drink in return for allowing him to observe him at work; he admitted to being less than honest about his purposes by telling the slaughterman that he 'came from curiosity'. In some cases, witnesses were unable to provide names, dates, or places for the sources of their 'facts'.[76] Some provided precise accounts of the gruesome slaughter of animals but they dodged requests for names of drovers, salesmen, or butchers who were the subjects of their testimonies. In some cases, even when the committee provided a list of names, witnesses refused to identify any one individual by name. Mills said that he 'did not come here to implicate any individual butcher', especially if it brought on 'an odium, nor expose [himself] to the complaints of butchers, and bring forth the indignation of a set of persons who I believe [were] as desirous to avoid cruelty' as he was.[77] Deference was still part of the English character, and as social barriers were becoming more and more transparent, Londoners were mindful of the need to protect relationships that might be useful in the improvement of one's social status or business dealings. These trusted relationships provided order and stability during a time of change and reform, and the witnesses were not about to sacrifice these relationships to the government.

It is not clear how Parliament selected the witnesses that appeared before the select committees. Dr. John Ramsbotham, an 'accoucheur' (a physician for pregnant women) declared that he was 'entirely ignorant' about the reason for his appearance in front of the committee. Apparently, one of his patients was married to a Smithfield butcher and the committee saw his relationship as an opportunity to inquire about the effect of Smithfield upon the family's health. Expecting criticism of the market in Smithfield, the committee was confounded by Ramsbotham's testimony. He denied that the smell of putrid meat was in any way harmful to public health.[78] The committee may also have selected witnesses whose testimony was based on evidence gathered from the worst types of slaughterhouses in the metropolis. Describing Whitechapel, one of the least respectable areas for animal slaughter and unsavory trades, Jeremiah Barrett, a founder, (person who works with metal) characterized it as 'one of the most wretched of the wretched places in the Metropolis'.[79]

Some witnesses appeared at the behest of others. Reverend Blackburn of Islington admitted that he was 'not at all interested in the alteration of the market ... and that certain persons asked him to testify because he had complained about the noise and the 'violation of the Sabbath-day'. He confessed, 'I am not a volunteer here; I attend because I was summoned'. Others like John Fowler, a half-pay lieutenant, had no interest in the market before learning about the inquiry but became passionate about cruelty that he subsequently observed. Fowler testified that he saw drovers with long stick and pikes beating animals our of 'wanton cruelty' as 'animals were tortured ... for twenty minutes, by three or four people'.[80]

Witnesses often contradicted themselves. The butcher Michael Scales rejected the idea that the facilities were cramped by pointing out that the slaughterhouses were built to accommodate large animals. He said that all but about four or five slaughterhouses in Whitechapel had wide shared alleyways that enabled animals to move between buildings and wide doors to accommodate the fatstock. When called back to testify a second time, Scales retracted his earlier testimony about wide doors and stated that ten slaughterhouses had no alleyways. Some witnesses gave incorrect information about the number of butchers in London or the number of animals in the market. Fiction was often stated as fact, and facts were slippery, often changing within the same hour.

Other witnesses brought their technical professions to bear upon the investigation. In his capacity as civil engineer, Mills rented an apartment in Smithfield and investigated the treatment of animals. He measured the space for tying up animals and came to the conclusion that the market could support only 1,170 oxen, a calculation that shaped his plan for a new layout of the market. He also calculated the number of cattle in the off-droves and side streets that did not pay tolls to the City because they were not tied up, proving that the limitations of space led to lower revenues for the City. He reviewed past records of City tolls and discovered that only 821 oxen were tied up, not even utilizing the full capacity of the market space. The observations and the conclusion that the market was too small were, according to Mills, based upon 'mathematical certainty'.[81]

Some witnesses added gruesome details to their testimonies, suggesting that the witnesses engaged in courtroom theater to persuade the committee to a point of view. In his account of the slaughtering practices of Whitechapel, Mills described how one animal required seventeen blows before expiring, after the slaughterman broke its tail, 'jumped upon its loins', and poured water into its mouth until it stood up again to receive its final blows.[82] References to these seventeen blows appeared throughout the testimonies, as if they represented a common practice among butchers.

Most of the complaints were based on observations of the market as it appeared during the Christmas holidays and Mondays when most of the trade took place. The implication was that the market operated at that capacity throughout the week, even though most observers knew that was not the case. Butcher Giblett was quick to correct the committee when they cited statistics from the Monday market as if they were indicative of the entire week, stating that the market statistics were, 'on an average, rather less' on other days.

The hearings themselves provide opportunities for understanding the role of evidence and raise the question of objectivity in the political sphere. Could it be that the select committee had already made up its mind and selected witnesses to corroborate its decision? The nature of the questions posed to witnesses suggests that the committee was seeking confirmation and authentication of a particular point of view. Witnesses such as William Darnton, a Quaker, and surgeon John Ludd Fenner, a member of the Society for the Prevention of Cruelty to Animals, predictably offered evidence concerning animal cruelty in favour of removing the market. Some Londoners who observed the debates by City officials and Parliament concluded that both bodies selected witnesses to support their position, which was not conducive to an unbiased debate. A group of Smithfield merchants and inhabitants wrote in 1834 that 'the Committee of City Lands had listened to the representations of a few publicans, salesmen and butchers, and that not a single person who was known to entertain different opinions ...'.[83]

Some of the witnesses, called 'Christian philanthropists', participated in the 'March of Intellect' characterized by Asa Briggs in his description of progressive reform during this period.[84] These individuals sought 'the facts' concerning their City and attended coffeehouse 'lectures' to become informed about civic issues.[85] Their concern about Smithfield came from a utilitarian ideology that advocated for more rationale systems and for a 'scientific' answer to social problems. They met in such places as the London Tavern and the Freemasons' Tavern to compare their observations and their impressions, of the problems associated with the market. Other civic improvers organized exploratory trips to the slaughterhouses of Whitechapel and other meat markets to gather empirical evidence in support of their impressions. These witnesses were informed more by idealism than by experience. Henry Jemmett, a land agent in Smithfield, admitted that his testimony was a result of 'having joined myself to some gentlemen who have taken the same view of the subject with myself; since that, I have paid more attention to it'. Several witness expressed their opinions as a 'general feeling'. One witness, Dr. James Alexander Gordon, confessed that his testimony resulted from 'sentiments expressed in common conversation. He indicated that his perceptions were not indicative of 'general opinion', just the opinions of his friends who came to his house.[86]

The butchers were typically offended by accusations from the 'philanthropists' that appeared disconnected from the realities of animal behaviour and slaughtering practices. The butchers, the 'practical men', those who worked in Smithfield, were the antithesis of the gentleman farmers who sought improvements in agriculture and the social reformer who thought animal slaughter too barbarous for modern times. One publication made this suggestion:

> ... in a free country like this, where individual interests are so plainly expressed, it is always prudent to consult them practically ... first before any attempt is made to enforce measures for the public interest in connection with any of the arts which may not have the sanction of experience ... practical men, such as farmers and butchers, have a right to be practically dealt with.[87]

After hearing all the evidence, the committee concluded that the 'necessity of due caution' prevailed. They cited 'much personal interest, confirmed habit, and inveterate prejudice' as the reasons for a deferred resolution to the complaints about Smithfield, and urged the City to adopt short-term remedies to ameliorate the difficulties associated with the market.[88] While the committee had gathered compelling evidence for removal of the market, its members concluded that no matter where the market was, the inconveniences would follow. They recommended that the City begin enlarging the space for the market and that traffic to and from the market through the main thoroughfares be further restricted during market hours. In addition, the committee proposed changes in market days that would even out the volume of traffic in the market.

Resignation and Response

In October 1828, after the House of Commons committee called its last witness, the City responded. The Committee of City Lands, charged with the responsibility for the City's markets, delivered a report to the Court of Common Council. The recommendation of the select committee in the House of Commons for an enlargement of the market became the central focus of the City committee and they once again began to look for land that would be suitable for this purpose. The committee also proposed to end the horse market that had generated frequent complaints about the 'bad characters' and frequent sales of stolen horses. The committee felt the horse market would not be missed and was 'not necessary for the public convenience'.[89]

In 1829, in order to accomplish these activities and changes, the City committee asked the Common Council to submit a bill to Parliament for approval so that the City could acquire the funds for the market improvements. A new market, Farringdon Market, replaced the Fleet Market and in 1829 opened near Smithfield. By the 1830s, the debate about the cattle market in Smithfield had defined the main issues that would be contested in subsequent bills and petitions leading up to its relocation. Concerns relating to congestion, public health and morality repeatedly surfaced in Parliamentary inquiries and led to consideration of larger issues such as the status of private property rights, government power and authority, and the stability of a society under pressure physically, morally and socially. Smithfield had become a reference point for rethinking the urban landscape in London.

Other Proposals and the Perkins Market

In 1832, a pamphlet written by a country meat salesman presented a proposal in that hinted at the path ahead in the next decade. A salesman for twenty years in the City, Stephen Munday declared that the market was 'the foundation and source wherein all the evils spring ... ' Slaughterhouses were the 'root of the evil'. His pamphlet suggested that the live cattle market in Smithfield be relocated outside the metropolis near other markets in Southall, Barnet and Croydon. Parliament could establish abattoirs or public slaughterhouses in the country near these markets and prohibit any slaughter of animals between those abattoirs and the metropolis.[90] A wholesale meat market west of Newgate could sell the meat from these abattoirs and Parliament could create wholesale markets in the west to sell country-killed meat. He was sure that the 'practical' men in the trade would see the wisdom of this system and eventually adopt it, recognizing that the new arrangement would 'reduce expenditure and promote trade ... and ultimately benefit the country at large'. His plan also included some innovative ideas such as the suggestion that farmers could use waste from the abattoirs as manure.[91]

Revealing his bias towards country-killed meat, he lauded the quality of the meat from animals 'taken quiet and cool' from the fields. Country meat, he said, kept longer, was 'in better order, with less waste, even in the hottest weather in Summer'. His proposal was prompted by his observation that the public was 'lethargic' about country meat and that if something was not done to revive interest in the meat it would 'become in time, nearly, if not wholly – extinct'.

Munday saw that the butchers would have to 'give way to the advance of public improvement' as they joined the "March of Intellect" adopted by the other London trades. The country butchers, he said, 'cared not one straw which way or how their goods are disposed of ... so that they obtain the best price'.[92]

Noting the estimated annual profit of £2,000 that the City gained from its operation of Smithfield, Munday calculated that the City could almost triple its income by converting its Smithfield space into a dead meat market. He attempted to assuage the Smithfield butchers and salesmen who might feel threatened by his proposal by suggesting that they could benefit by utilizing their connections with the country butchers to acquire higher quality meat for the London markets. Butchers and salesmen would be able to sell their meat in several new markets west of Newgate in an area ill-served by meat shops.[93]

One individual published another plan in *The Monthly Magazine* with the invitation for others to contribute their ideas to 'fill up the detail'. He suggested a new building at the centre of the market for the sale of meat, an upgrade from both Newgate and Leadenhall markets. All animal slaughter would occur outside a four-mile radius from the Post Office (near Smithfield) and every day of the week would have a specialized market: two days for meat, other days for vegetables, corn, flour, straw and hay. He allowed that there would still be a day for horses and cows, 'a partial evil', and Bartholomew's Fair would specialize in onions.[94]

Others brought forward alternative plans and utopian schemes for London's cattle market.[95] One proposed that the market be located in St. George's Fields. A literary magazine,the *Athenaeum*, accused the promoters of ties with *The Voice of Humanity's* abhorrence of 'slaughterhouses and the driving of cattle through the publics streets' while arguing for more slaughterhouses in the area south of the Thames. The publication suspected the promoters bringing the slaughterhouses of Smithfield that were 'positively injurious to the public health' to the area south of the Thames in order to raise subscription money.[96]

No event revealed the increasing anxieties about the initiatives of private individuals more than a bill for a private market in Islington. The Islington Bill of 1833 proposed the construction of a new market and abattoirs in Islington and the removal of Smithfield. A group of businessmen led by John Perkins initiated the bill, acting out of commercial interest and a desire to provide an alternative to the Smithfield market. Described as a reformer who was 'independent in mind as he was in property', Perkins spent his own money on this 'benevolent and gigantic undertaking' to alleviate the 'miseries to which the animal creation was unnecessarily subject'.[97] Newspapers portrayed Perkins as a 'Radical' who threatened a 'free, open, and unrestricted market, which is not merely convenient to, but promotes the interests of all parties'.[98]

Predictably, a group of butchers, salesmen and graziers met in Butchers' Hall to organize their opposition. Butcher William Giblett and salesman Richard

Hicks were especially outspoken. Giblett pointed out that the bill would certainly be against the public interest, contained a 'specious pretext', and was a 'mere job' for someone who sought a monopoly of the meat trade. Hicks was outraged at the 'grossest falsehoods' and 'base misrepresentations made against a useful class of tradesmen' circulated by publications such as *The Voice of Humanity* promoting the Islington Bill. In defense of leaving the market in Smithfield, Hicks pointed out that the select committee of 1828 had failed to find compelling evidence to show that 'the slaughtering of cattle was prejudicial to the health of the inhabitants'.[99]

Since most of the 1,500 butchers near Smithfield were in the retail trade, the butchers indicated they would refuse to use the Islington abattoirs. The butchers noted that Smithfield had 'taken centuries to establish, and which has [had] proved to the inhabitants of the metropolis, to the agricultural interest, and to the country at large, a source of affluence and wealth'. They were also optimistic about the City's efforts to continue with its improvements to the area. Benjamin Stubbing, a representative from the City and a butcher and salesman, outlined how the New Road, a project in construction, would eliminate the passage of cattle through Holborn and thereby mitigate some of the traffic congestion in the area. The butchers maintained that the removal of the market to Islington would deny them the advantages of a local, convenient site for their trade and represented a threat to private property and competition. The butchers and salesmen also objected to two cattle markets, and felt that as long as the market in Smithfield continued, another market in Islington would only confuse buyers and sellers. Charles Pearson, the City Solicitor, argued for one market, arguing that two markets would 'disturb the trade of a useful class of persons graziers and butchers' and 'would unhinge [their] relations'.[100]

In 1834, the debate escalated. The parish of St. Sepulchre reacted to the possibility that the market might be moved to Islington or elsewhere. Since the City paid the parish for land in Smithfield, the parishioners became concerned that they would lose an important source of revenue if the City market were relocated.[101] Concerned that the new market would disrupt tenants in Smithfield, almost two-dozen parishioners petitioned Parliament to assure a continuance of rent for their property. Parliament responded with the assurance that the City would continue to pay rent for any new public venture in Smithfield and, if the City declined to begin a new venture, surely new tenants would pay higher rates to the parish since the market would have removed elsewhere.[102]

Salesmen met in George Tavern to refute the assertion, appearing in various reports, that they supported a cattle market in Islington. They gave a 'most unqualified Contradiction to such Statement, and declar[ed] it to have been wholly unauthorized by us, and which has evidently been used as a means for advancing private interest against the common weal'. At the same time, a group of farmers and graziers presented a petition to Parliament against the Islington Market Bill and in August, the City applied to Parliament again to enlarge the market by purchasing surrounding property.[103]

Parliament's preference was for the bills proposed by the government and the city, not by a private individual. Perkins proposal provoked controversy and complications on multiple levels. The City came under attack for appearing to resist the removal of the market by putting forth an additional bill for market enlargement and Parliament sought a legal remedy for overruling the City's ancient charter for its market rights in Smithfield. A central complication of Perkins bill was the legal right of the City to limit other markets within seven miles (from St. Paul's Cathedral) proscribed in the market rights given by royal charter to the City of London. While the House of Commons avoided this legally nuanced issue, the House of Lords debated it in detail and agreed that since the right existed, it could be abrogated if the existing market was unable to be enlarged to accommodate the number of cattle. The new market could handle surplus demand, 'to supply the deficiency, but no more'. The Lords decided that allowing a new market within the seven-mile limit specified in the royal charter, required an act of Parliament. The City fought the bill, arguing that another market in Islington would be 'injurious to the old market, and therefore void'.[104] But, even after the City spent almost £7,000 to oppose the bill, held a celebratory dinner party when they mistakenly thought that the bill had been defeated, and invested £30,000 to enlarge the market, the Islington Market Bill passed in 1835.[105]

In 1836, Perkins opened his cattle market on Balls Road in Islington.[106] Perkins had been accumulating land since 1830 and had built the market by 1835. (In 1833, his market passed inspection by a group of 'scientific, literary, and professional men' including Sir Anthony Carlisle, co-inventor of electrolysis, and Dr John Haslam, The Mad Doctor). They were impressed by 'the spirit of the projector'. Optimism radiated from those engaged in the new market project. After one afternoon of hard work, the workers celebrated their success as they stood on top of one of the buildings, 'supplied with abundance of wine', singing 'Success to the Mart'.[107]

The appearance of the new market excited those on both sides of the debate.[108] In January, 1836, butchers, graziers and salesmen met to refute allegations that they had any interests 'beyond the advantages they will reap in common with all those who attend such New Market – viz., an opportunity of exhibiting the Stock consigned to them by the Grazier for Sale, in a proper and commodious manner, which it has been most satisfactorily proved cannot be done in Smithfield'.[109] No sooner had the meeting adjourned, than a boiler belonging to a steam engine at the Islington site used to construct iron rods for sheep pens exploded. The engine, 'blown to atoms, and the fragments scattered all over the market', killed two men and severely injured three others who were taken to St. Bartholomew's Hospital.[110]

Drovers, salesmen and butchers argued that Perkins's self-interest, largely viewed as monopolistic, threatened the public interests. It is likely that the main source of resistance came from the London butchers who refused to give up their private slaughterhouses. The 'self-interest' of Perkins was the main objection of those who eyed his market with suspicion. The Smithfield salesmen saw their market as 'true to Conservative principles', promoting the 'interests of all parties' and not satisfying the 'self-interest of one, the cupidity of some, and the speculative views of others'. The butchers argued that Smithfield enabled them to purchase cattle 'direct from the grazier' and 'as regularly sold the same day'. They suspected that Perkins' market encouraged forestalling and other abuses by middlemen, all threatening to raise the price of cattle for the butchers. Some Smithfield salesmen transferred their loyalty to Perkins' market and attempted to convince their fellow traders in Smithfield to do likewise, but without success. The *Times* remarked that a 'Mr. Lehaire, formerly a respectable salesman at Smithfield, was busily engaged in that market this morning, canvassing the butchers to 'come and buy' at Islington', but failed to get enough support. In May 1836, John Stimpson was unable to sell his cattle in Islington and, after waiting until noon without success, attempted to take his cattle on to Smithfield, but was not able to because the Islington Market insisted he cut the tails of his cattle before departing, indicating the cattle were already sold.[111]

Perkins's market hinted at what was to come almost twenty years later when the Metropolitan Market opened in Islington. It occupied fifteen acres, an open space located on the main road that drovers travelled with livestock on the way to Smithfield. Four areas separated the animals in the market place, which could accommodate 7,000 cattle and 40,000 sheep, a space much larger than Smithfield. Ten-foot-high brick walls enclosed the space that contained lairs with slated roofs 'supported by no less than two hundred forty-four plain Doric pillars'. Two water tanks fed pipes that directly filled troughs for the animals that remained in the lairs from one market day to the next. The spring-fed water troughs, 'at any season of the year, must prove a great relief to the cattle'.[112] A windmill powered the pumps that delivered the water into the troughs. 'Hard bricks' and drained pavements satisfied concerns about sanitation.[113]

The market incorporated many of latest designs for ironwork, drainage and lighting that had been developed by such engineers as Charles Fowler, who designed and engineered the new Covent Garden market during the early 1830s. Unlike the open market in Smithfield, Perkins's market was enclosed, representing the new market spaces that were appearing throughout Britain during this period.

In spite of the market's modern and technologically advanced design, sixty-seven salesmen fomented resistance against the Perkins market and refused to patronize the new 'innovation'.[114] The innovations that Perkins had built in the market included machines that could weigh animals, giving 'the exact weight of every beast', which threatened the practice of measuring by the eye or hand. Thus, salesmen and butchers were fearful that less skilled individuals could enter their business. Graziers who sold cattle directly to butchers without employing a salesman were also the targets of salesmen who saw that new practices might threaten their position in the market.[115]

As it turned out, Perkins's market failed as an alternative to Smithfield. On Friday, May 20, 1836, the comparison between Smithfield's sales and that of Islington illustrated the failure of salesmen, butchers and drovers to move their business northward. Further, it appeared that the sixty-one animals sold that Friday were carried over from the previous Monday as unsold stock. Perkins's salesmen purchased stock from graziers in Norfolk in order to sell them in Islington, but failed to anticipate the lack of support from those engaged in Smithfield.

Perkins seemed to have gotten off on the wrong foot from the beginning. Perceived to be interested in his own pecuniary gain, at the expense of the public interest, he further disenchanted those in the Smithfield system by attempting to obtain an Act of Parliament to close the market in Smithfield. This brash action further confirmed the damage Perkins might inflict upon the meat trade if he monopolized the cattle market.[116]

The City's efforts to discredit Perkins combined with the lack of support from those situated in Smithfield were fatal to Perkins' enterprise and the market closed seven months after it opened. Even his well-intentioned efforts to design a market engineered with technologies that would alleviate the problems of Smithfield were not enough to move the business away from Smithfield. It appears that Smithfield had to be closed first to eliminate widespread anxieties about multiple markets. In addition, the legal status of the City's trading rights was still not clarified to the satisfaction of many observers. The City began to look for other sites in response to a series of demands suggesting alternative locales. It would still take decades before political changes, public attitudes, and reform transformed the urban landscape to open the way for Smithfield's removal. Short-term remedies appeared more desirable both to the City and Parliament, deferring risk and in recognition of the entrenched habits embedded in the meat provisioning system.

As noted earlier, three main issues dominated the debate about Smithfield: space, public health and morality. In the following chapters, we examine these issues in detail and the technological changes that eventually facilitated the agreement in 1851 to relocate the market.

4 SMITHFIELD'S URBAN LANDSCAPE: SPACE IN TRANSITION

Today I chanced to pass thro' Smithfield, when the market was three fourths over: I mounted the steps of a door, and looked abroad upon the area, an irregular space of perhaps thirty acres in extent, encircled with old dingy brick-built houses, and intersected with wooden pens for the cattle. What a scene! Innumerable herds of fat oxen, tied in long rows, or passing at a trot to their several shambles; and thousands of graziers, drovers, butchers, cattle-brokers with their quilted frocks and long goads pushing on the hapless beasts; hurrying to and fro in confused parties, shouting, jostling, cursing, in the midst of rain and *shairn* [dung] and braying discord such as the imagination cannot figure.[1]

The select committees considering Smithfield's removal revealed an increasing public awareness of the influx of labourers into the city and the resulting congestion and competition for space. Office workers and tradespeople, street hawkers and pedestrians all shared the streets with animals on their way to market. This was untenable. Something had to make room for modern London and Smithfield's open space was tempting those who sought relief.

The social, technological, political and economic tensions of the first half of the nineteenth century pushed, prodded and reorganized London's urban geography. Humans and non-humans moved through winding, uneven spaces and streets that became wider, straighter, smoother, cleaner and brighter. Meat provisioning became mechanized through the application of steam and iron technology that engineered a modern landscape in ways that would compress time and space.[2]

Smithfield's nuisance value, both imagined and real, evolved out of its location and size. Urban growth, reform and technology descended upon Smithfield in its central location. Journalist Andrew Wynter, a London doctor who specialized in insanity, wrote this in 1854:

This scene, which has more the appearance of a hideous nightmare than a weekly exhibition in a civilized country ... is absurdly and disgracefully confined ... .[3]

Between 1800 and 1850, London's population grew from about 959,000 to 2.6 million. In 1837, metropolitan London encompassed twenty-two square miles and a population of two million. By 1900, London included one hundred twenty square miles and five million people.[4] The impressive if not meteoric increase belied some paradoxical trends. For example, between 1801 and 1851 the population per acre in the City remained the same and soon after declined. In the parish of St Sepulchre, where the cattle market resided, the population between 1801 and 1851 held fairly steady except for a 10 percent increase during the 1840s when the railroads transformed the landscape in that area.[5] These statistics concealed the suffocating density of animals and humans that descended upon the area as labourers came into the City to work and as animals and humans moved into and through the market in Smithfield.

Place, Position and Problems

The geographical location of the market shaped much of the debate about Smithfield. Its proximity to the centre of London created confusion and congestion; it meant that Londoners were constantly aware of the realities of animal slaughter. Because of the growth of wholesale markets in the City, many of those working in the live cattle market saw its central location as its most important feature. In a letter to Lord Russell, Thomas Challis, a London butcher, expressed his view that convenience was the traders' paramount concern and that 'the superiority of a central position' served the trades' interests.[6] Close to the slaughterhouses, retail meat market, carcass processing trade, banks and consumers, Smithfield was at the nexus of Britain's meat-provisioning network.

Angus Reach characterized Smithfield as a 'suburban field [that] has become an opening in the most populous city in the world. In Miltonic phrase, it is the 'very navel of the world. Narrow streets and swarming lanes branch from it like the threads from the central hold of a spider'.[7] But the arachnid was becoming troublesome to a population who saw the Smithfield market as an obstacle to commerce, civility, health and morality.

Several environmental factors influenced the original establishment of the area outside the Roman walls.[8] Antiquarian maps of London reveal a landscape that contained many elements that made the area a suitable location for a livestock market. Two rivers situated near the Thames formed a terminus for the network of roads and rivers that brought trade to and from London as long ago as the first century when the Romans occupied *Londinium*. At that time, the Fleet and Walbrook rivers flowed on either side of Smithfield, bringing water to animals and carrying away detritus to the Thames River.[9] The ebb and flow of food and waste carried on these water networks connected the market to a national and international provisioning system.

A network of roads connected the market to the countryside and beyond. The largest road, St John Street, fed the market from the north and the smaller roads channeled animals, humans and meat throughout the metropolis. To the south, Blackfriars Bridge created the conduit for animals travelling to the market from the south of London.

Smithfield's geographic identity was also reflected in its relationship to the City walls.[10] The location of the market outside the walls implied separation from the ordered society within. More than a physical boundary, the walls separated the legal and structured environment inside the walls from the unregulated activities of the market. The walls divided free society, freemen, the law, legal trade and guilds, from foreigners, outsiders and outlaws.[11] The market's proximity to the walls also implied its ancient roots in the established myths of London's creation, in medieval charters, knights and tournaments. The narrative of the City within the walls included Smithfield's history without.

'London' was the City within the Walls that included one square mile, or six hundred acres that included the City within the Walls and the City without the Walls (eleven parishes, the Inns of Court and Chancery, Blackfriars and White-friars precincts.) The City within the Walls had become 'one vast counting-house and warehouse', a 'vast mercantile emporium or factory' by the nineteenth century as most of the bankers and traders had moved to the suburbs. Farrington Without (created in 1394) near the City within the Walls, included Smithfield. Other designations of metropolitan identity included the City of Westminster and the Bills of Mortality. Fletcher presents this conclusion:

> The obvious imperfections of all these boundaries compels us still to seek some other, and to inquire whether, to the present day, there really has been drawn no boundary of the metropolis for any political or administrative purpose whatever which would mark, by its aptitude for some definite purpose, the limits within which comprised the whole of the population that can fairly be considered metropolitan in locality and in character.[12]

The confusion about boundaries combined with the embedded meanings of location within London's urban geography complicated a decision to uproot the market from Smithfield.

Renewing, Reforming and Redesigning Urban Spaces

After the Great Fire of 1666, Smithfield became increasingly congested as the City absorbed an increasing number of out-of-work labourers from rural areas. Londoners began to address the 'old tottering and dilapidated buildings' that 'almost def[ied] delineation' and the growing number of slums.[13] The ideas of Jeremy Bentham and evangelicalism fueled an enthusiasm for urban improvement and Smithfield was a logical target for such reform.[14] Utilitarianism would become a moral mandate for Victorian reformers who saw public and private markets as an opportunity to create greater utility for London's urban spaces.

Self-appointed city planners like John Gwynne produced plans that rationalized the design of London's buildings and streets to accommodate the pressing needs of an expanding population and a growing economy. Gwynn, born in 1713, a self-taught architect and engineer, applied his skills to de-Wrenify London buildings and was an articulate advocate of the improvement of several of London's districts, most notably, the City and Westminster. He thought that the cattle market had been 'obliged to be kept in Smithfield, or Smith's field, a field without the walls, near enough to the center of the metropolis to rend it convenient, but at the same time properly situated to prevent those inconveniences which at this time are so justly complained of ... ' By the early eighteenth century, the cattle market had become 'nuisance at once extremely dangerous as well as inelegant and inconvenient'. In a grand gesture of urban renewal, he recommended the construction of the Thames embankment, a sewer system and the removal of Smithfield.[15] Over a century would pass before his ideas reached fruition in London's modern urban landscape.

In the late 1700s, new and wider roads appeared in and around Smithfield to accommodate the increased traffic created by the appearance of cabs and hackneys. The replacements of the New Road (1756) and Blackfriars Bridge (1769) were attempts to ease the tension between pedestrians, animals and horse-drawn vehicles. Blackfriars Bridge was, and still is, the bridge over the Thames located off Farringdon Road and was the main route for animals travelling from south of London to the market. The New Road was intended to move the cattle from Oxford Street to an East/West route that would bring traffic to Islington where it would travel down to the market on St John Street.[16] These roads and bridges tested wrought and cast iron technologies that were useful in the design of railways and the covered market designs of architect Charles Fowler's Covent Garden during the late 1820s.

Additional improvement schemes surfaced to reduce congestion and to raise land values. *British Farmer's Magazine* pointed out that the City 'might nett [*sic*] much more from ground rents in a handsome street or square on the six acres upon which the legal and illegal market stands'.[17] In addition to new streets, these efforts included the removal of buildings, improved drainage and the building of railways and bridges. Several of these were in the Smithfield area, including Fleet Street, Clerkenwell and Holborn areas, and did much to lay the groundwork for increased rents and taxes sought by the City. A new post office opened in 1829 on St Martin-le-Grand, near Smithfield, increasing traffic down Aldersgate Road from the north.

Londoners remarked upon this energetic tearing down of buildings and digging up of streets. The *Builder* complained, 'No sooner is a pavement laid in concrete, and the way seemingly plain and permanent for years to come, than bands of navigators take possession of the tessellated granite, edge, pick and delve the almost adamantine crust and sink trenches for new rills of water or columns of gas'.[18] During the 1820s, The City removed much of the Saffron Hill area and extended Farringdon Road, preparing the area for later construction of rail lines and new housing. Throughout this period, the City covered over more of the Fleet River. Later, during the 1840s, the Clerkenwell Improvement Commission (1847) planned a massive rebuilding of the area surrounding Smithfield that would further break up old streets and build new structures along new thoroughfares.[19] The commission attempted to extend Farringdon Street through Clerkenwell Green but was unable to obtain the necessary financing and finally turned the project over to the City in 1851.

As a result of these projects and the impending incursion of rail lines, Smithfield was a space in transition and upheaval.[20] The public knew that the City was considering either an enlargement of the market or its removal. Businesses were aware that their future existence was caught up in the unresolved location of the market. Tenants were all too well aware that their homes were in the crosshairs, either as targets of rebuilding or acquisition by the City. Every time an action by the City resulted in a new traffic pattern or new hours for the market, businesses had to adapt. The debates in the City and in Parliament eroded any sense of permanence in the neighborhood and portended a questionable future that prevented new businesses and tenants from putting down roots in Smithfield. These events suggest that the landscape around Smithfield was open to renegotiation as local parishes, the City and Parliament deliberated over funding, technologies, politics, legalities and municipal governance. By the 1840s this loosening up of the ground, the stirring of roots, contributed to the opening of possibilities that the market could move during the next decade.

Space Reformed

As the landscape underwent renewal and rebuilding during the first several decades of the nineteenth century, markets also changed. Between 1820 and 1870, as the demand for food increased, Britain responded by expanding its market spaces and improving its landscape. The number of public markets decreased as they were replaced by individual retail activities that moved out of formal markets into the surrounding neighborhoods. Formal markets began to account for less and less of the total retail trade.[21]

Market reform situates Smithfield within a larger context of architectural design and institutional change. During the debate about Smithfield's location, market design changed from open, uncovered spaces to either market halls or enclosed, covered markets. The government's role as market regulator increased, and Parliament became more active in the development and design of public markets. The trend towards greater regulation became part of a growing acknowledgement of the government's duty to protect public interests such as free trade, public safety, access to food and public health.

Between 1801 and 1870, ninety-eight Parliamentary acts increased government control over markets, usually in the form of increased regulation. During the period between 1841 and 1850, when the Smithfield bill was considered for the last time, almost half of all the market reform bills passed.[22] Integral to these efforts to reform the marketplace was the redesign of the market space. Open markets became enclosed, and Smithfield appeared destined to move from an organic, open space to an enclosed, geometric space. Market halls, such as Covent Garden, took on these new forms where gates and tall brick walls surrounded engineered spaces and enclosures.

These new, orderly market spaces became part of the re-engineering of Smithfield.[23] Both the exterior and interior spaces of the market underwent change. The wholesale butcher Benjamin Stubbing felt that the removal of foot paths through the market and sheep pens on the pavement would open up additional space for traffic. By improving the use of the space, Stubbings observed, the City could provide more rails for tying up the cattle, adding to the capacity of the market.[24]

The size of the market space in Smithfield was hotly contested. Those that argued that Smithfield was too small presented abundant evidence about the effects of crowding on the operation of the market. Reformers argued that inadequate space caused drovers to abuse animals, the salesmen to miscalculate the value of animals, and damage to pens and railings. Some butchers argued they could not approach an animal on all sides in order to assess its condition and price it correctly. One observer, W. Pittman, wrote in 1826 that the 'crowded state of the market' provided the buyers and sellers an 'imperfect view of the animals', creating a 'disadvantage' to both when prices were incorrectly calculated.[25] Cattle salesman Charles Merritt saw the problem in Smithfield as the result of the 'misarrangement of the market', that could be redressed by an enlargement of the market. He thought that the mere addition of half an acre would solve congestion along with the removal of sheep pens, which would allow cattle to be tied in the market instead of being put into ring droves outside the market.[26]

These new market designs included market halls that changed the structure and appearance of markets in Victorian London. An architectural expression of the growing Victorian consumer culture, market halls transformed food markets into spaces that combined both pleasure and consumption, instilling order to a previously uncontrolled and undisciplined space.[27] They emphasized public safety, sanitation and orderly commerce. Innovations included central clock towers, enclosed and drained areas for animals, and engineered passageways that moved people and animals without harm to each other. These new market spaces created predictable patterns for movement and reassured middle-class shoppers that the market was safe and convenient.[28] Market halls engendered a community of consumers who were pleased to engage in their shopping rituals in a new, ordered marketplace, sanitized and respectable. Enclosed by walls, these new structures featured improvements in light, drainage, pavement and ventilation, and utilized new technologies such as cast iron and glass construction.[29]

Within this larger context of reform was the idea of replacing the large public markets with smaller regional markets outside London. The prospect of building such markets to take the load off Smithfield was considered but dismissed because of the complication of the City's charter for market rights within seven miles of the City walls.[30] Some observers suggested dividing Smithfield into several markets around the periphery of London, thereby dividing one large nuisance into several tenable nuisances.[31] Several proposals arrived in Parliament and the City for the division of Smithfield in this way.

Those in the livestock trade, including butchers and salesmen, were unimpressed by these proposals, and many were ardently opposed. Butcher Giblett calculated prices for his meat based upon the quantity of stock in the market. A single market, rather than multiple markets, facilitated this process. While he did not actually walk through the market in order to gather his market intelligence, he gathered information from salesmen and relied on his own observations in order to determine his prices.[32] The retail butchers preferred to see all the market animals in one location because of the particular requests of their customers and 'nobody but themselves' could make the best selections for their clientele. On the other side of the issue, some butchers, like the wholesale butcher Edward Bartram, bought sheep wherever he found the best animals. He patronized other markets if he could not find a good deal in Smithfield.[33] The markets in the periphery of London were just far enough away from London as to not be considered competitive markets. Benjamin Stubbing, a wholesale butcher, felt the graziers would not know where to send their animals if there were more than one market and that the resulting confusion 'would materially injure all the trade of London'. Benjamin Stubbing worried that multiple markets would disrupt the market system for years to come.[34]

Salesmen disliked the proposals for multiple markets since they feared that buyers would compare prices and force the salesmen into price fixing. The salesmen also worried that fewer customers would attend the separate markets, lessening the competition for sales. The salesmen felt that it was important to know the whole of the market at any given time and that separate markets would make this extremely difficult. They argued that, in order to operate in fairness to the consumer, it was necessary for the buyers to know the quantities of animals, and the prices of byproducts and live and dead meat at one moment for the entire market.[35] The salesmen in Smithfield connected the provinces with the market and each salesman had his own network of relationships within the provinces that they felt were able to create the 'best market' for their customers. Salesman Merritt said, 'such is the inclination of every grazier to send where he considers the greatest number of buyers ... the choicest buyers'. He was convinced that even if multiple markets were established to replace Smithfield, after six months they would fail, returning the cattle market to its singular position in Smithfield. Salesman Guerrier said, 'The greater the number of purchasers we have around us the better for the sale'. He said, 'Both buyer and seller have an opportunity to purchase and sell the article to the greatest advantage, the purchaser goes with an opportunity of a greater choice, and the seller with a better opportunity of getting a market'.[36] The principles of Adam Smith seemed the accepted model for the market's operation, although the resistance to multiple markets belied a fear of free market competition.

Multiple cattle markets would also require changes in cattle traffic in the metropolis. No substitute for Smithfield would entirely eliminate the drovers and cattle on London streets. If a market were to be located north of London, cattle would still need to cross through the metropolis from Kent and Surrey. (Some cattle passed from Smithfield to Portsmouth and Maidstone where they crossed the English Channel to European markets.)[37] All proposals that entailed a northerly site for a new cattle market or any arrangement of sites north of the Thames still had to contend with the need to move cattle through the metropolis. Grazier and salesman John Warmington, an advocate of 'subsidiary' markets, explained how at least one-eighth of all cattle in Smithfield arrived from the south of England, especially for those droves that traveled from ports such as Portsmouth. The surgeon John Fenner felt that four markets in the suburbs of London would eliminate the need to drive animals through the City. Graziers were not typically against removing the market a few miles outside of London as long as there was only one market and that there were no additional market days since they disliked the idea of having to make additional trips to and from the market.[38]

Moving markets farther away from the City had other ramifications. Salesmen and butchers depended upon the banks located in the City to process cattle sales, payments and remittances. Smithfield was near cattle banks, the Bank of England, the Post Office and the offices of the country banks. A recurring objection of salesmen to the market removal was the potential for delayed payments. By moving the market farther away from the banks, it was likely that owners of cattle would not receive payments the day after a sale. Butcher Stubbing suggested that remittances would have to wait longer because of the late hour of the market closing and the time required traveling to a bank. If a draft was unacceptable to the seller, then the buyer may not have time to acquire the cash required to pay for the animal. Stubbing thought that locating the market farther away from the bank 'would be the ruin of many people'. But this objection never gained traction in the select committees. Some witnesses seemed unimpressed by an increase in the distance between the market and the banks. Even Stubbing confessed that the banking issue was 'a very small point'.[39]

In the context of these efforts to rearrange and relocate the cattle market, individual entrepreneurs attempted to interest the City and Parliament in replacing Smithfield with their own markets. James Mills presented two plans: one was for a market west of Highgate-hill, located near the North Road on a hill with adequate drainage; the second was to be near the Battersea Bridge, convenient to cattle coming from the south of London. Surrounding abattoirs would operate much like the Parisian system; four abattoirs would serve both markets. His plan would replace all livestock slaughter within the City with slaughterhouses around London connected through an oval circuit. Barges and carts would deliver meat from the slaughterhouses to the metropolis during the night to avoid congestion on the streets during the daytime.[40] Like several of the other proposals made by well-intentioned individuals, Mill's system was insensitive to the butchers' fierce sense of independence that fueled their resistance to public slaughterhouses. Other proposals surfaced, such as one that featured a market in East London at the edge of the Thames and another proposal that would establish four markets on the periphery of the metropolis so that animals entering the city from any direction would not have to traverse the city to the market. All failed to capture the imagination of the public or of Parliament. Suspicions of personal gain, monopolistic practices, and interference established relationships, similar to those that arose when John Perkins built his market, persisted during the 1840s.

Space, Enlarged and Improved

When it came to debates concerning the size of the market, perceptions often did not correspond with the realities. Urban reformers generally felt that Smithfield's capacity was inadequate to feed London's population and that its growing traffic problems were untenable. Even before the nineteenth century, the City made efforts to address the concerns about Smithfield's size. In 1794, the City acquired land from the Mayor of Rochester to widen the area along Long Lane between the market and Aldersgate Street.[41]

The public had widely varying concepts of how much additional space was required to eliminate the problems associated with Smithfield. Some suggested half an acre; others double or triple the space. Salesman Charles Merritt, who sold both sheep and cattle, thought half an acre adequate.[42] In 1828, the select committee inquired about the outer limits of the need for space and asked if there were such a thing as too much space for the market. Salesman John Warmington argued that too large a space inhibited the drovers from controlling the animals. It was unlikely that those that worked in the market could come to an agreement concerning the need for more space.

Ongoing efforts to expand the cattle market in its current location were problematic and collided with changes in land values, existing slums, the City's desire improve the space for existing businesses in Smithfield, and the harmful effects of the market cited by reformers. Just the issues related to the land alone complicated the debate about removing the market. Current residents were fearful of any change that would entail the removal of residences or businesses in order to add land to the market. Some of the witnesses in 1828 felt that the City ought to purchase the additional land and that it would not cause the City any financial hardship since the public believed that the City had ample funds to invest.[43] Others, such as butcher Stubbing, felt that the City was all too willing to invest excessive amounts of money in urban improvement projects, inferring that the City lacked financial discipline. And the City's proposals for enlargement, which consisted of adding two or three acres to the market at a time, seemed feeble in comparison to the images of streets filled with hundreds of animals waiting for space in the market.

The City added some space along Long Lane in 1815 and between 1833 and 1835, it spent almost £25,000 to enlarge and improve the market.[44] Between 1848 and 1849, it spent almost £7,000 more to add more sheep pens and pavement. It pointed out that while the market originally accommodated 100,000 cattle each year, by the early nineteenth century 150,000 cattle were crowded into the market every year.[45] After Peel lowered and eventually removed the tariffs on foreign livestock in the 1840s, livestock imports began to arrive in Smithfield, moving the annual totals closer to 250,000 cattle. In 1853, 277,000 cattle filled Smithfield, two years before its removal to Islington.[46]

Over the decades of debate, the City had succeeded in enlarging the market to include six and one half acres, far less than the twelve acres promoted by many of the reformers. Many of the houses on land that the City wanted to purchase were leased to individuals or businesses. The purchase of land became complicated by the length of lease contracts and often put land out of reach at the time the City's plans included specific land purchases. The City argued that it owned the land because of the royal charters for trade on the Smithfield site. Others, such as Mills, saw the City's ownership limited to the gates, hurdles and other structures that it used to operate the market.[47]

The City often came under fire for its role as landlord, appearing to force tenants to live in houses filled with animals from the market. One issue of *Punch* in 1849 amused its readers with an account of City lodgings in Smithfield with 'bestial advantages: On the Level with our Kitchens is where they keep a Quantity of Bullocks. And Level with the Parlours they keep a Quantity of Pigs &

Calves. And level with our First floor they keep a Quantity of Sheep ... and Underneath all of these sheds there is a large Cavity, of which they Slaughter a Quantity of Pigs, Both on Sundays as well As Other Days'. *Punch* also took aim at the City tenements called, Greenhill Rents, where the author suggested that 'a sufficient number of Corporation worthies' should live in the buildings, 'the more stolid with the bullocks; the more stupid with the pigs and calves; and the more simple with the sheep'.[48]

Some butchers were keen supporters of an enlargement of the market and presented petitions to the City for remedies to their tight quarters. They also wanted water for the cattle standing in the market, better paving in the market, and some alterations in the layout of stalls and pens. Some salesmen were not as convinced that space was the problem in Smithfield; when asked if the difficulties in sorting and controlling cattle would be alleviated if there were more space, salesman Warmington would answer that space was needed only 'in some measure'.[49] The graziers were desirous of additional space to allow them to send more animals to market; in their view, limiting the market to the existing space would restrict landowners in the country from any increase in live stock sales. Generally, most felt that the market would operate more efficiently in a larger space. The City Lands Committee, which later became the Markets Improvement Committee, continued its interest in enlarging and improving Smithfield.

The opinions of these individuals in the Smithfield meat provisioning system illustrate how a change in one part of the system could impact the entire system. Indeed, an enlarged market space had ramifications throughout the system. A removal of the market had even greater significance since a new location implied a restructuring of traffic to and from the market but also a consideration of greater capacity in the marketplace. What about traffic?

Traffic – Human, Animal and Carriage

As London's population increased, so did pedestrian, bovine, ovine and equine street traffic. During the months of peak market activity, which included November through December, roads and approaches surrounding Smithfield were filled with droves of cattle from the early morning hours until the afternoon, coming and going from the market. According to at least one observer, the cattle were 'wedged together in one compact mass'.[50] The greatest conflict between cattle and carriages appeared to occur between four o'clock in the morning until noon on Monday. The traffic on the old narrow roads suffocated pedestrians, impeded commerce and ignited accusations of animal cruelty. Drovers collided with hackneys, wagons delivering goods to warehouses were unable to proceed through the City, and the wet and slippery ground was hazardous to horses with carriages in tow and to pedestrians attempting to make their way to and from the

City. Workers, especially those who had recently arrived from the countryside, were affronted by the images of physical and animal force in the midst of their new lives as Londoners.

Animals and pedestrians competed with vehicles in the narrow streets surrounding the market. During the 1820s and 30s, new forms of transport joined the hackney coaches and stagecoaches, crowding the streets even more.[51] Omnibuses and cabs, all horse-drawn and all joining the increasing pedestrian traffic on the narrow City streets, contended for space in Smithfield.[52] Cattle salesman Guerrier had been 'driven down against [his] own beasts in consequence of the carriages coming in'.[53] Timber and coal wagons that traveled from east to west across Smithfield often encountered droves. The wagons seemed almost as dangerous as the animals at times, and some argued for the redirection of the wagons over a removal of the droves. One Londoner complained that animals injured humans more than humans injured animals.[54]

Many of the streets surrounding Smithfield were narrow with sharp corners, problems for both long wagons and drovers. Animals, by nature, resist moving through areas they cannot see, so drovers had to use pressure to move them around blind corners. The area around the Old Bailey and Ludgate Hill were examples of these narrow areas and caused considerable consternation to pedestrians, businesses and drovers.

This scene of confusion and mayhem on the City streets was assembled by the convergence of at least seven streets that brought pedestrians, animals, hackney carriages, carts and wagons into and through the space. These streets operated as conduits of beasts, humans, and their freight night and day. The public imagination about Smithfield was filled with images such as the one that appeared in the *Times*. In Smithfield, ' … the drovers may often been seen clambering, with lighted links in their hands, over the backs of the beasts, in places where it has not been possible to leave a free passage between the animals … remind[ing] one of Milton's or Dante's account of the regions guarded by Cerberus [the three-headed dog that guarded Hades] than of the orderly arrangements with which the business of a civilized community is usually conducted'.[55] These scenes, described with florid details in the press, became emblematic of urban chaos rejected by Victorian moral sensibilities.

The confusion on the streets around Smithfield also frustrated local merchants. Some businessmen in Smithfield refused to live nearby, insisting that it was too dangerous and noisy. A druggist on Giltspur Street, Robert Barron, claimed that he feared for his family's safety as his wife and children passed through the market. He said that his neighbors had a 'general dislike to the continuance of the market'. Thomas Pritchard, an oil merchant in Smithfield, shared similar feelings of dislike for the market. His wagons could not move oil to and from his warehouse, which strained his horses because they were forced to frequently stop and start with their heavy loads. But since his was a wholesale business and unrelated to the meat business, he submitted to the necessity for congestion around his place of business and felt that the removal of the market would have an insignificant impact upon his business.[56]

Business owners in St Bride's Wharf, near Farringdon Street and Blackfriars Bridge, testified about the traffic problems caused by cattle passing through their neighborhood. John Pocock, a businessman at St Bride's Wharf, complained about injuries to cattle and accidents involving teams of horses transporting goods through the same streets occupied by cattle. He said, 'Our men have run over a beast's foot, and we were jambed [*sic*] between large droves of beasts'. Charles Hopper, a coal merchant, complained about injuries to his horses and injuries to sheep encountered by his horses; he found it necessary to avoid the Smithfield area and to travel out of his way in order to carry coal to his customers.[57]

During the 1830s, the City imposed regulations to address the congestion in the market during peak hours. It mandated that passageways be kept clear in the market, that barriers be erected at the ends of streets where animals were entering, and that the use of off-droves be eliminated. The Lord Mayor, under pressure from the Smithfield inhabitants, agreed to limit traffic on several occasions after the traffic problem was 'represented in such a manner that he condescended to accede to it'.[58] Newspaper reports of the City's efforts to remediate problems such as traffic often contained irony, mindful of the City's loss of political clout in solving such matters.

Newgate, the nearby retail meat market, was extremely congested because of its narrow streets and the invasion of carts and baskets used to convey meat into the market. The butchers were just as guilty in some cases of adding to the traffic-related danger when transporting carts of meat through the markets. Butcher Giblett admitted that even though he admonished his men to drive slowly, he 'had many accidents', including once when a 'lad of mine, a very careful driver, killed a horse'.[59] Shrugging off the select committee's suggestion that that meat slaughtered outside the city be transported to the London market in carriages, Giblett asserted that accidents caused by animals and drovers 'are so few compared to the very many instances of persons who lose their lives from the fast driving of persons'.[60] Butchers had to be careful not to overly criticize the congestion in the streets if they wanted the market to remain in Smithfield.

Often the criticism of butchers centred on other businesses that impeded the flow of buyers into Newgate. The butchers tended to resent the incursion of vehicles during the peak market hours and some felt that the removal of such vehicles as 'brewers drays' would so greatly improve the traffic flow in the market that the 'trade at large would be happy to contribute every thing [*sic*] to have that blessing'. William Clay, a woolen draper, said, 'it is utterly impossible, the carriages going through they are jammed in so that they cannot do any thing [*sic*]'. Salesman Merritt spoke of the congestion caused by men who used drays to convey goods. He noted how they would run over people, shove animals, and operate with impunity.[61]

Salesmen, such as Merritt, and others who worked in Smithfield, joined those who passed through and around the market to reconsider how man and beast should occupy London's increasingly modern space. The increase in commerce and traffic collided with the outdated infrastructure, one that was in the process of being impinged by a transforming new technology, steam and its ability to propel even more people into the metropolis upon steel rails.

The Iron Beast

In 1844, William Turner presented the Royal Academy with his painting, *Rain Steam and Speed – The Great Western Railway*, an impressionistic tribute to the work of Victorian engineers like Isambard Kingdom Brunel, who had completed a bridge over the Thames River in 1829. The painting portrayed how steam, speed and railways perforated the metropolis with tunnels, stations and tracks. Victorian railways represented an amalgamation of the sciences of steam, metallurgy and engineering. New transport networks led to radical changes in the seasonally driven meat provisioning system. Promoters of new railway companies saw railways as the solution to the cries for relief from traffic congestion and this required a reconstruction of the space that Smithfield occupied.

The Victorian railway was the engine of commerce that entered London's landscape throughout the years leading to the removal act in 1851.[62] Beginning in the 1820s, steam technology and railways made inroads on, above, and below London's landscape, providing the possibility for meat to arrive on London's dinner tables from farms at a greater distance. The economies of scale made possible by transporting cattle and meat from the country, would keep prices low and provide higher quality meat. Technologies that built the London railway network evolved out of the need to transport an increasing amount of food to London's growing population at lower costs and at faster speeds.[63] The timely arrival of railways shaped London food provisioning activities both by reducing congestion and by increasing delivery speed and distances between the market and production. The transition away from live cattle to meat represented this shift as the transportation costs of meat influenced a cost/benefit tradeoff by the mid-nineteenth century when it was more effective to send meat to Newgate, especially mutton, by rail.[64]

Dodd makes much of the arrival of railways. He begins one section of his book, entitled *Rapid Transit An Aid to Food-Supply*, with the declaration, 'Time is money!' Dodd acknowledged that food transportation relied on the economies of speed because of the distances between production and consumption and the perishable nature of food. He explained how 'food becomes too costly when a high freightage was added to the original value ... in many articles of animal and vegetable produce, speedy transport is essential to cheapness on other grounds. Further, the deterioration of produce (meat) lowered prices and added to the necessity to find means of transporting meat close to the point of consumption where the carcasses were butchered at the point of sale to the consumer'.[65] Dodd captured the relationship between the location of the market, transport, meat, pricing and quality.

Others would follow with similar calculations of the economic considerations of transportation speed and markets. Dionysius Lardner, a nineteenth-century science writer and economist, produced *The Railway Economy* in 1850, an insightful book about the economics of speed and transport relative to various commercial products. He clearly articulated the problems associated with meat distribution. 'A part of the cost of transport consists of the interest on the cost of production chargeable for the time elapsed between the departure of the article from the producer and its delivery to the consumer'. He particularly addressed the exigencies of food: 'Numerous classes of articles of production become deteriorated by time, and many are absolutely destroyed, if not consumed within a certain time'.[66] Lardner recognized the depreciated value of animals while they travelled to Smithfield as they suffered injuries and lost weight. During the summer, heat only hastened this deterioration. Cattle salesman Merritt said in 1828 that he lost up to £3 for each animal that had been bruised or injured. John Cramp, a Whitechapel butcher, estimated that losses incurred by injury to animals was £62,400 a year, at three shillings per head for cattle and beasts and six pence per sheep as both a retail and wholesale butcher.[67] Aware of these experiences in Smithfield, Lardner came to this conclusion:

> To convey ... live cattle from a great distance, not only speed but evenness of motion is indispensable. Now these two requisites cannot be combined by any other means than the application of steam-engines upon a railroad.[68]

Both Lardner and Dodd recognized that technologies that increased the speed and uniformity of meat transport would change the Smithfield system. As with other food markets, Smithfield was 'so much governed by the circumstance of distance, that the whole country round London was easily separable into zones or annular belts, in which the different operations of milking, calf and lamb fattening, butter-making, cheese-making, and pork-fattening, were respectively carried on'. These 'annular belts' extended to Scotland, Ireland, Wales and continental Europe by the 1840s.[69] The network of drovers' roads intersected those belts, channelling cattle to market, sometimes utilizing canals and steamboats in order to shorten distances and increase speed.[70]

Railways began competing with drovers to bring cattle into the market at Smithfield by the 1840s. In 1845, members of the City's Common Council contemplated a rail connection between the Kings Cross rail terminus and Farringdon Street. By 1847, it took one day to transport goods by rail from the countryside, a trip that required three days with other transport.[71] In 1849, half of the animals sold in Smithfield that year arrived at the market by railway; by 1854, two-thirds arrived by rail. Estimates for 1853 indicate that 39,187 tons of meat arrived in London by rail.[72]

Up to the 1840s, railways concentrated on long-distance travel and had stopped short of inter-City transport. Suburbs, such as Islington, were still isolated, outside of the transport system in the City. A Royal Commission in 1846 declared, 'railways should not at any time be allowed within the central area'. And the lack of a central metropolitan authority to plan such a railway was an impediment to any rail line that might have linked Smithfield sooner with long-distance lines.[73]

While railway construction was gathering momentum, so were investors in new stock companies that would utilize the steam locomotives to build railways. The 'Railway Mania' of the 1840s encouraged by laissez-faire policies of the government and abundant credit created intense speculation in railways.[74] The City and railway entrepreneurs saw railways as a way to improve urban space and commerce and to link the long-distance rail lines to the City.[75] Investors in railway companies often included landowners, engineers, reformers and bankers. Charles Pearson, the City solicitor, was an enthusiastic reformer whose interests embraced the metropolis, the City, and a desire to ameliorate the lives of urban workers who daily traveled to and from the City.[76] Pearson worked against the packing of juries, the association of Roman Catholics with the Great Fire, and the resistance of the Bar to the admission of Jews. For a while, he even became a proponent of a controversial and unproven atmospheric railway, a railway whose motive power depended upon compressed air that was incompatible with other railway systems. Pearson proposed a central terminus that would bring passengers from the City to the country on the Great Northern, Great Western and North Western lines. He wanted a 'cheap conveyance' for the working class so they could escape the city. One thousand butchers in the area wrote petitions in favour of Pearson's proposal.[77] The line would pass through the area between Kings Cross and the Holborn Bridge, carrying food items to the wholesale markets. He also discussed removing the meat market at Newgate, notorious not only for its loathsome slaughterhouses but also for its proximity to the gruesome but popular executions of prisoners at Newgate prison.[78]

Parliament authorized the incorporation of the Metropolitan Railway in 1853, but after considering and modifying the plan for the railway, the company shareholders had difficulty raising funds for construction, in part because of the

Crimean War and the high cost of money. Charles Pearson put up £200,000 to reinforce his commitment to his plan for transport between the City and the suburbs. And in 1859, after the market moved to Islington, Pearson finally got the City to invest in the Metropolitan Railway.[79] Although the rail lines in the Smithfield area were not completed until after the removal of the cattle market from Smithfield, the activities related to their construction impacted land values, the determination of alternate market sites, and the meat trade in general.

Railway line construction transformed the area around and underneath Smithfield, and re-oriented meat markets towards long distance provisioning and a greater reliance on meat than on live animals. These events linked Smithfield into the re-engineered landscape, replacing animal networks with iron and steam networks that increased the speed of provisioning from ten miles per hour to forty-five miles per hour.[80]

Ephemeral Space: Sound, Light, Air

Subliminal space entered the debate through the visual, aural and olfactory senses. While the railways ran under and through Smithfield, the atmosphere in the market drew the attention of reformers and entrepreneurs. Guided by notions of public health and safety, light, air and noise provided Londoners with sensorial experiences of Smithfield. The unpleasant sights, odour and noise of the market included blood flowing in the streets, the sounds of goading animals, the appearance of physical harm done to the animals, the smell of rotten offal, and the sounds of humans and non-humans contending for space. One observer portrayed the scene during the early morning hours on a Monday lit by 'the dim red light of hundreds of torches, a writhing part-colored mass, surrounded by twisting horns, some in rows, tied to rails which run along the whole length of the open space, some gathered together in one struggling knot'. There were 'acres of living wool, or roods of pigs' skins ... a universal ferment among the beasts'.[81] These elaborate descriptions of the market scenes by writers such as Dickens and reformers who sought empathy for their causes shaped public perceptions of Smithfield as a public space.

The press consistently portrayed the Smithfield as a site characterized by dark images of savage drovers waving flaming torches in the faces of terrified cattle.[82] Because the drovers brought the animals into the market during the dark, early morning hours on Monday, they used torches for illumination. The darkness that surrounded these market activities contributed to the contentious nature of Smithfield's location. Londoners were concerned about safety, the sounds of animal and drovers disturbing the local inhabitants who lived near the main drovers' roads, and the obscured views that salesmen had of the animals when they assessed their value in the poorly lit spaces, causing 'egregious blunders', and the alleged cruelty inflicted upon animals.

The boundaries of day and night, light and dark, have drawn scholars to explore the meanings of Victorian space in connection with safety, morality and gender. By the 1840s, many City streets used gas lamps for illumination in combination with oil and candles.[83] Gas created new boundaries between light and dark, consumption and violence, both shaped by shadow and light created by gaslights. Londoners reacted in different ways to the new technology for illumination: some feared the new shadows and foreboding atmosphere created by gaslights; others saw the lights as part of urban improvement, a symbol of modernity. Chris Otter's study of the politics and light in Victorian Britain suggests that London butchers saw gaslight as a way to mask unwholesome meat.[84] Butchers may not have welcomed 'improved' lighting of the market space as it illumined already contested practices of their trade.

The gaslights in Smithfield opened up those gloomy spaces that Dickens wrote about in *Oliver Twist. Walks Through London*, written in 1817, noted that Smithfield has a gaslight in the centre of the cattle market.[85] The effect of gaslight could have been to illuminate the chaos and blood, possibly exaggerating and drawing the public eye to spaces normally dark, shadowy and indistinct. Gaslight heightened the imagination, sometimes creating unsettling images of the market's activity. The extension of daytime social life as a result of gas lighting brought Londoners into Smithfield beyond regular market hours, offering the opportunity to view the vagrants, filth and disarray behind the scenes.[86] The installation of gas lines also contributed to the upheaval in London streets. Lack of regulation led to a chaotic laying of pipes and random inspections as the competing gas companies laid down lines throughout the City.[87] Ongoing railway projects often led to the same ground being dug up multiple times in the process of engineering London's landscape.

Other atmospheric conditions affected perceptions of the activities in Smithfield. Warm temperatures in summer brought problems for the butcher who had to contend with the need for speed in delivering meat faster after slaughter, since heat quickly spoiled the meat. For this reason, the close proximity of a slaughterhouse to the market was critical. Butchers could not kill on Sundays but would kill around mid-night on Sunday in order to have meat for Tuesday from animals they purchased on Saturday. Animals purchased on Mondays could be slaughtered during the rest of the week for meat sales through Saturday. These practices resulted from changes in air quality and determined a butcher's price and the quality of his product.

Butcher Giblett and others preferred not to move meat immediately but rather to allow a few hours, for the meat to 'set ... or to be in a fit state to be carried'. But because of the distance between his slaughterhouse and the market, he sent his meat without any setting time in order to avoid decay in hot weather. During warm weather, Giblett described how the meat was 'in actual motion from before it is dead till it gets into the pot'. By moving the meat so quickly from slaughter to the plate in order to avoid spoiling in hot weather, a butcher compromised meat quality by not enabling the meat to absorb seasoning such as salt.[88]

Air was also thought to contain miasma – a unhealthy vapor that contained pollutants that transmitted disease, according to Victorian medical theories. Public health reformers saw the air in Smithfield as a possible source of cholera epidemics. The public, moved by what it saw, smelled and heard in the market, brought their impressions to the select committees in Parliament, decade after decade. Catapulting the environment even further into the debate was the issue of sanitation. London's sanitation reformers were becoming increasingly aware of the negative public health consequences of the blood, filth and contamination emanating from Smithfield.

5 'A GRATEFUL ODOR RUNNETH ROUND': PUBLIC HEALTH AND SMITHFIELD

Filth of all hues and odors seem to tell
What streets they sailed from, by the sight and smell.
They, as each torrent drives, with rapid force
From Smithfield or St. Pulchre's shape their course,
And in huge confluent join at Snow Hill ridge,
Fall from the Conduit prone to Holborn Bridge.
Sweepings from butchers's stalls, dung, guts, and blood ... [1]

Along with the battle for space in London was the emergence of science as a means of understanding public health. Victorians such as William Whewell, John Stewart Mill and Charles Darwin contributed to the development of knowledge as a science and as a means of understanding the physical universe. The gradual development of science from avocation to profession occurred during the late Victorian period, leaving the early scientists to develop their own methods and theories while knowledge was still incomplete and fluid. Smithfield became entangled in the shifting theories about sanitation and disease.

Jonathan Swift was not the first to take notice of Smithfield's association with urban squalor. As early as the fourteenth century, the live cattle market became embroiled in the debate concerning sanitation and disease in London.[2] By the nineteenth century, public health was a project for reformers who saw connections between poverty, morality and mortality in London's urban landscape. Epidemics and social reform made Smithfield a target for urban sanitation and public health reforms.

Londoners were aware of the detrimental effects of the influx of rural workers and immigrants into the City, crowding the streets and threatening an aging infrastructure.[3] Dickens and other popular writers filled London periodicals with images and prose describing the smoke, fog, traffic and filth in the streets. Public health played on a public conscience that rejected these images as anomalous to a civil and modern city. Critics of the market pointed to offensive trades, those associated with the meat trade, as contributors to the moral and physical degradation of the urban landscape around Smithfield.[4]

Not only did livestock slaughter around Smithfield produce a grisly and polluted space, but these associated businesses also contributed to the filth. Tripe boilers, soap boilers and knackers' yards contributed to the nuisance value of Smithfield.[5] A member of the Royal College of Surgeons, Dr Bushnan, testified that the 'hoofs of horse and of oxen lie strewed, mingled with heaps of bones, dry and moist, emitting effluvia which only such putrescent material can exhale'. In Cock Lane, one encountered 'animal interiors', noxious smells, and 'death-bearing gases, polluting the air of the whole vicinity'.[6] Between 1800 and 1840, knackers and a distillery added to the scenes of debauchery, brothels and prostitution. Both Turnmill and Cow Cross streets contained slum areas with dilapidated buildings, including tenements with inadequate sanitation.

By the 1840s, publicans, innkeepers, salesmen, butchers, merchants and porters filled Smithfield. Joining neighboring hospitals, priories and Newgate prison the landscape around the market was rife with both pollution and death.[7] Eating houses, saddlers, bellows makers, butchers, harness makers and a wide range of small manufacturing trades occupied adjacent streets. All them depended upon the skins, offal and hides of animals slaughtered by butchers mostly located in the Newgate market area near Farringdon Street.[8] On St. John Street, the main artery from Islington to Smithfield, there was a Quaker Meeting House (keeping a watchful eye on those abusive drovers), butchers, public houses such as the Black Bull, coffee rooms and a few whip makers. There were three butchers and a tripe dresser (one who boils tripe for human consumption) on Cow Cross Street. The Smithfield butcher shops were described by contemporary observers as the 'conduits and the pipes' that distributed meat 'over the whole surface of the metropolis'.[9] Illicit and legitimate businesses existed side by side.

Sharp's Alley, near Cow Cross Street, was a different story. All of the six businesses on Sharp's Alley were considered offensive: two butchers, three violin string makers and one horse slaughterer (Jack Atchelor, 'horse slaughterer to Her Majesty and the Royal Family').[10] Horsemeat provided most of the food for London's cats and dogs.[11]

In 1848, Richard Grantham, a sanitary reformer and civil engineer provided an overview of the trades that drew upon the live cattle market. Aside from the meat, the animals provided the following: Blood for blood-puddings, 'clarification of syrups and other dense fluids, for sugar refining', manure and in a dried form for 'prussiate of potass'; intestines for strings used in clocks and musical instruments (that drew the 'delicious tones with which Paganini drew tears from his audience'); fat for tallow candles and in soap making; skin for leather, parchment and vellum; hair for mortar, cushion and mattress fillings; horns for cups and glass substitutes; hoofs for charcoal; bones for sizing, handles, knives; manure; marrow for perfumes and hair grease.[12]

In addition to these unpopular trades, persistent pandemics pushed Smithfield into the vortex of sanitation reform. Four cholera epidemics descended upon London during the nineteenth century.[13] Two occurred between 1830 and 1850. On February 9, 1832, during the first epidemic, ten cases of cholera appeared in Smithfield and caught the attention of local reformers. All ten cases proved fatal by the end of that week. The Fleet River was so polluted that observers thought the river was the cause of cholera in the nearby Clerkenwell Prison.[14] By the end of the year, London had lost over 4,000 of its inhabitants to the disease. A second epidemic rolled into London between 1848–9. London's sanitation became the concern of hospitals, the City, Parliament and the inhabitants of the City who saw a correlation between the disease and the accumulating garbage in City streets, particularly near Smithfield, 'the foul blot upon the fair face of the City of London'.[15] The re-occurrence and persistence of the disease brought together Londoners across political and social boundaries. And the lack of a definitive medical response pushed Londoners to view the disease as divine retribution for sin, immoral behaviour and poverty. (The belief that cholera had religious meanings may also have retarded progress towards an informed medical response to the disease.)

Within the context of the unrelenting and tragic cholera epidemics, an urban sanitation reformer, Edwin Chadwick, surveyed London during the 1840s and brought the decaying and putrid landscape to the attention of urban reformers and the government. He laid the groundwork for improvements in sanitation technology that influenced the City and Parliament as they deliberated over Smithfield's future. Chadwick, not known for being diplomatic or modest, described himself as 'the most prominent ... of obscure civil servants, who, in the quarter century after Bentham's death carried their Master's principles into practice'.[16] A proponent of the Benthamites, a group of social reformers that followed the utilitarian philosophy of Jeremy Bentham (1738–1832), Chadwick represented the rational city, the 'greatest good for the greatest number', as his model for London as a way to mitigate the deleterious social effects of poor sanitation. A passionate and tireless civil servant, Chadwick argued that there was a link between the diseases, sanitation and poverty. He spent hours visiting towns and observing the living conditions and social practices of England's inhabitants. A crusader for the eradication of disease as a means of moral improvement, he often ignited resentment from his colleagues because of his unrelenting and sometimes tedious and dogmatic insistence on fastidious detail. He overlooked the nuances of the embedded need for local autonomy and the nation's inclination for laissez-faire government. Some of his colleagues characterized his career as 'a set of blundering escapades'.[17]

The 1834 Poor Law Amendment, the result of work of a commission led by Chadwick to investigate poor laws, reflected Chadwick's belief that poverty and sanitation were correlated and that by improving sanitation fewer of the poor would live out dismal lives in poor houses at the expense of towns and cities. His recommendations, presented in his Sanitary Report of 1842, *The Health of the Towns Commission of 1844–45, and the Commission of Inquiry of 1847*, were not implemented because of his unfortunate inability to secure the trust and leadership required to unhinge the parishes from local control.[18] He also collided with the political tensions between local improvement acts, private bills and public acts. Local authorities resisted and resented Chadwick's efforts to centralize political power over any metropolitan plan for ameliorating sanitation in London.[19] But he did introduce an empirical map of the relationships between poverty, sanitation and disease that was to contribute to the development of sanitation reform.[20] Chadwick's work induced select committee witnesses to consider the Smithfield market as a cause for disease and poverty.

Chadwick's declaration that 'all smell is, if it be intense, immediate acute disease', reflected the general perception that the malodorous activities surrounding Smithfield were a source for contagious disease.[21] London's drainage system, composed of an antiquated network of pipes and cesspools, was linked to the inadequate drainage that select committee witnesses observed in the areas where butchers resided around Smithfield. The witnesses saw the cattle market as a site of 'deformity', 'underdrained' and 'ill-ventilated'. Some medical doctors said that cholera lingered longest in the areas around Smithfield.[22]

Cesspools near slaughterhouses presented the greatest threat to public health, in their opinion, because the effluvia were pumped to the surface before draining to the Thames.[23] Some Londoners were concerned about a connection between typhus fever and the activities of the slaughterhouses, even declaring that the connection was factual. The surgeon Fenner claimed that 'It is the general opinion among the best informed of the faculty, that typhus fever comes most frequently from such causes'. But science would not cooperate when tested in the select committee rooms. When confronted by his interlocutors about his statement concerning the connection between typhus and slaughterhouses, Fenner contended that his conclusion was based upon theory, but only 'upon the best established theory'.[24]

Observations of poor drainage contributed to the theories about the causes of cholera, and the drainage in Smithfield and around the meat markets was especially suspect. The miasmatic theory, similar to Chadwick's 'all smell ... is disease' theory, became the popular view of those looking for the cause of cholera. Although contested, this theory persisted until after Smithfield's removal.[25]

The air surrounding the market was saturated with the smell of blood and slaughter, particularly during the sultry summer months. In 1847, Angus Reach wrote that Smithfield was an incubator for typhus, where 'the ghastly monarch of crowded cellars and squalid lodging-houses – for heaps of reeking offal, have 'Stifled the air, till the dead wind stank; ... a very abiding-place and a home for pestilence ... ' Some tolerated the butchers in Newgate, Leadenhall and Whitechapel, but others repudiated the visible and odiferous filth that flowed from the private slaughter cellars and rooms associated with the butcher shops.[26]

Reformers in favour of improved sanitation and those who objected to the slaughterhouses on the basis of animal welfare joined forces in opposition to the slaughterhouses.[27] 'The Sanitation Question', investigated in 1848 by Grantham, became the focus of these reformers concerned about the relationship between Smithfield and public health. As one writer in the the *Farmer's Magazine* explained, 'The butchers trade of the metropolis must, of necessity, join in the mark of improvement; for to stand still in these steam-going times is absolutely impossible'.[28]

Solving the sanitation problem in the 1840s and 50s was complicated because of the web of multiple regulatory committees, each lacking the political power to engage in a metropolitan-wide solution. And although much has been said about laissez faire economic policy during this period, the government was already exerting its power on the local level to improve the urban landscape. The Metropolitan Buildings Act of 1844 was an early effort to make it illegal for 'offensive or noxious' businesses to operate within fifty feet of other buildings or vacant land, unless licensed. The act contained clauses that removed private cattle slaughter in London beginning thirty years after passage of the act. (In 1900, there were still no public abattoirs in London.)[29] The prohibited businesses were 'slaughterers of Cattle, Sheep, or Horses', and soap, tripe, blood and bone-boilers. Although erratically enforced, this act was intended for Smithfield, with its 'noxious' businesses.[30]

But not everyone was convinced that Smithfield was unsanitary. Some argued that Smithfield was 'a system wherein the blessings of health were preserved and promoted'. The City of London Central Markets' Association defended the site, stating that popular opinions about public health were speculative and 'contradicted by facts'. However, the City put forth a proposal to improve the existing market by the construction of a new drainage and sewage disposal system and the removal of 'objectionable neighborhoods'. It also proposed the removal of underground slaughterhouses and the construction of a public abattoir, washhouses and other 'decided ameliorations'.[31] One select committee witness in favour of improving the existing site said, 'I should say that, taking one day with another, the area of Smithfield is one of the purest sites in the center of London'. Mr Fortescue, a registrar of births and deaths for the Smithfield district, presented evidence that mortality for the area was similar to other areas in the metropolis.[32] Butcher Cramp assured a select committee that the 'filthy state' of Whitechapel was wrongly cited as being the cause of contagious diseases. George Brown, a surgeon and apothecary, who lived in Rotherhithe, south of the Thames and outside of the City, practiced medicine near Leadenhall Market. He, too, rejected the idea that markets caused diseases and thought the markets were 'healthy as in an other part' of the metropolis.[33]

Some physicians cited the healthful benefits of Smithfield, noting that the market was an open space, providing light and air to Londoners compressed by narrow, crowded streets and tenements. Dr Jordan Roche Lynch, a member of the City's Common Council, testified that the market was 'a blessing to the neighbourhood' because it was an open space, making it 'more wholesome than if it were choked up with buildings'. Dr George Burrows of St Bartholomew's Hospital also contended that having Smithfield in its present location provided open space that had healthful benefits for the patients in the hospital and that the residents of Smithfield were 'better off with the market as it is at present, than they would be if there were rows of houses built upon the site'.[34]

Perceptions that the area around the cattle market was healthful and sanitary continued to counter the descriptions of Smithfield written by Charles Dickens representing the area as foul and harmful to public health. Charles Harris, a surgeon who lived near the Leadenhall market was convinced that 'children were more healthy there than in many parts of the environs, or in the City itself'. Exhibiting pride in his own neighborhood, he felt that the poor physical appearance of some of the butchers came from their drinking habits rather than their trade. James A. Gordon, a doctor at London Hospital, also felt that butchers did not suffer from their working conditions, although he did consider them suspect, and would 'look very narrowly to the state of the butcher when he came to be examined'.[35]

In contrast to these testimonies of the healthful environment around the cattle market, cholera had raised suspicions about Smithfield as a source of the disease. The recurrence of cholera (the epidemic of 1848–9 caused more than twice as many deaths than the 1831–2 epidemic) and the tenacity of the miasma theory that linked the putrid air of Smithfield with the disease contributed to the pressure felt by the MPs to pass a removal bill. Parliament had also enacted additional sanitary measures that would impact Smithfield. The Towns Improvement Clauses Act of 1847 mandated the inspection of slaughterhouses, the registration of existing slaughterhouses, and the licensing of all new slaughterhouses.[36] The act required that butchers have paving stones, adequate underground drainage, 'capacious cisterns', with 'self-acting apparatus', and good ventilation, with daily removal of blood and offal. The statute requiring the licensing of new slaughterhouses appeared to place a monopoly in the hands of those butchers who already possessed slaughterhouses. (It would take another twenty years after the closure of Smithfield before the Public Health Act of 1875 would restrict private slaughterhouses in London).[37] In 1848, the City passed a regulation that would require an inspector to review all existing slaughterhouses and to inspect meat to see if it was 'unwholesome'.[38] No slaughterhouses were actually closed, nor were the slaughterhouses located in cellars affected. This regulation only covered activities within the City, not outside the City's jurisdiction. The City placed its own inspectors in the meat market in Newgate and in Leadenhall. Whitechapel and smaller private meat markets did not have inspectors until later since those markets fell outside the City's jurisdiction.[39]

In addition to proposals for new sanitary practices for animal slaughter around Smithfield, reformers promoted the construction of public abattoirs with the same entrepreneurial fervor as they had proposed new cattle markets. The reformers believed that private slaughterhouses were implicitly unsanitary and compromised by the pecuniary interests of the proprietor butchers. Andrew Moseley, an architect and District Surveyor of Fulham, proposed an elaborate system of abattoirs and underground pounds for storing live animals waiting to enter the market. His plan included a central roadway with abattoirs on either side, each with its own passageway to large underground cellars that could accommodate almost 25,000 sheep in eight and one-quarter acres. Criticized for proposing an enlarged version of a typical butcher's shop with a cellar for killing animals, Moseley responded with details concerning how he planned to drain manure, blood and entrails in Smithfield through two sewer lines, approximately twenty-five feet above Farringdon Street, one from Smithfield Bars and the other from Long Lane, into the odiferous Fleet Ditch. Moseley was confident that his plan would remove debris from the abattoirs by using the existing sewerage lines. He also designed an elaborate system of cast-iron columns to support the market space over the underground areas. These columns would ventilate the underground area through air passages hidden in the hollow columns. The abattoirs would be full of clean air, purified by 'passing the whole of the air through fire before it escapes to the atmosphere; the fire [would] tend to create a current, and draw the foul air from the abattoirs, and also will purify it before it passes into the atmosphere'. Sunlight would illuminate the underground space as it entered through lenses placed at the apex of the supporting arches, and he planned to use Arnott's ventilators to regulate the temperature inside the storage areas, the same technology implemented later in the Islington Metropolitan Cattle Market. Invented in the 1830s, Neil Arnott's ventilators provided heating with 'smoke consuming fireplaces' that burnt coal and used a valve to prevent smoke from entering a room.[40] Mr Moseley's plan was ambitious and prescient in terms of the technologies utilized in the late 1840s, but resistance by the butchers made it unlikely that abattoirs would replace private slaughterhouses. Indeed, Moseley's proposal never surfaced again. The issue of public versus private slaughterhouses became conflated with public health even though the issue was clearly associated

with the modernization of the meat trade and the butchers's view of their right
to personal property and their trade. As with many other aspects of the Smithfield debate, the boundaries between interests overlap, change and often include
multiple and sometimes conflicting issues. The public versus private slaughterhouse was only one of those instances.

Other individuals surfaced to propose plans for public abattoirs. James
Hakewell, an architect, came up with a plan based upon the Parisian model for
his proposal that consisted of ten public abattoirs around London's periphery.[41]
One country meat salesman proposed that animal slaughter move to the country, eliminating the necessity for urban slaughterhouses. He suggested that such
a move would result in the 'purification of the atmosphere ... during the present
awful pestilential disease (the cholera) now raging in every neighborhood ... '
His plan utilized the railways as the means of transport of dead meat to London,
a system already gathering steam as railway companies purchased land in London for their new lines.[42]

Richard Grantham, a civil engineer, proposed a public slaughterhouse
owned by a joint stock company where butchers could rent space for their own
use or utilize the services of 'Company servants'. Located outside the metropolis,
the Company would remove the activities of private butchers from the City.[43]
Grantham was critical of the butchers, admonishing them to take more notice
of mounting pressure to reform the trade. He said, 'it is well known that those
most interested, the butchers, have taken a very few steps toward endeavoring
to improve the present system of slaughter-houses, to meet the just demand of
the public, in order that a better and less objectionable plan should be instituted, and that they are too confident that no interference with their trade can
take place, and are certainly not aware of the state of public opinion upon the
questions'.[44] His sharp criticism of the butchers' trade belied his general support
of the trade. Grantham had studied the French system of abattoir construction
and concluded that it would not work in England. His proposal appears to be a
pre-emptive attempt to allow butchers to own the slaughter business as a stock
company rather than for those outside the trade to own slaughterhouses.

Thomas Dunhill, an architect, proposed a new market near King's Cross that
included abattoirs for use by London butchers. He emphasized the proximity
of the railroads to the site as the main strength of his model in addition to his
conviction that public abattoirs would improve sanitation and address animal
welfare. Although he had 'not been a great while in practice', he prepared a model
for his new market and investigated both the existing Smithfield area for possible
enlargement and designed the Kings Cross market as an alternative. When challenged by the select committee in 1847 about potential acceptance of his plan
by the butchers, Dunhill said that he was aware of two concerns of butchers,
that of 'submitting to another party, over whom he has no control', and 'that of

doing it himself at his own place'. The committee pointed out the unlikelihood of a butcher forfeiting the use of his own property for the use of a public facility, but Dunhill was sure the butchers would agree to his plan 'when they saw the manifest advantages it possessed'. Revealing his own prejudices against butchers, Dunhill declared that it was not wise for the select committee to consider 'the prejudices of the butchers ... at the expense of the public safety, the health and morality of this great city, and every consideration of humanity and decency'.[45] The butchers consistently opposed the plans for public abattoirs and denied the accusations that their private businesses were unsanitary and inhumane. But these reformers revealed the oft-contentious relationship between the butchers and the public. On one hand, consumers needed the services of the trade but sometimes resented their practices or at least desired that they find other ways to perform slaughter that would not impinge upon public health or their perception of a re-imagined, civil urban society. (This complicated relationship between meat producer and processor and the consuming public persists today and is the topic of contemporary reformers and food activists.)

The delayed arrival of a central administrative body for London hindered solutions to the sanitary problem. The first administration of public works, the Metropolitan Board Works, arrived in 1855, but it did not gain effective control of the improvement of the sewage system until 1858, seven years after the Smithfield Act, when the Thames Embankment project began under Joseph Bazalgette's leadership.[46] A comprehensive solution to the sanitation problem in Smithfield would not arrive until the appearance of centralized municipal governance, after the market relocated.

Anxieties about centralized administrative and political power persisted in London, making it unlikely that Parliament would impose government-administered slaughterhouses or abattoirs. The suggestion that the government build public slaughterhouses not only defied a tradition of private slaughterhouses and private property but also suggested a potential government monopoly of the meat trade. Defending property rights, Andrew Spottiswoode, the Queen's printer, reminded the House that the market was the property of the City and it was his grave concern that others not be privy to disposal of another's property.[47]

In 1848, the replacement of eight local sewer authorities by the Metropolitan Sewer Commission was evidence of progress towards a centralized, municipal response to the 'sanitation question'. A potential government monopoly of the meat trade concerned the general public who doubted Britain's ability to feed such a rapidly growing population. Debates about protectionism and the role of government to intervene in the food trade continued throughout the 1840s as the government began to reconsider tariffs and move towards free trade policies. A cautious attitude persisted as MPs were worried about reforms that might affect the urban food supply. Some Londoners were concerned that the Irish potato blight could become the English blight and lead to a food crisis. Cholera and public concerns about Smithfield's role in causing outbreaks only raised the stakes for addressing the 'sanitary question' in London.

Concern about the unsanitary private slaughterhouses along with a general distrust of the government and monopolies infused the debates with skepticism concerning the transference of slaughterhouses from private to public ownership. Public abattoirs threatened the butchers who believed the new system would 'place the trade in the hands of the few men of large capital' and that 'numbers of the public would go without a Sunday's dinner in consequence of the inability of the butchers to procure an adequate supply in time'.[48] The butchers feared that meat would spoil or become unavailable because of the distance between outlying abattoirs and their butcher shops. The number of meat carts would multiply if slaughter occurred at a distance from their dead meat markets, further clogging the streets and adding even more inconvenience to the inhabitants of Smithfield.

Butchers argued that they were the most qualified to safeguard public health, but it was not easy for butchers to police themselves.[49] Keeping the market clean was problematic since the space was filled with animals, horses, hay and straw. Benjamin Stubbing, who was at one time a Commissioner of Sewers, stated that Wednesday was the only day when it was possible to clean the market space.[50] Butchers also felt that they might lose the opportunity to sell offal if the presence of animal entrails became illegal. Since offal had retail value on the market, butchers felt that any public slaughterhouses would remove the offal before the butcher could acquire it for sale, thereby interfering with their businesses. Public slaughterhouses threatened a loss of quality and profitability, and the London butchers held out for their own businesses in spite of public pressure.

In contrast to those who had testified about the healthful atmosphere around the cattle market, others protested. Those who lived around Smithfield resented the unsanitary conditions imposed upon their neighborhood by the private slaughterhouses. The owners of Greenhill Rents, located near Smithfield, maintained that the slaughterhouses limited their ability to attract tenants. The 'shocking stench' particularly from animals kept in nearby Ram Inn Yard caused residents to complain and rats drawn to the slaughterhouses attacked the foundations of the houses let by Greenhill Rents. A local physician warned the inhabitants that the smells from the slaughterhouses was 'enough to cause a fever'.[51]

Observations such as these filled the select committee rooms. Most of those testifying at the 1828 Committee hearings cited their observations at Whitechapel and described blood and entrails flowing throughout the streets. Henry Jemmett, who latter testified about the tormented animals and uncontrolled detritus filling the streets of the market, canvassed the dreary slaughterhouses of Whitechapel to observe if the butchers complied with the sanitation regulations.[52] The butchers declared that they washed down their slaughterhouses after killing animals and that any appearance of blood in the streets was only the residue left from the cleansing process. In his defence, Thomas Warre, a slaughterman, said the gutters and underground drains were kept clean and that slaughter debris was carted away.

Some of the butchers criticized the City for not addressing the needs of sanitation. Michael Scales, a wholesale butcher who lived near Aldersgate, complained that the sewers installed by the City in the street near his butcher shop were inadequate to convey the refuse from his slaughterhouse. After the City rebuffed his offer to clean the sewers himself, he asked the City to rebuild the sewers so they could function properly, but the dysfunctional sewer remained in place. Scales testified that the regular schedule for cleaning the streets was not adhered to, leaving bloody water to flow through the streets. His testimony revealed the possibility that the City's self-interest was not always allied with that of its market, and that the City's rhetoric about improving the market was sometimes inconsistent with its actions. Scales also suggested that the City officers were apathetic when he described how they summoned him about his sewer 'half a dozen times', but failed each time to attend the summons.[53] This negotiation between private and public interests – the butchers who wanted to preserve their right to private slaughter and the public that wanted regulation, inspection and improve sanitation – persisted throughout the first half of the decade. Both public and private interests were wary of meddling with a provisioning system that was apparently working.

The butchers continued to hold their ground. Butchers both inside and outside the butchers' guild presented petitions to the City and to Parliament in an effort to get their voices heard. Out of seventy-three witnesses called to the select committee in 1847, only four were butchers and they were not active in Newgate, the primary market closest to Smithfield. The select committees recognized the entrenchment of the London butchers and eventually surrendered, stating that 'compulsory enactments by which cattle could only be slaughtered under the superintendence of public inspectors, would be repugnant to the feelings of Englishmen'.[54] Protected by statutes that discouraged the construction of new, competing slaughterhouses, London butchers resisted any interference in their trade that would threaten their independence and private property. Butchers continued to shun abattoirs until late in the nineteenth century, and even then none operated in London.[55]

While Londoners railed against private slaughterhouses, they also expressed concerns about the effect of 'unwholesome', spoiled and diseased meat upon public health.[56] This threat to public health occupied doctors and scientists who were beginning to assimilate the ideas of organic chemistry and its relationship to food. In 1849, the *Farmer's Magazine* described how the area around Smith-field was 'poisoned by blood and garbage; the quality of the meat that we daily eat is deteriorated by the ill-usage which the animals undergo whilst alive, and by the faulty accommodation for cleansing and dressing it when dead'.[57] Salesmen were accused of selling diseased meat to the butchers who then sold the meat to 'compilers' of black puddings and other low-grade sausages and soups by the poor.[58]

Mired in multiple understandings of contagion, physicians and amateur scientists explored connections between human and non-human health. Some reformers felt that consumers should become more aware of how to assess the quality of the meat in the market and to make sure the meat was not 'too dingy or too bright'. Treatises appeared that described how to determine the wholesome-ness of meat in the market and health officers confiscated meat they thought was diseased, but sales of diseased meat to sausage and soup makers continued throughout London.[59]

To mitigate the problems of spoilage and the potential of associated public health risks, butchers turned to slaughtering animals more frequently during the summer months because of the difficulties of keeping dead meat fresh. New-gate sold a large amount of country-killed meat, especially mutton and veal brought by rail to London. Mutton survived the heat more than beef and was often slaughtered in the country from Surrey and Kent and sold as dead meat.[60] Because the summer months were particularly challenging, butchers used pack-ing materials to inhibit spoilage.

Charles Whitlaw, a well-travelled 'agriculturist', studied 'the physiology of botany as applicable to the purposes of life, particularly to the rearing of live-stock and medicine, scrofulous and glandular diseases'. (He also operated two steam baths, probably some sort of medicated Turkish baths that were popular in Victorian London.) Whitlaw's plea for attention to this matter was motivated by his concern that the increase in diseases in London was 'showing other nations our growing weakness', and might therefore have more nationalistic implications for England.[61] The link between national cleanliness and national power joined other constructions of British identity such as the consumption of beef and Brit-ish livestock breeding practices.

The consumption of wholesome meat as an indication of national vitality became part of the argument for those who wanted to reform the meat trade without tampering with a functioning meat provisioning system. While visit-ing New York, Whitlaw observed the city's slaughterhouses and knew of similar activities in Boston and Philadelphia. Consistent with food theorists of the time, Whitlaw believed that anyone who ate meat containing decomposed fat would suffer a 'bilious attack almost immediately'. He cited the work of Dr Hamilton, the president of the Hunterian Society, who, on his deathbed, exacted a promise from Whitlaw that he would find the cause of the increases of diseases, including cancer, in London during the preceding fifteen years. After considering the London gas works as the cause of these diseases, he fell upon the butchers of London as the culprits who slaughtered diseased animals. German sausages even came under fire. He maintained that the butchers in poor neighborhoods 'compiled' working class fare such as 'German sausages, polonics, saveloys, and black puddings' from animals in 'a more advanced state of disease'.[62]

As foreign livestock arrived at British ports in increasing numbers, Smithfield became a collecting point for animals from unknown sources, often carrying diseases from foreign farms. Inspectors at ports did their best to ascertain the health of animals, but diagnoses of animal diseases were inconsistent and the transference of diseases from human to non-humans was only speculative. Some physicians and reformers suggested that the consumption of diseased or spoiled meat could cause human disease The two livestock diseases that were most common at that time were foot and mouth disease and pleuro-pneumonia. In 1841, five physicians at St. Bartholomew's Hospital sent a petition asking the City to require a veterinary inspector for the horses sold in Smithfield after they observed several deaths of patients inflicted with glanders that was contracted, they believed, from the horses in the market. After consideration by the City, the petition went unheeded, in spite of the committee's concern about the danger to public health of this human to non-human contagious disease.[63]

By the time Parliament began to consider another bill for the removal of Smithfield in the late 1840s, many observers of the market felt that many slaughterhouses had improved, detracting attention away from the move to construct public abattoirs. Still, the public and the press continued satirizing and criticizing Smithfield for its visible and unsanitary slaughterhouses. In 1848, *Punch,* mocked those who contended that Smithfield was somehow a salubrious neighborhood. The 'Song in Favor of Smithfield' was to be sung by Mr Dixon, a resident of Cripplegate Ward, 'father of thirteen or fourteen children', and a resident of the Smithfield neighbourhood for fifty years.

> The Field! The Field! The old Smithfield!
> To none in sent 'twill ever yield;
> Without a mark, without a bound,
> A grateful odour runneth round;
> It gets in the nose, it tickles the eyes,
> Or underneath the mouth it lies.
> I'm in Smithfield! I'm in Smithfield!
> I am where each disease is heal'd,
> With the smells above, and the dirt below,
> And animals wheresoe'er you go.
> If an ox should send one an awkward leap,
> What matter! I fall among the sheep!

I love, oh, how I love to inhale
The odors wafted on every gale,
When some mad bullock towards the moon
Is tossing aloft some hapless loon;
Who, after quitting the world below,
Come back again with an awful blow.
I ne'er was on Margate's dull sea-shore,
But I loved old Smithfield more and more,
And backwards flew to her dirty pens,
As chickens seek their parent hens;
And a mother she was and is to me,
For I was born in Bartholomee.
The oxen were active with hoof and horn,
In the noisy hour where I was born;
And the drovers whistled, the butchers swore,
As the dogs kept barking more and more;
And ne'er was heard such an outcry wild
As welcomed to life the Smithfield child.
I've lived since then in London town,
Till my hair has turned to grey from brown,
With power the rural fields to range;
But I never Smithfield wish to change;
And Death, when it summons me to sleep,
Shall find me 'midst oxen, pigs, and sheep.[64]

6 NECESSARILY CRUEL? BEEF, BRUTES AND WOMEN IN SMITHFIELD

'Mr. Bovington's blood ran cold as he witnessed the cruelty ... tremendous blows were then repeated on the nose, neck and horns, till the tortured animal could turn ... 'I can't lay all the blame on the drovers. What can they do? If they have got one hundred beasts to wedge into a space only big enough for seventy, they *must* be cruel'.[1]

Along with the modernization of sanitary systems, other changes were circulating. Attitudes towards animals, both wild and domestic were challenged by new meanings of civility and Victorian morality. During the 1830s and 1840s, child and animal welfare became a social issue that had ramifications in Smithfield. Child welfare concerns led to factory reform that in turn led to a rethinking about the treatment of non-human animals. In a way, both human and non-human welfare became central to the Smithfield debate. And this amalgam of social concern was also a gendered concern as women increasingly entered the masculine space of Smithfield. The feminization of Smithfield by animal welfare reformers and by women – who entered the Smithfield neighborhood to shop – points to another way in which London became a modern urban landscape.

According to at one least London journalist, drovers in Smithfield were brutal, immoral and indecent characters.[2] He was not alone in his observations. During the 1850s, Dickens wrote a series of articles in *Household Words* that satirized Smithfield, using a character named Mr Bovington to articulate the worst scenes in the market. In these articles and in his novels, Dickens argued his view that the market bred immorality and threatened the very civility that Victorians associated with their modern city.

By the late eighteenth century, the scenes of drovers thrashing bullocks, animals bitten by overzealous herding dogs, and butchers' stalls spewing entrails were familiar to most Londoners. The reaction had been building for decades as a new civility gradually emerged to complement rising incomes and the modern imagination of what it meant to live in a civil society. Victorians had become associated with an ethos that acquired greater force each decade, as a 'religion of humanity' displaced traditional religious issues.[3] Reformers who gathered to debate Smithfield's location combined utilitarianism with this secular theology in their efforts to improve both themselves and their world. This intense ethos came through the arguments presented in the select committee reports across multiple social classes, arguments that juxtaposed the realities of provisioning a city with the ideals of secular humanism.

Three moral issues that arose from this ethos surfaced in the select committee reports. The first, animal welfare, was an unrelenting and emotive argument. The committee reports tell a story that, if taken literally, suggest that animal cruelty drove the animals out of the City.[4] Witnesses provided evidence in 1828, 1847, 1849 and 1850 to defend their opposition to the treatment of animals in Smithfield with exhortations that appropriated animal welfare either to justify the market's existing location or to promote the removal of the market. Some observers cited public apathy towards the activities in Smithfield as evidence of a general acceptance of brutality towards animals.[5] This led to a discourse about animal welfare that was complicated and often contradictory. A deeper reading of the committee reports reveals that cruelty had multiple meanings. While the treatment of animals in Smithfield improved during the period leading to the market removal, significant changes in the laws regarding animal welfare did not occur until after the market moved to Islington.

A second issue concerned the effects of the violence inherent in the meat trade, such as animal slaughter, upon the morals and character of those involved in the meat trade. Some reformers felt that brutality and daily contact with blood and filth corrupted and otherwise abased the moral character of drovers and butchers. Further corrosion of character occurred when drovers and salesmen worked on the Sabbath, eliminating the possibility for religious observance and subsequent moral redemption. Members of the clergy often saw these professions as degrading and represented butchers and drovers as victims of a commercial system that precluded self-improvement.

The third issue concerned conversations about gender that suggested that Smithfield was an unsafe space for women, in both a moral and a physical sense. Women were allegedly at risk in and around the cattle market, which impeded their access to shopping areas and public spaces in the center of the metropolis. Witnesses reported that women were subjected to the immoral influence of the market where drovers blasphemed and pickpockets prowled through the market into the shops around Smithfield. Those that supported the removal of Smithfield argued that the relocation of the cattle market would enable women to enter the public spaces in and around Smithfield without fear of being contaminated by an impure environment.

Animal Welfare

By the time the select committee met in 1828, Parliament already had responded to calls to address the 'barbaric' and 'inhumane' practices of drovers as they brought animals into Smithfield. In March 1774, James Hodges, Town Clerk of the City of London, wrote about the petition sent to the Common Council by the parishioners of St Sepulchre, requesting the City to address the movement of cattle from the market in Smithfield to the butchers by drovers. They complained of the drovers' behavior and the 'weapons' they used to exercise 'wanton cruelty' upon the animals 'who otherwise would be very tame and quiet naturally'. At the same meeting, the Common Council considered a petition sent by salesmen and butchers concerning the allegations made against them by the parishioners.[6] The Council was concerned primarily for the safety of the inhabitants of the parish whose lives were threatened by accidents caused by the 'Barbarity and Inhumanity of ... Drovers and their Assistants, who are a disgrace to Humanity and a Reflection upon the good Order of Government'.[7] The petition claimed that drovers were guilty of 'unnecessary' cruelty, cruelty that could be avoided by employing more rational or humane practices that would eliminate the need for violence. The violence and disorder perceived in Smithfield, caused mostly by driving cattle in a confined urban space, were worrisome to a population that was filling London's narrow streets at an increasing rate.

Three months later (June 1774), Parliament passed 'A Bill to Prevent the Mischiefs [*sic*] that arise from driving Cattle, within the Cities of London and Westminster, and the Bills of Mortality'. The Act prohibited drovers from 'the unskillful [*sic*] and cruel Manner in which cattle are driven from Smithfield market', required drovers to wear a badge, and specified the length and circumference of a drover's stick. Further, no nails or spikes could protrude from the stick. These measures were intended to prohibit 'improper driving' and to prevent accidents to those in the market, both human and non-humans. Penalties included the forfeiture of 'goods and chattels, prison time, and hard labor', if terms of punishment were abrogated.[8] In 1777, the Court of Aldermen decided to limit the congestion of animals in the market by staggering the hours allocated for cattle and those for sheep, calves, lambs and pigs. All animals left in the market outside of their specific market hours would be confiscated and kept in a field for later redemption in return for payment of penalties.[9]

The call for laws that would address animal cruelty gained traction in the first decade of the nineteenth century. Lord Erskine, an eloquent Scots and lawyer, brought the first bill for the protection of animals to Parliament in 1809. Although he raised important issues, his bill never passed into law. Known for his infamous defense of Thomas Paine and an eclectic community of animal friends (dogs, birds and leeches), Erskine delivered a speech in the House of Lords, creating an association of biblical 'dominion' with a more nuanced moral 'trust':

> ... I am to ask your Lordships, in the name of that God who gave to Man his dominion over the lower world, to acknowledge and recognize that dominion to be a moral trust.[10]

Speaking of domestic animals, Erskine eschewed any thought that animals had rights, but stood firmly on the belief that animals were property and ought to be protected on the same basis as would be necessary for the protection of any capital asset. Referring to post-horses, horses ridden hard for the purpose of delivering mail, Erskine further articulated the dilemma that would confront legislators and the Victorian moralists as they debated Smithfield. Erskine raised the question: How would the legal magistrates tell the difference between perceived abuse of animals used for slaughter as they proceeded along their 'melancholy journeys to death in our markets' from unnecessary cruelty, that inflicted by persons of immoral character?[11]

Another decade passed before Parliament responded with further regulations. In 1822, Richard Martin, a member of the Irish Parliament who subsequently played a role in the formation of the Society for the Prevention of Cruelty to Animals (SPCA), proposed a bill that was the first act to specifically address the accusations of animal cruelty in Smithfield outside of the regulations for drovers enacted in the late eighteenth century. Martin's bill, titled 'An act to prevent the cruel and improper treatment of cattle', passed on July 22, 1822.[12] Intended to protect horses, his bill was rebuffed by David Ricardo (the political economist and Whig MP) who dismissed the importance of protecting horses because 'so many barbarities prevailed in fishing and hunting, and other species of amusement, it was idle to legislate without including all possible cases'.[13] How could the MPs distinguish between the treatment of animals used for sport from animals used for consumption? Some witnesses at the select committee testified that they thought Martin's Act had lessened the amount of cruelty in Smithfield, but cattle salesman Merritt felt that Martin's Law was of no help in regulating the market as it was rarely enforced. Once while observing a drover striking a bull, Merritt reminded the drover of Martin's Law only to witness the drover's complete disregard of his warning as he continued to exert 'wantonness' with his charge.[14]

Despite the large number of witnesses that addressed questions about slaughterhouses and animal welfare, the select committee in 1828 declined to recommend any changes to the regulations concerning animal cruelty or the operation of slaughterhouses. The testimonies of witnesses revealed that the perceptions of what was cruel were ambivalent and contested. Animal cruelty was often misunderstood, or at least inconsistently understood. Some Londoners during the early nineteenth century believed that cruelty was a matter of degree, intent and circumstance. Distinctions between the types of cruelty, involved in the production of food for the metropolis resurfaced throughout the testimonies of butchers and consumers and revealed multiple interpretations 'necessary' and 'unnecessary' cruelty.

Necessary or Unnecessary Cruelty?

Witnesses who called for punishment and regulation of drovers and butchers resisted the intrusion of government into the affairs of these 'practical men' who delivered millions of pounds of beef, mutton and pork to their tables. This paradox reflected the ambivalence of the age and the tension between the desire for improvement and a reluctance to upset the order of the system of trade and distribution that kept the machinery of commerce in operation. One writer in the *Chamber's Edinburgh Journal*, saw no evidence of excessive cruelty as drovers moved their animals within the City.

> ... you will presently see that numbers of animals march in, take up their positions, and in due time march off again, with a dispatch, regularity, and order which, under the circumstances, must be considered perfectly admirable. Now and then, to be sure, a silly sheep, at odds with destiny, will bolt suddenly off with a dog at its heels' but whatever speed may be put forth, it finds, alas! No egress from the perplexing maze of pens in which it is involved; and very soon, in obedience to the cry of 'Turn un – turn un', is made to retrace its steps, and rejoin its Norfolk or Southdown companions. Perhaps too, a recalcitrant calf, obstinately inimical to conversion into veal, whilst gently led along by a halter, starts off with the boy in charge, and is with some difficulty restored to his place in quadrupedal juvenile society'.[15]

This description of the activities of drovers differs from vivid descriptions of cruelty in *The Voice of Humanity* and suggests with some humour that there was an innate order in the machinery of commerce in Smithfield and involved only those practices necessary to function efficiently.

The dominion bestowed by God upon man for the use of animals offered a complicated ethos for the graziers, salesmen, butchers and consumers of meat who saw animal cruelty as an unavoidable necessity for the orderly operation of the market. Necessary cruelty was, for them, implicit in the meat trade. The natural behavior of animals, the process of bringing them to and from the market, and the act of slaughter contained violence and cruelty that could not be avoided, according to many graziers, drovers and butchers. Even those unassociated with the market saw the inevitability of some cruelty. William Darnton, a bookseller in Smithfield who daily observed the activities in the market, felt that the cruelty he saw was 'inseparable, in such a city as this, in conducting the animals through it ... ' He saw this cruelty as unavoidable as long as animals were driven through city streets. Gurney, the bill broker, felt that 'London will at all times entail acts of cruelty, but much more or much less according to the arrangement'. William Hickson, a shoe ware-house owner in Smithifield, felt that some cruelty was unavoidable in the cramped quarters of Smithfield and resulted from the 'anxiety to get as great a number of cat-tle as possible into as small a space as possible'.[16] This overriding sense of practicality and compromise mitigated the desire to remedy acts of cruelty. But while respect-ing the market system, reformers gathered evidence, wrote petitions and implored the select committees to protect the welfare of animals in Smithfield. The City was sympathetic to the claims of those who accused the butchers and drovers of cruelty and responded with added supervision of the market by its officers.

But others were not so sympathetic and instead defended their actions. The nuances of the meanings of cruelty were evident in James Mills' testimony when he decried the violence and inhumanity of drovers who goaded their cattle while stating that butchers were 'as humane a set of men as any in London'.[17] Consist-ent with Mill's portrayal, the testimonies of the London butchers were defensive and attempted to deflect the accusations of reformers. Butcher John Cramp said, ' ... most certainly, I would not allow cruelty'. Butchers were more likely to accuse salesmen and especially drovers of cruelty. Thomas Warre, a slaughter-man, defended his trade with outrage. Responding to the testimonies of other witnesses accusing slaughtermen of flaying live animals, Warre, offended, said, ' ... you do not suppose we begin to skin them alive; a man would sooner have his hand cut off than skin one alive'. William Collins, a cattle salesman, challenged the image of butchers as evil, unfeeling and violent characters, '... the butchers are a very different class of men from what they are supposed to be; they are men of feeling, and they would discharge a man if they thought he committed an act of cruelty'.[18] These views demonstrate the perspective of those in the butchers' trade who behaved with their own sense of integrity and within the boundaries of their particular moral norms. They also reveal the multiple layers of meaning given to the concept of cruelty by the different interests in the debate.

Those outside the trade wrote advice and moral guidelines for the butchers' trade with the intent of improving the overall practices and character of butchers. Sometimes the advice came from unexpected sources. James Plumptre, an actor, wrote 'The Experienced Butcher, Shewing the Respectability and Usefulness of His Calling, The Religious Considerations Arising from It, The Laws Relating to it, and Various Profitable Suggestions for the Rightly Carrying It On' in 1816.[19] Invoking the Bible and including both hymns and poetry, he provides practical advice on raising animals for slaughter, slaughtering, preparing meat for the mar-ket and setting prices, all within the context of Christian morality. Through the writings of those such as Plumptre, England's culture of improvement attempted to palliate the morals of some of its more contentious tradesmen.

The behaviour of butchers was indeed contentious. In the butcher shops around Smithfield, the practice of throwing or sliding a sheep down a board into a dark cellar before slaughter was an offense often cited by animal welfare reformers. Cellars evoked images of darkness and poor ventilation, all foreboding symbols that only confirmed the worst fears of those who perceived the meat trade as a grisly, immoral and inhumane business. Still, some witnesses defended the cellars stating that 'it is a very wrong impression that as a cruelty, it is by no means so; they are put down with caution, and then killed and brought up again; just as many are thrown down as are wanted'.[20] Did these arguments suggest that the butcher was immoral and brutal or not? To some, the violence was inherent to the business of providing meat to the populace. Only a few decades after the select committees met in 1828, vegetarians would cut through the ambiguity suggested by these earlier debates by advocating a rejection of all meat as a means of addressing animal welfare.

But the butchers continued to be defensive. Butchers often insisted that injuries to animals occurred before the animals entered the market. These butchers felt that carriages and wagons in the streets caused most of the injuries to animals. Collins said that he saw animals 'with their claws taken off by the drays', two-wheeled horse-drawn carts.[21] Cramp said, 'I am convinced that a great deal of the damage done to the cattle is from the carriages'.[22] The rhetoric of 'damage', not 'cruelty', reveals the butcher's sensibility regarding animal welfare. Warre argued that bruises and other injuries of cattle resulted from the animals fighting with each other, not from blows inflicted by drovers.

William Hickson, shoe warehouseman, stated that necessary cruelty was 'owing to the situation itself; the men themselves, and the salesmen ... '[23] He insisted that cruelty and damage to the beasts arose out of battles between the beasts themselves. Hickson attributed accidents to the separation of animals from their herd or flock; when these beasts were denied their 'attachment to each other', they would run wild through the market space. He admitted there were no 'serious accidents' other than bruising from being kicked by an animal and only one death per year.[24]

Some of the witnesses called to testify to the committee cited the practices of Jewish butchers who slaughtered animals according to Mosaic Law. These butchers cut an animal's artery with a large knife rather than rending a blow to the head of an animal with a pike or bludgeon. Some viewed the slaughtering practices of Jewish butchers as more humane. Moses Asser, a Jewish meat inspector and slaughterman in Whitechapel, considered cruelty 'necessary', but not desirable. Asser believed that he and his slaughtermen did 'not use any cruelty towards the animal, by which means we have a very sharp knife to do this operation'.[25] Animal sympathizer John Ludd Fenner saw the Jewish method 'the easier possible death'.[26] Abraham Silva, a Jewish slaughterman in Whitechapel unapologetically described how he used a knife to cut the throats of cattle and how he inspected his meat according to the requirements of Jewish law. A seal of inspection was affixed to the meat after slaughter for the Jewish market. In effect, Jewish slaughtermen had a system of meat inspection before the City's meat inspection system became operational.[27] Silva saw no conflict between the fact that he was both an inspector and a slaughterman. He said that 'force and violence' were sometimes necessary as a practical matter to get the animals to enter a slaughterhouse.[28]

The butchers' view of cruelty rested on the concept that animals were property, as Erskine had argued earlier. Butchers saw it in their self-interest to care for an animal's welfare in order to preserve the animal's value. Through careful handling of an animal before and after slaughter, they could preserve the value of a carcass. Butcher Cramp said that he had seen 'the prime part of bullocks so deteriorated, by the bruises inflicted', that he had £15 returned to him in consequence of loss on ten oxen. He estimated that his losses were 'the enormous sum of £62,400 [sic] per annum'.[29]

Some butchers appeared oblivious to public criticisms of slaughtering practices. James Asser, a former butcher, was unrepentant about how he treated animals in the past. He admitted to 'unnecessary cruelty', such as cutting apart meat from an animal not yet dead. Suggesting his own lack of culpability, he said that he was not sure if an animal moved at all after death, a surprising admission considering that his work daily entailed close contact with dead animals.[30] Asser was more concerned about upsetting his master than mistreating animals. John Warmington, a grazier and salesman, had worked in Smithfield for at least thirty-five years when he testified before the select committee in 1828. His opinion was that 'Some violence is necessary to cause the cattle to get into a situation to be handled'. His view was similar to others who felt that in order to do their job with minimal harm to the animals, it was necessary to be forceful. He was more critical of young boys who ran about the market causing disruptions, throwing rocks at the animals, pulling tails, and generally interfering with the drovers who were in the process of gathering their stock into groups for the market.[31]

In some cases, groups of young men engaged in 'bullock-driving', or 'bullock hunting', the practice of stealing animals out of droves while the cattle were awaiting entry into the market. These 'bullock-hunters' carried clubs and often injured animals. The salesman and carcass butcher Stubbings indicated that this practice had mostly disappeared by the 1820s and had been forbidden by the laws of the late eighteenth century.[32] Butcher Scales described a practice called 'waking' cattle. Drovers would ask young boys to 'wake' the cattle, by beating them so that the animals would become agitated. This treatment exercised the animals to such a degree that by the time the butchers handled the animals, the animals would be more docile. Scales said that he often intervened, but in fact efforts were probably ineffective since the practice did render the animals easier to handle. Another practice, called 'Bull Hanks', caused considerable disapproval in Whitechapel.

This practice involved selecting a single animal out of a drove, driving it to distraction until the animal was exhausted, and then ending the whole nefarious affair by hitting the animal on the head, presumably to end its misery.[33]

Thomas Slocombe, the only drover called as a witness in 1828, had worked for over thirty years in Smithfield. He argued that drovers were practical men, using force to control the space between humans and non-humans in the City. He rejected accusations of egregious cruelty and said he had never seen such behavior as 'waking' cattle. Slocombe felt that drovers had become less violent towards their cattle in response to recent regulations and increased pay. At the same time, he acknowledged some cruelty was necessary in order to control the animals in the off-droves.[34]

Some witnesses felt that animal cruelty was unnecessary in all cases. These individuals were often members of religious or social reform associations such as the Society for the Prevention of Cruelty to Animals, (SPCA), organized in 1824, the Association for Promoting Rational Humanity, and the Religious Society of Friends (Quakers).[35] The SPCA campaigned for the removal of Smithfield, and its members were vocal critics of its practices. John Ludd Fenner was also a member of the SPCA and whose activism motivated him to report drovers without badges to the magistrates. He visited other markets in England and was aware of how animals were treated elsewhere. In his opinion, Smithfield was the worst offender, with drovers who were 'in the habit of inflicting such cruelty as to make them mad [the cattle]'.[36]

Many witnesses argued that the limited size of Smithfield was the principal cause of animal cruelty. The off-droves appeared to be the site of most of the cruelty, as the animals were gathered in the narrow streets and left untied, often beaten by the drovers to keep them from escaping into other parts of the City. Witnesses such as the woolen merchant William Clay suggested that in a larger market space, animal cruelty would all but disappear. He observed that about two thousand cattle could comfortably occupy the existing space, without much harm.[37]

Some witnesses who knew little about animal behavior made ill-informed suggestions for improving animal welfare. Thomas Christie, a businessman, thought that if the animals 'were arranged properly ... beating them on the head to keep them together, would be avoided'.[38] *The Working Man's Friend and Family Instructor* suggested that small flags be installed in Smithfield to guide the sheep instead of 'the goad and bludgeon'.[39] Farmers and drovers knew that by placing animals within a confined space, either through a narrow chute or into a corner of a barn, increased the likelihood of controlling the animals. A herding dog was particularly adept at this practice. Without the pressure of confinement, herding animals panicked and fled the drover's control into surrounding streets, out of control and prone to sustaining and inflicting injury. But the reformers still cited both the dogs' herding behavior and the cramped space as cruel treatment of animals.

Critics like Christie lamented the length of time animals were left in the market after arriving fatigued following long journeys on dusty roads. Sometimes animals remained in the market into the afternoon with little food and water, which Christie viewed as unnecessarily cruel treatment.[40] Butchers had a very different view: It was common practice to withdraw food from an animal before slaughter since death was inevitable and the presence of food in an animal's gut compromised meat quality.[41] These practical matters were of no concern to the well-meaning reformers who were influenced by the images of withering animals left in the market. Cattle salesman Warmington felt that the amount of time that cattle stood on the hard pavement in the market caused more harm to the animals than the drovers. His interest was one of pricing animals and would have wanted animals to sell quickly rather than lingering late into the afternoon. Consident with his role as salesman, he thought that long droves were actually better for an animal since they allowed time for the animal to become accustomed to the herd and to gradually become more docile.[42] But contradictions continued to weaken the arguments of the animal welfare advocates. The elite reformers seemed to object to the animals standing in the market and those who worked with the animals countered with their views of practical considerations that would reinforce the status quo.

The off-droves and ring droves were most often cited as a cause for cruelty. Because it took repeated efforts on the part of drovers and dogs to get the animals into these narrow spaces and in the desired arrangements, the resulting mayhem drew the attention of the reformers. Some observed the practice of drovers who hobbled sheep by tying up one foreleg to prohibit an escape. On the other hand, Merritt, the cattle salesman, believed that if cattle were individually tied in the market, then the chaos of moving a purchased animal through the other animals on the way to the butcher would be greatly ameliorated.[43]

Joining the reformers protesting unnecessary cruelty towards animals were farmers and graziers who felt that cruelty lowered the value of their animals in the market. A broadside circulated in 1835 around Smithfield by graziers and farmers concerned so many cases of animals cruelty in the cattle market that Smithfield was 'so much disgrace on the metropolis'.[44] Two drovers were cited in the broadside, accused of 'goading a poor beast until they knocked out both its eyes'. A police report cited in the broadside noted that the complaint against the drovers made by Mr Sebo, a butcher, described a quarrel between two salesmen over their spaces in Smithfield. As the salesmen argued over the space allocated to them by the Clerk of the Market, a drover attempted to claim space for one of the salesmen, and the animals 'suffered dreadfully'. Richard Hicks, an officer from the City, held the salesmen responsible for the abusive treatment of the animals, not the drovers. The broadside illustrated the extent of blame for the cruelty in Smithfield. The farmers and graziers implicated drovers, butchers and salesmen in their protest against the treatment of their animals.

Wide ranging views of what constituted cruelty and whether it was necessary or not proved to be only a distraction to the debate about Smithfield's location. The issue of location and cruelty intersected when reformers argued that improved and enlarged quarters for the animals would improve the treatment of animals. And those in the market took their positions relative to their interests in the meat trade.

Immoral Spaces

In addition to their concerns about animals, social reformers attacked Smithfield for its effect upon humans. Secular and non-secular reforming institutions stepped in to fight against what they saw as immoral behavior and practices in Smithfield.[45] They argued that the work of drovers and butchers engendered moral depravity and promoted the profanation of the Sabbath because of market preparations in Islington on Sunday to prepare for the Monday market. The reformers were also concerned about the contamination of individual morality by the pollutants of filth, violence and blasphemy. When it came to the live cattle market, many of the same organizations that objected to the treatment of animals in Smithfield – the SPCA, the Association for Promoting Rational Humanity, and the Quakers – joined forces with the Lord's Day Observance Society (LDOS) in the effort to jettison Smithfield. Evangelicalism and Methodism did much to connect religiosity with self-improvement across social classes.

The Monday market required drovers and related trades to operate on Sunday as a result of the need to bring animals into the market early Monday morning from Islington. Because some wealthier Londoners came to the meat market on Mondays, butchers slaughtered animals on Sundays in the Smithfield area and in the neighborhoods around other meat markets, such as the Clare and Hungerford markets.[46] Church and parish officials in Islington protested against the drovers and salesmen in their town on Sundays, alleging that these men drank too much in the taverns and disrupted the religious activities of parishioners. Cattle salesman William Hebb and the banker Joseph Pocklington commiserated about the plight of drovers and salesmen who were unable to rest on Sunday because of the need to get their animals to market. One drover was 'extremely sorry he had not been in a place of worship for twelve years.'[47]

The repeated efforts to change market days hinged, in part, on the desire to allow drovers the opportunity to observe the Sabbath. A change from Monday to Tuesday for the market would potentially enable drovers to attend church. If the market were held on Tuesday, those employed in the market would not need to work on Sundays but instead could keep the Sabbath and work on Mondays for the Tuesday market. Salesman Merritt thought that of the seven hundred employed on Sunday, five hundred would not need to work if the market was moved to Tuesday.[48]

Reverend Daniel Wilson, vicar of Islington, argued that Smithfield had 'brutalizing effects ... such as to produce upon the minds of the keepers of the public-houses and the drovers themselves, the very worst moral effects'. Wilson complained that cattle droves got in his way to and from church and that the market was a threat to 'quiet and orderly families'. He described the public houses in Islington, such as the Pied Bull (located near Wilson's residence and frequented by drovers), as a source of 'the noises and blasphemies all through the Sunday night'. Some observers called drovers 'fierce ... savage tribes'. Reverend John Blackburn, a dissenting minister from Pentonville, spoke of the market as 'very offensive' and maintained that the presence of cattle was a 'violation of domestic tranquility .... and of the Lord's-day'.[49]

Residents of other areas along the cattle routes objected to the noise and behavior of drovers and animals.[50] Reformers described drovers shouting oaths and providing a base moral example to families who lived along these cattle routes. Dr James Alexander Gordon, a physician from Finsbury Square, complained about 'the screams of the drovers ... it is a well-known fact, that any individual coming from the country is unable to sleep for several nights'. The 'violent imprecations' of drovers caused concern not only to the public but also to merchants who felt that such behaviour discouraged families from entering the market. Darton, a Quaker, described how the arrival of sheep on Sunday nights in his neighborhood of Holborn created collisions between Sunday evening church goers and the sheep in transit.[51]

Some witnesses diluted the association of these objectionable activities with Smithfield by stating that bad language and noise could follow any market, no matter where located and what size.[52] One City official, Alderman Lucas, said in 1837 that a great effort had been made to include the argument of humanity as a reason for market relocation, but he believed that a change in location would have no effect at all upon the characters of drovers.[53]

The idea of carousing drovers and salesmen contrasted with more traditional images, complicating the argument of the reformers.[54] Some periodicals depicted drovers as rural, virtuous professionals walking along country roads, knitting socks as they returned from the market. Licensing practices instituted by the City reinforced the belief that drovers possessed appropriate moral qualities. The requirements for a drover's licence included character references that vouched for trustworthiness and fine moral character. Some Londoners defended the moral reputations of drovers. The bill-broker, Gurney, sympathized with the drovers who appeared to him as at the mercy of the extreme circumstances of their labour, 'toiling in the sun all the day' and faced with moving excitable animals through unnatural urban spaces. Once, when he saw a drover hitting an animal with 'a sort of bravado', he attempted to help the animal by placing his hat over the animal's eyes in order to calm the beast.[55] While critical of the behaviour of drovers, witnesses like Gurney appeared to understand that droving was not any easy job and that these individuals were engaged in doing a thankless task.

Similar to the early animal welfare bills, the effort to encourage drovers to attend church and become better Christians failed. Bills proposed to change market days to enable the observance of the Sabbath failed in 1828, 1848, 1849 and 1850. A law proposed in 1832, designed to prohibit cattle driving on Sunday, failed to pass. And in 1856, a Sunday Trading Bill failed after a public riot in Hyde Park.[56] If Smithfield was to move, it would take other causes than moral reform to uproot the market.

Women and Cattle: Dangerous Spaces

Victorian anxieties about urban space and gender would also shape attitudes towards the market. As Erika Diane Rappaport argues, shopping became a new leisure activity during the first half of the nineteenth century.[57] This new visibility in public spaces often brought a certain anxiety on the part of men who observed women in social spaces unfamiliar to them. Men who observed women who shopped in 'halls of temptation', had similar concerns about the safety of women shopping near Smithfield who were frightened by market cattle.

In the case of Smithfield, men often appeared more concerned about the cattle discouraging traffic to their shops rather than the safety of females. Unlike the emerging shopping areas in the West End, Smithfield was not a space for shopping as a leisure activity. Instead, women shopped for food in the meat markets surrounding Smithfield. These women were working-class women for the most part, servants or providers for middle class families.

Some select committee witnesses argued that Smithfield was particularly offensive to women and should be removed in order to protect the pure and moral status of the ladies. The select committee reports pointed out instances when ladies became the victims of the activities in the market. Darton, the bookseller near Smithfield, described how women avoided shopping in his area on Mondays and they were 'in great terror' of Smithfield. In addition to the sights surrounding the market, the reports suggested that the sounds of the market could have a terrorizing effect, upsetting the nerves of women. Women often witnessed bloodied animals, distressed cries of animals, and harsh blows inflicted by drovers upon their cattle.

The advent of gaslights in the market space, discussed by Lynda Nead, created a 'confusion of space'. This new light altered the impressions of the market, adding the flicker and shadow of gas lamps to the other Smithfield sensations.

Nead points to the effects of gas light on the market, stating that 'The butcher's uncontrollable, unguarded gas flare expresses a form of insanity that is taking place on the streets of the metropolis'. Andrew Wynter called Smithfield a 'hideous nightmare' and other journalists, such as Dickens, appropriated the dark, dangerous sensations of Smithfield in their literature.[58] One observer complained that Smithfield at night was when 'rapine and murder prowl in the lanes and alleys'.[59] These images appeared in periodicals read by women and appropriated by men for the purposes of reform and relocation.

The subjection of women to animal cruelty was a particularly egregious offense to men who viewed women as helpless victims in the face of moral corruption and potential physical harm. Jeremiah Barrett, who lived in Barbican, reported that his sister saw a sheep's eye dislodged, as it 'hung down by the vein, which very much distressed her, in fact made her quite ill to the next day'. Likely a Quaker who attended the Quaker meeting house on St John Street, Barrett also complained that the ladies could not come to the evening meeting because of the 'abuses and the oaths' of the drovers. Salesman Warmington offered his view that Smithfield was frightening for women who 'are apt to apprehend danger where there is none'. Robert Padmore, who worked in an ironmonger's shop, reported that women stayed away from his shop on market days, and some were injured by passing animals.[60]

A Smithfield bookseller, John Bumpas, complained that 'not less than 100 ladies ... take shelter in my house' to escape the danger of cattle in the streets. He noted that a woman who was ill passed through the Smithfield area one afternoon and was almost run down by a drove: 'In all probability' her husband 'would have lost his wife, and seven children their mother'. Bumpas also complained that ladies avoided passing through his neighborhood on market days. He had several windows broken and knew of a lady whose 'life was sacrificed' after being run down by cattle coming down Hatton Gardens.[61] These remarks by men attending the select committee meetings suggest that they feared that Smithfield threatened the moral and physical character of women whose presence in public spaces as consumers was contested and unproven.

These moral considerations drew upon the religious and secular roots of the improvement and reform years. Pushing against tradition and the practicalities of meat markets, reformers contributed to the growing public opinion that was in favour of removing the market, but the multiple meanings of cruelty and the embedded practices of Smithfield continued to complicate the debate. By mid-nineteenth century, the reformers joined other Londoners who had become impatient with the City and Parliament as both institutions continued to grapple with legal issues and the resistance of the meat trade. In 1847, a new select committee convened to consider removing Smithfield, and the ground under Smithfield began to shift.

7 THE FINAL ACT: 1840–55

By 1840, the concerns about Smithfield's size and location, public health and morality contributed to a general consensus that something had to be done. After the select committee concluded its consideration of the bill to remove Smithfield market in 1828, improvement and removal were still the only two options. The City had modestly increased the size of the market to six and one-half acres, reorganized the space, removed dilapidated buildings and improved drainage. The effort to establish a market in Islington had failed.

Change and reform evident during the early removal bills accelerated, bringing steam, iron and other technologies to engineers and entrepreneurs who sought ways to solve problems caused by London's increasing population.[1] These innovations challenged the durability of London's urban landscape and institutions. The political landscape had begun a gradual democratization and more diverse voices were heard in Parliament. Londoners, many of whom were now middle class consumers of Smithfield meat, saw themselves as 'civilized' and empowered to improve their city. The Whigs had gained power in Parliament and the Corn Laws had ended, allowing competition from foreign markets. And the sanitation question was yet unresolved as cholera continued to invade the City. The old order of business struggled to adapt to a new, mechanized and timely system of provisioning London. The new system demanded 'orderly arrangements' and rationalized systems as part of the discourse of reform as the City and Parliament struggled to protect the operation of a free market and society.[2]

Even though the City had spent the 1830s improving the market, the press portrayed the City as solely occupied with its business interests, including those of the publicans. The press criticized the City for its inability to take action, bound by old traditions, inertia and languishing power amidst growing pressure for a centralized administrative body for the whole of London. These critics reminded the public that the revenues from the cattle market were not significant enough to motivate such obstinacy and admonished the Common Council for ignoring its own business interests and thereby being guilty of 'inattention, or something worse'.[3]

The City continued its efforts to improve Smithfield and surrounding neighborhoods. In June 1840, Charles Pearson appealed to the Markets Improvement Committee (MIC) to regulate Bartholomew's Fair, citing the transfer of ownership of the market from the Crown to an attorney general, Sir John Rich, in the sixteenth century as the legal basis for City regulation of the space.[4]

The fair had continued to attract hawkers and pickpockets as crowds absorbed the antics of dancing bears, wrestlers and other odd displays, such as the use of steam to hatch baby crocodiles. Critics accused the fair of 'giving the profligate and abandoned opportunity to debauch the innocent' and 'endanger the public peace'. A visitor to the fair in 1825 had seen a mermaid, dwarfs and a 'mare with seven feet'.[5] The fair was an eyesore, offering 'debaucheries and mayhem' in an already contentious space. Pearson also continued to promote his idea of a central rail terminal in the City and attempted to raise money for the Metropolitan Railway. Other rail lines were approaching the periphery of London with new terminals opening throughout the 1850s and 60s.[6]

Critics continued to call attention to the alleged illegality of City's proposed expansion of the market. Those in favour of removing the market felt that the original royal charter only allowed for the trade rights in a four and one-half acre space. Richard Hicks, Chairman of the City's MIC, argued that the market originally covered forty acres and that any enlargement of the market could extend up to the ancient boundaries.[7] The question of the City's legal right to additional land continued to complicate proposals by the City to further enlarge or improve Smithfield. The City held its ground, arguing instead that it possessed the legal right to acquire additional land for public benefit.[8]

Newspapers and periodicals widened the debate about the market. The *Times* continued to berate the City, accusing the aldermen of self-interest, while the City's aldermen accused the newspaper of viewing the inhabitants of Smithfield as the 'special objects of [its] tender care'.[9] The *Citizen* attempted a more conciliatory view, urging the City to be more forceful in its response to critics. And some Londoners wondered why the market was continually well attended when Smithfield was allegedly so vile and unhealthy.

Parliament Reconvenes: Select and Royal Commissions

Select committees and a royal commission took up the debate between 1840 and 1851 when the bill passed to remove the market. In 1847, 1849, 1850 and 1851, the select committees heard from hundreds of witnesses who contributed their own personal observations, advice and evidence for consideration of each bill to either improve or remove the market. Although the arguments were similar for each bill, the emphasis on issues and the selection of witnesses varied somewhat from the bill under consideration in 1828. Recurring issues included

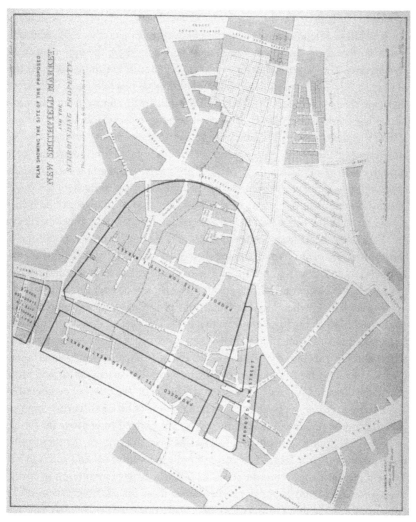

Figure 7.1: The City's plan for an improved market in Smithfield.
1850, Standidge and Co.

the size and location of the market, the deleterious effects of the market upon public health, and allegations of animal cruelty and immorality. In addition to the select committee meetings, other groups met in coffee houses, taverns, trade association halls and in the Guildhall to address the provisions of bills as they arrived in Parliament. By the time Parliament convened in 1847 to consider the removal bill, the denouement of Smithfield live cattle market was irreversible.

In spite of the gathering momentum of public opinion, the opponents were unrelenting. They argued that the government should not 'interfere with this market so injuriously as, in the opinion of almost all practical men, will utterly dislocate this great system of demand and supply, will remove from this most important market a large body of its competing customers, and will divide and scatter that demand which insures its supply, eventually causing a reaction which will seriously affect the supply itself'.[10] The ideas of Malthus lingered, even though evidence of increased agricultural productivity and ample food supplies appeared to contradict the skeptics. But as mid-century approached, the provisioning system of London had weathered technological change, public health crises and an influx of workers into metropolitan London that somehow all got fed. Parliament became emboldened to act and the opponents were outdone by the improvers, intent on modernizing their great city. The Great Exhibition was to open in 1851, putting London on the world stage for all to see, and making the Londoners even more self-conscious about their modernity, or lack of it.

In March 1847, the House of Commons proposed a select committee and appointed both Whigs and conservative MPs; the select committee consisted of mostly reform-minded individuals. Lord Morpeth, a public health reformer who was responsible for the Public Health Bill of 1848, suggested that although the issue was of utmost importance to the metropolis, Parliament should move cautiously. Thomas Wakley, a surgeon and founder of *The Lancet*, considered by some to be a radical, suggested that although most of his constituents opposed the creation of such a select committee, he felt obliged to approve its formation since the inquiry 'would give full satisfaction, not only to the metropolis, but to the country at large'. The anti-Catholic, pro-universal and suffrage MP Edward Prothroe supported the committee on the basis of his interest in changing market days from Monday to Tuesday to allow for the observation of the Sabbath. Lord Henley, Conservative MP, wanted the government to 'take the matter into their own hands.[11]

William Ormsby-Gore was a conservative landowner from Shropshire and Morpeth and a Whig who had supported the reform bills. William Taylor Copeland, a Lord Mayor of London in the 1830s, was a mechanical innovator in the potteries industry and an investor in railway companies. Sir Robert Grosvenor was also a public health reformer and a member of the Incorporated Society for Improving the Condition of the Laboring Classes. While the committee appeared to consist of mostly reform-minded individuals, it appointed two agents to question witnesses, one to represent those in favour of the market removal and one to represent those against removal.[12]

The 1847 bill was for the removal of the market 'to some appropriate site, comprising an area of not less than twelve acres, and the establishment of abattoirs in the vicinity of London'. Over seventy witnesses passed through the committee room, including butchers, farmers, engineers, salesmen, merchants, physicians and City officials. The select committee met throughout the summer of 1847 and concluded that it was impossible come to a decision with too little time to consider the overwhelming amount of information provided by the witnesses.[13] By the end of the session, the committee recommended to continue deliberations during the next session of Parliament the following year.

The public and the press continued to exchange opinions concerning the status of the market in Smithfield. In December 1848, an inhabitant of Smithfield wrote an article in the *Farmer's Magazine*, exhorting the publication to join in the battle to remove Smithfield. The magazine responded by excoriating the 'monopoly which the Smithfield salesmen enjoy' and the violence, recklessness, savage treatment of animals that the 'graphic force of truth' conveyed to the public.[14]

Meanwhile, after Perkins' Islington market closed and he passed away, his three sisters took possession of the land and became interested in selling the enterprise.[15] A group of investors gathered in 1848 to establish a joint stock company for the purpose of re-establishing Perkins' market. Called the Islington Cattle Market and Abattoir Company, the new market gained support from Parliament and assured its shareholders that Smithfield would close, insuring the financial success of its new venture.[16] In possession of Perkins' assets and the market facilities, the group argued that their company would overcome previous objections by combining public and private interests. The public investors, they argued, would attract reformers who wanted changes for the public good and the 'other class of supporters' would include those who thought they could make the enterprise profitable. Since earlier objections came from those who feared that Perkins would have a private monopoly of the live cattle trade, this new venture was promising.[17] Meanwhile, the market served as a grazing area for cattle traveling on to Smithfield.

While the company sought investors, the City was very much aware of statements made by witnesses in the House of Commons and convened its own session in the Court of Common Council. During the spring of 1849, J. T. Norris, a printer from Aldersgate Street near Smithfield, made a strong case for moving the market, while Mr Anderton (a member of the Court of Common Council) felt that the market's central location was its greatest asset and that moving it would disrupt commerce in the metropolis. He criticized the prospectus printed for the joint stock company to re-establish the Islington market, accusing the investors of being speculators interested in exploiting the public. Anderton disparaged the investors, stating that they were proposing profits similar to those sought by gold-seekers in California. He proposed that the market remain in Smithfield, where it was more profitable than panning for gold. Anderton advised the Common Council to ' ... maintain the market as long as they were able to do so, and until they were interfered with by the Legislature of the country'. The Council was inclined to follow Anderton's advice. Seemingly tone deaf to the rising imprecations in the select committee, the City continued its own prevarication within the Markets Improvement Committee and the Common Council.

Other Londoners expressed their support to the Common Council of the City's desire to improve the existing market. William Jones, a physician from Berkeley Square, believed the market to be a 'blessing to its locality', and a butcher, George Godson, felt that cruelty was expressed towards the animals in Smithfield was 'much more in imagination than in reality'. But other Londoners opposed the City's apparent complacency. One told the City that 'the expirations and exhalations from the cattle were most inimical to the health of all parties residing in the vicinity; the very air was contaminated by the expired breathing of the thousands of animals, and the fetid stench which arose from the excrements was also highly prejudicial to health'.[18] The City continued its discussions about ways to further improve the space beyond its efforts to provide officers to supervise the drovers and butchers and to improve drainage systems within the market.

While the press reported these meetings, Parliament called for another select committee to continue deliberations concerning the removal bill. Some MPs felt that the wording of the bill was prejudicial and suggested that a decision had already been reached to remove the market. After changes in the wording of the preamble of the bill and the membership of the committee, Parliament authorized the select committee to begin work during the summer of 1849.[19]

Almost seventy-five witnesses testified before the committee, including butchers, physicians, and sixteen police inspectors. Salesmen, local business owners, graziers, a civil engineer and professors, also filed in to remonstrate against the continuance of the market in Smithfield or to argue for improvements for the market in its current position. By June, the committee resolved that 'the continuance of a market for the sale of live stock in Smithfield is proved by experience to be attended with serious inconveniences and objections, and that it ought to be removed'. The members noted that the City had made improvements to the market but, 'the inconveniences referred to [would] not admit of prevention'. The committee wanted an expansion of the market to account for future growth of the meat market and to maintain the healthy benefits of open space. Other resolutions included the recognition that the metropolis could only accommodate a single market, located near transport facilities (railways and waterways). It also called for meat and abattoir inspectors, larger lairs and a change from Monday to

Tuesday as the first market day of the week.[20] In spite of all these remonstrations and accommodations, the market went about its business. Indeed, the intransigence of the old Smithfield system kept the cattle market in its ancient location.

The committee's recommendations met an indecisive Parliament. Concerns about timing and inconsistent evidence provided by witnesses stalled the bill. In July 1849, Parliament concluded that although the space in Smithfield was too small, efforts should continue to find accommodation for additional space and improvements. In spite of the pressure applied by reformers, the allegations of animal cruelty in the market failed to convince Parliament that animal welfare could be improved by a relocation of the market. Instead, Parliament supported the committee's recommendation that,

> ... while we are sensible that all cruelty must tend to degrade and brutalize its perpetrators, and that anything dangerous to health is an evil great in proportion, not only to the density of the population around, but also to its poverty and consequent inability to take precautions or obtain remedies for itself, we cannot disguise from ourselves that in every city, how civilized soever it may be, occupations must exist whose details are disgusting, and that no arrangement can separate the infliction of death on so many thousand animals from some practices painful to contemplate, though it is comparatively easy to exhibit evils and to counsel change.[21]

MPs admitted that even a city as civilized and modern as London had to tolerate undesirable trades and practices in order to feed its empire. Growing laissez-faire economic policies and the desire not to interfere with a functioning market system trumped the improvers. But even this statement condoning the status quo failed to quell the effort to move the market.

In November 1849, four months after the committee delivered its recommendations, the Queen appointed a royal commission 'to report upon Smithfield market, and to inquire into the state and management of all markets in the City of London for the sale of meat'.[22] Queen Victoria may have well become impatient with the parade of select committees designated to deliberate on Smithfield market. She asked the royal commissioners to review the recommendations made by the select committee of 1849.

Members included the Under Secretary of State George Cornewall Lewis. Son of a baronet, Lewis was a liberal politician who had become an MP after an academic career at Eton, Oxford and law school. He worked hard to unravel the issues of poorhouse reform and was the object of Chadwick's ire when Chadwick was passed over as a member of the poor law commission in favour of Lewis. After a scandal involving mistreatment of prisoners at the Andover workhouse, Lewis left the commission in 1847 and ran for a seat in the House of Commons, which he won.[23] Frederick Byng, also a member of the House of Commons, had the unfortunate nickname 'Poodle' either given him by Lady Bath and the Duchess of Devonshire who remarked about Byng's curly locks ...

or because he made a striking impression upon Londoners with his daily walk with a black French poodle. Early in his career he was a member of the Foreign Service and a Gentleman Usher to the Privy Council while he was member of the Smithfield Commission. Byng, seen by his peers and the press as a dandy, appeared in London periodicals in feathered breeches.[24]

Other commission members included Richard Owen, the Hunterian scientist, comparative anatomist, and founder of the British Natural History Museum and Matthew Wood, the son of a hop merchant and former Lord Mayor of London, who worked as a lawyer on behalf of the railroads before becoming the Queen's counsel in 1845.[25] Wood was a member of the Fishmonger's Company and a liberal orator, successfully sentencing 'the Coggeshall gang' in a contentious trial in 1848, just before his appointment to the Smithfield Commission.[26] Harry Verney, also a liberal, was a friend of George Stephenson and was a follower of evangelicals such as William Whewell. Issues that gained his support included the repeal of the Corn Laws and the abolition of the slave trade. All the members of the commission were liberal politicians, even 'Poodle' who was a member of Brooke's, the prestigious social club for Whigs.[27] In defense of accusations that the committee was prejudiced towards removal, MP Mackinnon insisted that the committee members were 'fifteen honest and honorable men'.[28] His deflection of criticism of the political makeup of the committee seemed inadequate, leading others to question the objectivity of the entire process.

The press continued to demand that the royal commission take action. A letter in *The Theatrical Journal* requested that the press 'step out of their regular course and endeavor to remedy the evil ... thereby giving an impetus to public opinion and benefit society in general'. The inhabitants of Clerkenwell wrote the paper requesting that the commission take swift action to remove the market so that sanitary reform could proceed. Another letter to the editor referred to the City's plan as a collection of 'abominable jobs'.[29] Pressure to act was becoming intolerable; something or someone had to give.

The royal commission completed its work and wrote a final report on May 24, 1850. The impact of increased quantities of imported livestock was unclear and the commissioners expressed their concern about British suppliers. Commission members noted the increasing demand for meat in the metropolis but acknowledged that supply had met demand. The commission knew of increasing quantities of animals and meat arriving by rail. These encouraging developments complicated the arguments about the future space requirements for the live cattle market.

The commission continued to acknowledge the beneficial aspects of Smithfield's centrality to the metropolis and its connections with the main thoroughfares coming from all directions. But it also criticized the market for obstructing traffic through and around the City.[30] The commission concluded that the market in Smithfield could not be improved and that it was insufficient to provision a city of the size and importance of London. Thus, the commissioners took the position that the market should be removed, not improved.

The commissioners noted that there were several proposals for other sites but refrained from recommending any specific location. They thought that the new cattle market should be paid for and managed by the City with the needed sums of money required for such a venture to come from additional market tolls. Further recommendations concerned the meat markets: Newgate should be closed and the City should erect a new meat market in the existing Smithfield space. Public slaughterhouses should be built and private slaughterhouses should be annually inspected and licensed. And market hours should change to alleviate traffic congestion within the City.

While its recommendations were comprehensive and more decisive, the royal commission worried about the negative impact of such recommendations, stating, ' ... we are not unmindful of the loss of custom which this measure would entail upon certain classes of retail dealers resident in the neighborhood. It is with sincere regret that we recommend any change which would be attended even with partial and temporary loss of trade ... but such local diminution of mercantile profit are the necessary, though undersigned, consequences of all extensive improvements, which alter existing traffic and communication'. They held out an olive branch to the City, suggesting that the property in Smithfield would increase in value as a result of the removal of the market. The City quickly responded with a statement supporting its own plan to improve the market and indicated that a new meat market to replace Newgate was part of its own improvement plan.[31] Thus Parliament was emboldened to act and the City was provoked to resist.

The City's Response

Parallel with the deliberations underway in Parliament, the City had been occupied with its own response to the mounting pressure to remove the market. The City's MIC began meeting in October 1849 to respond to a petition from several butchers, graziers and salesmen who opposed the removal of Smithfield.[32] All three groups supported the improvement of the existing Smithfield by expanding the size of the market space. The MIC met to discuss three City markets. Led by Chairman Henry Lowman Taylor, the committee requested the City Architect, J. B. Bunning, to prepare plans for the markets in Smithfield, Newgate and Leadenhall.[33] As an afterthought, they requested a plan of Farringdon since the area had also been a market and was adjacent to the Newgate market. Bunning provided multiple plans for the City's improvement of Smithfield. The City was moving forward with its plan for the cattle market to remain in its ancient location.

Guildhall was abuzz with new plans and ideas for ways to modernize the market. In November, the MIC heard from seventeen petitioners who supported the improvement of the market. Salesmen, graziers, butchers and bankers argued that more space would increase the number of cattle in the market by eight hundred to a thousand and increase the number of sheep by five or six thousand.[34] The additional space would come from the area to the west of the existing market and adjoin Victoria Street. Smithfield bankers, Joseph Pocklington and W. Wiggerstaff, and salesmen John and William Collins, John Giblett, William Guerrier, Charles Burrell and John Low, George Jacomb, a butcher, W. Johnson, a wine merchant and E. S. Caley, an 'agriculturalist', attended the meeting along with William Shank, the Clerk of the Market at Smithfield. Pearson, as City Solicitor, represented the interests of the City (and perhaps the Metropolitan Railway). The petitioners indicated that they would be willing to pay higher tolls to generate the funds necessary to expand the market rather than see the market remove to another location. Some of the petitioners would complain about the higher tolls once the market removed to Islington. They were aware that the market for meat was growing and that the railroads were replacing the wagons that had previously brought meat to London. The petitioners also pointed out that because of the increase in foreign cattle coming to Smithfield, the metropolis would require wider streets as part of the improvements. And to address concerns about traffic congestion and concerns about space limitations, they suggested that the sheep hurdles could be temporarily taken down to provide more space for cattle.

The group gathered for the purpose of promoting the enlargement of Smithfield was not necessarily united on all issues. There were numerous areas of contention regarding the market operation, use of ties, rings and off-droves, but the petitioners were united in their desire for more space. Shank informed the committee that since August 1849 the Monday market took in 4,500 to 5,000 cattle and 30,000 sheep. About 22,000 to 23,000 sheep and 2,750 cattle were tied up in the market at one time. Thirteen hundred cattle were in off-droves. He thought he could reorganize the existing space to accommodate up to 4,800 cattle. Bunning incorporated these suggestions into his new designs for the market and surrounding streets, indicating newly organized areas that could be enlarged to accommodate more animals.

Realizing the potential for the Crown to scoop the City's effort to address the needs of Smithfield, the committee asked the Court of Common Council for permission to inquire about the royal commission and to coordinate the activities of the City with those of the Crown. The Council resolved to dig deeper into the City budget so that it could provide Bunning with the resources to develop plans of other sites for an enlarged Smithfield, including details of property costs and terms. The Council also asked the MIC to create a deputation for the purpose of meeting with the Crown concerning its efforts. Chairman Taylor and committee members Dakin, Hicks, Low and Hall became members of the deputation. On a chilly December 11, the deputies visited the royal commission on Downing Street and offered information that they thought might be helpful to the government's deliberations. The commission requested the deputies to provide the 'facts' about the market and information about the City's legal right to operate its markets, including all information about the City's desire to improve or enlarge Smithfield. In exchange, the deputies asked for all information about the government commission but deferred from offering any compromises without more funding and support from the Common Council. The royal commission urged the deputies to acquire such power so that the commission could continue to be apprised of the City's interests and activities.

The City increased its engagement with the government by assembling more information about the market. At its next meeting, the MIC assigned members to gather information on the City's legal rights to the market, the finances of the market, and plans of Smithfield and Newgate. It also prepared a statement of the advantages and disadvantages of leaving the markets in its current location. Salesmen in Newgate contributed by preparing a report of meat sales from 1839 to 1849.

By the beginning of 1850, the MIC had received additional powers from the Court of Common Council and increased its own membership. All reports were delivered to the royal commission and Bunning produced plans that would allow for 5, 000 cattle and 30,000 sheep in pens. Plans for an enlarged market included areas for a meat market and slaughterhouses. Deputy Hicks came up with plans for an enlarged Newgate market. Chairman Taylor urged the MIC to seek more support from the Common Council as it prepared to meet again with the royal commission. Armed with plans and calculations of the additional market tolls needed to expand Smithfield, the MIC deputation met with the royal commission in an attempt to deflect the government's attention away from a recommendation that would remove the cattle market. The deputation found innovative ways to sweeten their proposals. In order to alleviate the traffic in the roads leading to and from the market, the deputation recommended a toll for animals that left the market after seven in the morning to discourage animal traffic on the streets after the influx of commercial traffic in the morning.

The City took a broad view of the improvements in and around Smithfield. While the deputation reported back to the MIC about its meeting with the royal commission, the MIC was hard at work on plans to improve Holborn Hill and the area around Newgate market. The committee was aware that the improvement of Smithfield market would include the demolition of a number of old buildings in the area. The MIC had proposed some of similar area improvements to the royal commission, including a connection between New Street and Victoria Street in order to ease the flow of traffic. Meanwhile, costs for these improvements were increasing and the City recalculated the increases in tolls required to finance the project. Bunning amended his earlier estimates by stat-

ISOMETRIC VIEW OF PROPOSED IMPROVEMENTS IN THE NEIGHBOURHOOD OF SMITHFIELD.

J. B. BUNNING, ARCH TO THE CORPORATION OF LONDON. 1851.

Figure 7.3 James Bunning's proposed improvements to Smithfield, James Bunstone Bunning, George Hawkins, John King & Co., 1851.

ing that the meat markets improvements would cost not £141,000 but instead £177,000. Bunning was also working on specific operational improvements to the market such as a new apparatus for the cattle lairs that would make it easier for salesmen and buyers to pass between animals.

The City prepared its petition for a bill in Parliament for the improvement of Smithfield. The MIC worked with the Court of Common Council on the various plans, costs and tolls for improvement, not removal of the market. In order to promote its plans, the committee approved funds for advertisements, printing and publication of materials to explain the benefits of their plan to the general public. To ameliorate the sanitation problems, the City proposed to elevate the area so that waste would pour into a reservoir at one end that would connect with a nearby sewer tunnel. Other improvements in the City plan included an expansion of the market to include twelve acres, the removal of 'offensive' trades and 'haunts of immorality and pauperism', limits on cross traffic through the market, regulations pertaining to cattle that might enter the market during business hours, redesigned streets, better lairs with feeding troughs and water sources, a public abattoir and officers who would supervise drainage from improved drainage systems designed to deflect effluence away from the Thames and the surrounding neighborhood. The plan also proposed removing Newgate meat market to a new location on Victoria Street. And to address public concerns, the City included housing for the poor, public baths and an elegant water fountain. Well aware of the costs of such a grand plan, the City proposed to finance the improvements through its own debt. The increase in tolls, the City argued, would only be one penny per hundredweight of meat.[35]

In November 1850, the City placed a notice in the *London Gazette* indicating its application to Parliament for the City's enlargement and improvement bill for Smithfield.[36] To promote its bill, the City formed The London Central Markets' Association (also called the London Market Protection Association) to support the continuation of the London markets in their present location, the compensation for losses if the market relocated, the integration of recommendations of the Sanitary Commission, and the protection of consumers and producers from the imposition of taxes and tolls. The Association proposed that a new market in the same location would remove old slum buildings and modernize thoroughfares. Promoting the image of the City as a champion of modernized sanitation, the Association proposed an improved, hygienic slaughterhouse and the removal of the 'contiguous abominations' such as the knackers (workers in the business of buying old or injured horses for slaughter and sale) and bone collectors. It defended the City by arguing that descriptions of unsanitary conditions were often exaggerated and contested. George Borrows, a physician from St Bartholomew's Hospital, stated that Smithfield 'is one of the purest sites in the centre of London'.[37]

Others would step up to defend the City's plan. Thomas M. Challis, the meat salesman in Newgate and skin and leather salesman in Leadenhall, became an articulate advocate of the City's efforts to improve the cattle market in Smithfield and was treasurer of The Central Markets' Association. In a letter to Lord John Russell, a member of the select committee in Parliament, Challis argued on behalf of free trade and the consumer. Quoting Peel's definition of a free market, 'the right to buy in the cheapest and to sell in the dearest market', Challis railed against the removal.[38] He accused Russell of betraying his own free market principles, pointing out that that the government's plan would inconvenience buyers, increase the number of middlemen who would add to the cost of meat and upset the relationships embedded in the old system. How could it be possible, he asked, that the citizens of London would barter their right to free trade on the basis of a 'minor question of insufficiency of space?' Challis argued that the self-interest of the graziers, salesmen, butchers would not combine to give any one group 'a pecuniary advantage'. He accused the committee of shunning farmers, encouraging middlemen, adding costs, and raising prices. Challis saw these additional costs as a tax on food, an anathema to a growing population needing cheap and plenteous food. Challis continued,

> ... in a central market-place, where there is the variety consequent on a great demand and a large supply, each buyer will have the opportunity of purchasing the article that suits him best ... ' The extra expense incurred by butchers going to and from the live cattle market would indeed be passed on to the buyer. And, since at least one-third of all the cattle bought at Smithfield travelled over Blackfriars Bridge to feed the burgeoning population south of the Thames, moving the market to Islington would only increase the distance cattle would need to travel to reach those markets.[39]

He argued against the 'great cuckoo cries of the day' and criticized their 'unscrupulous zeal and persevering cupidity'. He was resentful of those in the committee who relied on theories instead of the realities of the market and the advice of those who had spent their lives buying and selling cattle in Smithfield.[40]

The comments of Challis and the opinions of the merchants of the market had made their impact in time to be included in the City's proposed Act for the Improvement of Smithfield. On Christmas Eve, the MIC met to discuss Challis' request for space on the Cheapside area of the market so that he and his Association could display the model of the proposed improvements while lecturing on the merits of the proposal. The MIC agreed to release their model for public display, stipulating that the Association would have to make good on any damage to their prize promotional piece.

The Association's publicity was effective: Letters from the public began arriving at the committee meetings along with requests for copies of their plan. The City's Central Markets Association wanted copies of Bunning's models and plans so it could display the materials at the upcoming Smithfield Prize Cattle Show. The Christmas cattle show was attended by thousands of people eager to see the huge cattle on display and undoubtedly presented a timely opportunity for the MIC to promote its plan to a wide audience. Others in the trade continued to make arguments against the relocation of the market. In *An Appeal to the British Public of the Abuses of Smithfield Market and the Advantages of a New Central Cattle market Fairly Considered of 1850*, George Jacomb, a butcher, argued for the City's proposal to improve the existing market. He warned of 'pseudo-philanthropists who used patriotism to exaggerate the abuses and 'monster nuisance' of the cattle market to 'benefit the public – by enriching themselves.'[41] The appeal criticized those who were most offended by the animal traffic in the crowded streets of London and 'who covet the seclusion which has selfishness for its motive and exemption from the inconveniences of busy life'. Jacomb urged those who wanted to be shielded from the hubbub in the City to instead seek rustic tranquility in the 'untraversed wilds of a primitive district'. Leaning towards hyperbole, he reinforced the importance of Smithfield in Britain's meat provisioning system by stating that Smithfield's central position in the city would attract the support of the growing industry that fed an expanding British empire.[42] Placing Smithfield in a global context, Jacomb appealed to British identity in the broadest sense.

Agreeing with Jacomb, some of the inhabitants of Smithfield expressed their concern that the removal of Smithfield would open up Smithfield to outsiders, 'foreigners', who would purchase land in Smithfield and then later benefit from higher land prices. Those in favour of the City's plan believed that the removal of Smithfield from the City centre would signal the beginning of a pattern of other market removals. Both the expected arrival of outsiders and the disintegration of the old market system insinuated instability within the changing landscape of modern London.

In early 1851, the City's Central Markets' Association was still campaigning for a new, improved market in Smithfield. Members met at a coffeehouse with their model of the improved market and promoted Bunning's design. James Acland, the Association's secretary, circulated petitions to gain support of the market.[43] Lord Russell and Sir George Grey agreed to meet the Association on Downing Street in February and the Association members returned to the Guildhall with the news that in spite of Bunnings' artful design and the impressive model, the government intended to pursue a bill for the removal of Smithfield. The bill would not include a recommendation for a new site for the market; the government appeared uninterested in reviewing any proposal from the City. In February 1851, during a meeting in the House of Commons, Sir George Grey brought in the bill to remove the market and indicated that the select committee to consider Smithfield market had ignored the City's proposal.[44]

Before enacting a bill for removal, Parliament took stock of all the bills pending that related to Smithfield's fate. It was still considering the bill (called the
Islington Market Bill) for incorporating the Islington Cattle Market and Abattoir Company that wanted to re-open Perkins' market along with another bill
for a cattle market at Hornsey. The public, realizing that Parliament was committed to the relocation of the market, inundated Parliament and the City with
proposals for alternate markets. Some who opposed the relocation submitted
their plans for improving Smithfield and were anxious about the impact of any
plan upon their lives, businesses and land. At this eleventh hour, reformers were
piling on to get their ideas heard, hoping to take advantage of a sense that Parliament was ready to act.

Hoping to get Parliament to take an interest in the City's plan, the MIC
obtained copies of the existing bills and continued responding to proposals for
improvements, including those from Major Cresswell of Northfleet, Kent who
offered suggestions concerning ways to fireproof the new buildings in Smithfield.
Inhabitants worried about the impact of the City's plan on their own property:
An anxious typesetter wanted to know how the City would treat his building
during the improvements. The churchwardens of the parish of St Sepulchre wondered about the loss of rents from buildings that the City planned to remove.

This was not a class conflict in the sense of a battle between workers and the
Corporation of London, the City. Petitioners often switched sides and some took
unexpected positions. Businessmen often argued against improving the market
and butchers sometimes wanted the status quo and other times wanted the cattle
market to be improved. In March, a group of businessmen called a special ves-
try meeting in St James to consider the preparation of a petition to Parliament
outlining their objections to the City's proposal to improve Smithfield. Richard
Hicks, a cattle and meat salesman and a member of the MIC, led the meeting.
He addressed the concerns that the City would raise tolls in order to pay for
the improvements. One critic called Bunning's design for improving the market 'absurd, impractical', and thought the City had outgrown its ancient market
rights.[45] The businessmen felt that the City's plan for traffic restrictions made no
sense; its improvements were too expensive and in order to acquire the necessary
land, it would remove over five hundred houses, four schools, a parish churchyard
and the West London Workhouse. Hicks said that ten thousand people would
lose their homes. They scoffed at the City's unrelenting promotion of Smithfield's
'salubrity' and centrality and suggested that if the City had truly considered the
location of the dwellings of most of Smithfield's butchers, it would have located
the market in Trafalgar, a location more convenient for the west and east end
butchers. These accusations stemmed from a growing disrespect and impatience
directed towards the City whom the public saw as increasingly irrelevant, holding
meetings out of phase with public concerns and revealing the loss of political trac-

tion in the empty halls of Mansion House. Frustration at the City's inability to exert leadership or to control the political process emerged from multiple fronts. Critics displayed outrage at the City's taxation of meat (through tolls) while the City allowed the market to continue as 'one of the greatest nuisances that ever disgraced a civilized society'.[46] Some saw the representatives in the House of Lords who agreed with the select committee to move the market as possessing the 'insolent communism of interested adventurers.[47]

The City's bill was in the hands of Parliament and was about to be read in the House of Commons. The City's efforts to publicize its plan continued as it sent copies of Bunning's isometric plans going to clubs, including the Farmers' Club, the Institute of Civil Engineers, merchants and MPs. One supporter of the City's plan bought fifteen hundred copies of J. Stevenson Bushnan's pamphlet, 'Moral and Sanitary Aspects of the New Central Cattle Market as Proposed by the Corporation of the City of London', and sent them to members of the committee and Parliament.[48]

The City made several more attempts to engage Parliament. The MIC decided to send a petition to Parliament in opposition to the removal bill and indicated that it would remove objectionable sections from the City bill to enable a more favourable reading. It sent a letter to five members of Parliament to request that all the bills concerning the market be sent to the same select committee in Parliament so that each would receive fair consideration. In Parliament, petitions arrived daily in support of and in opposition to the bills before Parliament. The MIC encouraged its own members to submit petitions and was keenly aware of the need to influence public opinion; one hundred and thirty-three petitions in favour of the City's plan reached Parliament. The MIC paid subsequent visits to Mr Grey in the Home Department for the purpose of promoting the City bill and to learn about the progress of the government bill.[49]

In April, 1851, Parliament had decided to drop consideration of the City bill and to move forward on the government bill to remove the market. Discussions leading up to that decision considered the public and private nature of the bills, the necessity to follow through on the recommendation of the royal commission, and futility of proceeding with two bills that fairly contradicted each other. The select committee refused to entertain the City's proposal to improve Smithfield and instead prepared a final report that recommended that Smithfield be removed from the City.[50] Undaunted, the City continued to promote its bill and argue against removal.

Several MPs were wary of the provision in the government's bill for a government commission that would operate a new market. Others were concerned that the bill omitted the determination of a site for a new market, since the location of a new market would raise important considerations of proximity to the meat markets and orientation relative to the cattle driving routes. The MP

Joseph Hume, a radial and proponent of universal suffrage, was on the side of the City. He argued that with the government rejection of the City bill, it might as well abolish the City. Hume warned, 'Where was this system of centralisation to end?' He felt that the rejection of the City bill signaled the first time that the government had 'violated all the rights of a corporation'.[51] Could it be that these concerns marked London's turn towards modern, centralized metropolitan governance? In all likelihood they did and the latter half of the century brought an institutional changes that would bring together the broader interests of a modern London that had outgrown the insular world of the City.

In May, the select committee in Parliament decided that the only parties that should be heard relative to the opposition of Parliament's bill would be the butchers, the City, the inhabitants near Smithfield, St Bartholomew's Hospital, and a representative of the merchants in Smithfield, wine merchant, William Johnson.[52] During a meeting in the House of Commons, the Butcher's Company petitioned the select committee. Sergeant Wrangham, a member of the select committee, offered the provocative argument that the butchers have no right to petition since their objections concern their private interests not the public good.[53] This allegation did not deter Mr Kettle, a butcher, who pointed out that Smithfield is a butcher's only legal wholesale market and so to interfere with Smithfield is to interfere with their right to trade.[54] St Bartholomew's Hospital wanted a guarantee that no buildings would be erected on the land vacated by the market and the local inhabitants asked for compensation for the market removal (They were denied). Some wanted the government to hold the City accountable for reforms in the new market if it continued to operate the cattle market in a new location. The select committee altered some clauses to extend the City's market rights and to provide for a regular public audit of the City's funds if the City managed a new market.

By now, two government bills, the removal bill and the Islington Market Bill were in Parliament. In June, Bunning reported that the select committee refused his testimony in opposition to the government bill, inciting the City's counsel to recommend that Bunning withdraw from the MIC. Eventually, Bunning did testify although the City and the butchers did not. More than ever, Parliament shaped the debate about the bill to relocate the market, allowing selected petitioners and including prejudiced MPs to participate on the select committee and in Parliamentary debates.

Letters continued to arrive from individuals who had their own ideas about the market, its location and operation. Some offered suggestions for a new location of the market to Nothing Hill, Plaistow and the North Woolwich Marshes, which were 'politely acknowledged'. While the House of Lords moved slowly, stumbling on legal process questions, the Lord Mayor of the City agreed to appear in opposition to the bill. New clauses appeared in the bill to compensate the City for the removal, but were later removed. Finally, on June 24, the bill passed after a third reading with a vote of 81 to 32.[55] On August 1, the act received royal assent and the next day, after months of campaigning for its own bill, the City received news that the act had passed into law.[56]

Objections continued but the Metropolitan Market Act closed the live cattle market in Smithfield and removed the market to another site outside the City.[57] The Act appointed five government commissioners to build and manage the new market with broad powers to collect tolls and to manage the market and the activities of the drovers. Licenses were required for all slaughterhouses in an attempt to enforce previous statutes designed to license new slaughterhouses.

The Act gave the City six months to decide to continue to maintain its ownership of the market rights for the live cattle market to be located elsewhere. If the City elected to execute the Act, the City would have three years to design, build and open the market in the new site. This provision exemplified the collaboration of Parliament with the City as Parliament provided the political engine to move the market at a time when the City was unable to forward its own proposals. Considering the legal issues concerning the City's trading rights, the concerns over public property, and the loss of political power on the part of the City, this collaboration was a pragmatic solution for this decades-old urban 'nuisance'. And, without a centralized municipal authority in place, Parliament was the still the only political and legal entity that could orchestrate a metropolitan-wide project.

The Act to relocate Smithfield confronted the City with a sober message. The City's political power and ability to govern the metropolis was weakened, challenged by Parliament and marginalized in spite of the City's efforts to rally support among merchants, butchers, graziers and the inhabitants.[58] Outside of the municipal reforms bills, the City had continued with its traditional governance practices, confident that it could manage reforms from within the City. Newspaper and magazine articles suggested that the public had become weary of the City's 'incoherent argument' and an 'alternation of braggadocio and hothouse facetiousness which so eminently mark the baffled and despairing advocate'. Although some had been encouraged by the City's bill, they thought it had come too late and had been 'born of the ghost Apprehension'.[59] While the City had endeavored to convince the public of the merits of its bill, it had failed to convince a public that had become distrustful and impatient. As David Owen pointed out, 'The City seemed to be the sole survivor from the bad old days; and its archaic institutions, its financial confusion and its smug professions of virtue were all out of place in the mid-century world'.[60]

The MIC invited salesmen and butchers to join them in consideration of the new act in order to determine how they should respond and the impacts of the removal. This was all the more frustrating for some MIC members, who, like Challis, believed that the problems associated with Smithfield would have long ago been remediated if only the government had allowed the City to proceed with the necessary improvements.

The Common Council reviewed the Act and considered the impact of the disappearance of the market from its historic site. The Council took its time and by January, the deadline arrived for the City to decide if it would continue with its trading rights in Islington. The MIC urged the Council to notify the government that the City would take the option designated in the Act for the City to continue to operate the market. Sensing the need for action, the Court approved the motion and the City quickly sent its representative to the Home Secretary, requesting plans and information regarding a new site for the market. Plans for new sites arrived both in the government's hands and in the hands of the MIC for consideration alongside the existing bill for the market in Islington that was still sitting in Parliament awaiting a hearing.

The MIC recognized that it had to commit to a new site for the market. Private individuals continued inundating the MIC with plans for new market sites. Mr J Carter appeared with plans but was dismissed since his plans included more than one market near London to replace the one Smithfield. They dismissed another plan, proposed by Mr W. Black because it was on the 'Surrey side of the River'. Mr W. Taylor proposed Waltham or Epping Forest. Sir Henry Jervis also wanted several markets around London, and the committee also rejected proposals for Ealing Common, Bow Common, Old Oak (Acton), Wanstead Flats, and Hammersmith. In all, the committee heard from individuals who proposed twelve plans for new sites. At the same time, the committee scrambled to learn more about the proceedings in Parliament concerning the Islington site. The Islington bill had been read once and was headed for its second reading while the City continued to oppose the bill.[61]

The passage of the bill stirred up interest from those who saw opportunities for land development, transport, and for their own ideas for where the new market should be located. By March 1852, at least twenty site proposals were on the table, some including land costs, and many accompanied by railroad representatives promoting the sites. The site of Old Oak Common gained support outside the committee and interested parties presented evidence to the committee in favour of the site, particularly individuals related to the railroads (North Western Railway and Great Western Railway). All were within about five to seven miles of the City. Engineer Thomas Cubitt appeared with his plan near Hornsey Wood on one hundred sixty acres. The solicitors for the owner of the Islington market continued their efforts to persuade the City to purchase the market.

Bunning presented plans for a site in Copenhagen Fields in Islington that consisted of fifty to sixty acres, expandable to one hundred acres and took the initiative to obtain the site at the most favourable terms and price.[62] But his efforts came under fire by the press that weighed in with its opinion about the City's selection of Copenhagen Fields. Dickens was one of those who expressed pessimism about moving the market to Copenhagen Fields in Islington. In *Household Words*, Dickens opined about Copenhagen Fields with houses 'as densely packed as they are in Cow Cross' and wondered about the wisdom of moving the market to a place where 'there will be as much trouble in getting the cattle in and out of the new market as there is to get them in and out of Smithfield, in spite of railways. There will be as large an acreage of population round Copenhagen Fields to be poisoned with stench and disgusted with bad language, as there is round Smithfield'.[63]

The MIC remained convinced that Bunning's proposal for Copenhagen Fields was the best option. It decided not to consider the proposal from the Islington Cattle and Abattoir Company unless the offer was unconditional and less expensive. In April, the City negotiated with the Islington Cattle Market and Abattoir Company and offered £90,000, pending approval of the Court of Common Council. The Islington company was eager to sell its market and negotiated with the City, offering £112,000. In spite of the effort to reach an agreement, the City preferred its own Islington site and informed the Secretary of State of their intention to proceed with the Copenhagen Fields site, stating that if the land could be purchased for a 'reasonable sum' that they would purchase the site. The market so presciently built by Perkins decades earlier became irrelevant, in spite of its modern technical innovations and existing buildings. Perhaps the owners were too uncompromising about their selling price, terms of administration, or perhaps the City wanted its own imprint on the new market under terms it controlled.

Bunning returned with the news that eighty acres in Copenhagen Fields could be purchased for £750 per acre, an astoundingly higher price than originally stated. Undaunted, the committee proceeded with negotiations and met with Walpole to present its plan. By May, 1852, Walpole agreed to accept Copenhagen Fields as the site for the new market and the MIC gave Bunning permission to negotiate beyond the sixty acres. In June, the City purchased the sixty acres at Copenhagen Fields and began to obtain the title for the land. By September, Walpole gave the MIC formal approval of the Copenhagen site.

Already the City had to defend its selection of the market site, confirming Dicken's prediction that the new market would be as odious to Islington as the old market had been to Smithfield. The inhabitants of Camden Town, near the new site, objected to 'the disgusting object' being 'plumped down again in the midst of the streets, immediately the policeman's eye was for a moment off it'. The petitioners accused Walpole of betraying the public trust and invading a settled neighborhood with the notorious Smithfield nuisance. *The Builder* alleged that the site had inadequate water supplies for the market.[64] *Punch* decried the effort of Parliament to remove the market 'away from the heart of the City, and [to] lay in down in the bosom of an elegant little suburb, is something like extracting a carbuncle from a groggy old gentleman's nose and transplanting it to a delicate young lady's cheek'.[65]

The committee also heard a supportive petition put together by those who lived near Copenhagen Fields, but the committee concluded that the evidence presented by those in opposition to the site was unconvincing. Preparations for the construction of the market began by placing cornerstones on the property and beginning a survey. The committee got the Clerk of the Works at the prison to guard the property and further negotiations led to the acquisition of a few more acres in the surrounding neighborhood to complete the market. In 1853, the City ordered that Copenhagen House, located on Copenhagen Fields, be demolished to make way for the new cattle market.[66] Throughout 1854, the City, builders, engineers and hundreds of suppliers and contracts occupied the site to erect the new market.

On the first day of June 1855, George Grey, Whig Home Secretary, signed a notice that appeared in the *London Gazette* signifying that the City had complied with all the provisions in the 1851 Act. Grey designated June 15th as the opening day for the new Metropolitan Cattle Market and declared, ' ... from that day Smithfield market will cease to be a market for the sale of cattle and horses'.

The celebratory scene at the opening of the Metropolitan Cattle market on that rainy June 15th in Islington brought together both public and private interests in an expansive space fitted with iron railings, covered lairs, flowing troughs, and graded walkways. The City, elated and somewhat relieved, gathered to celebrate the 'splendid and useful work', so designated by Prince Albert.[67] The corner stone laid at beginning of construction of the clock tower in 1854, testified to the stabilizing effect of the combined efforts of both the City and Parliament.

Not surprisingly, the removal to Islington was not popular with the London butchers. They complained that they would have to travel the two to three miles to the market, making it even more difficult to preserve the wholesomeness of their meat.[68] Some Londoners maintained that that the butchers were not fairly consulted during the Smithfield debates. One writer expressed regret, stating that ' ... in a free country like this, where individual interests are so plainly expressed, it is always prudent to consult them practically ... first before any attempt is made to enforce measures for the public interest in connection with any of the arts which may not have the sanction of experience ... practical men, such as farmers and butchers, have a right to be practically dealt with'.[69] Butcher Giblett rejected the idea of moving Smithfield to Islington, likening the move as removing 'the thorn out of the foot of one neighborhood and put[ting] it precisely in the same situation in another'.[70]

The significance of the removal inspired the muses of London periodicals. One wrote in the *British Farmer's Magazine* that, "The Great Globe itself' has not another field of six acres to place in the scales with Smithfield. It will be long before so many historical associations surround the new market in Copenhagen Fields as those that arise with the very mention of its name'. Both Dodd and the writer for the magazine wondered how long it would take before Londoners could 'place a proper estimate upon the Herculean task here performed, or to appreciate the benefits which they have gained by the change'.

The changes had been seismic. The upturning of the urban landscape, the 'bricks-and-mortar revolution' brought on by the removal of buildings and streets, the incursion of railway lines, the incision of pavement made to receive gas, drainage pipes, and soon, electricity lines made the uprooting of Smithfield a possibility. Technology redefined the old Smithfield system to create faster, far-reaching channels of distribution for livestock and meat. Spring-carts and other new, agile and fast vehicles, enabled butchers to move quickly between the abattoirs to their butcher shops. The 'machinery of the market' was to be steam-powered, transforming the organic meat provisioning system to the mechanized, from the urban to the suburban.[71]

The removal of Smithfield changed the meat trade. The younger butchers would arrive in Islington with little patience for the old adage, 'A current of cold air will blow the stench from meat'.[72] The changes in the division of labour within the Smithfield system integrated and combined the practices of farmers, drovers, salesmen, butchers and bankers. The 'jack of all trades' model, the subdivided system of labour in Smithfield would become a simplified, integrated system made of the 'industrial fabric' brought on by a 'more scientific state of things'. Individual laborers could dispense with the 'brute force' of the former market and utilize machinery with the eventual elevation of laborers to better occupations. 'The moral and physical *status* of the cattle market of the British Capital [would be] placed on a level with her own commercial greatness and magnificence'.[73]

New weighing devices would enable farmers to obtain consistent payments for animals sent to multiple markets, including Smithfield. The measure of the market was its ability to 'return the greatest weight and best quality of butcher-meat, creating at the same time the least obstruction to the traffic in the streets'.[74] The use of liquid manure manufactured at the new market would enable farmers to improve their pastures. The proximity of the lairs at the Metropolitan Cattle market in Islington removed the necessity of driving animals through the streets to the slaughterhouses. Money takers would be superseded by the telegraph companies that would communicate market transactions between buyer and seller throughout the countryside. The speed and accuracy of trading transactions would bring the market and consumer closer together. The engineered sanitation systems and ventilation devices in the new market removed the 'brute force and devilry' in the old system.

Most understood that cruelty would continue and that the squalor of Smithfield would continue in Islington. During the same month that the bill became enacted to remove the market an article appeared in *Chamber's Edinburgh Journal* expressing the realization that many aspects of the nuisance would continue. The new market would be a 'change for the better; yet it may not to be amiss to remark, that the danger of cruelty to the animals themselves, or which we have learned so much, will be rather increased than diminished by the change, inasmuch a the supervision which a jealous, antagonistic public exercises upon Smithfield will be to a great extent withdrawn. It may affright the human imagination to picture to itself wretched, tortured animals battered to death, amidst filth and darkness; but to the poor beast itself it is the same thing, whether the blows be dealt in a dark cellar or in an open, freely-ventilated abattoir'.[75] In 1856, William Perry, a drover bringing cattle to the new cattle market in Islington, was caught hitting an animal 'with great violence, using a very thick stick, and without any apparent cause'. An officer from the RSPCA charged the drover who resisted. Aided by his friends, Perry knocked the officer to the ground and 'kicked his legs and body' while his friends held him down.[76] Incidents such as this did not suggest that animal welfare reform had benefited from the removal of the market from Smithfield.

The inhabitants of Islington continued to complain to the City about the driving of cattle through the streets during church services on Sunday. At a meeting of the Common Council, Deputy Lott 'expressed regret that the chairman of the MIC had not allowed the government to have the new Metropolitan Cattle market hung round their necks, instead of advising the corporation to undertake its construction, as it was patent to all the world that it would be hung round their necks like a millstone for ever'.[77]

Ultimately, the public interest, and private interests accommodated one another, but not without a struggle and not without lingering anxieties about the centralization of metropolitan governance. Some Londoners were conscious of the identity of their nation as a model of self-government and reflected on its impact upon the battle to remove the market. One observer felt that even though 'self-government [had] its dark sides', it was that principle that accounted for its political and commercial greatness. Self-government also contributed to the length of the debate as England negotiated 'hostile and vested interests …. in a tender and cautious manner'.[78]

In the case of the new market, the 'public spirit' overruled the individual interests of the butchers who resisted the removal. As the Prince Consort had said at the opening of the Metropolitan Cattle Market in 1855, the 'splendid and useful work ... undertaken by public bodies, and carried out to success by public spirit', occurred through a 'very lingering and painful struggle'.[79]

But the bigger story is that the struggle over the location of the cattle market revealed the anxieties and concerns about the modernization of London. Smithfield was the anvil upon which modernity forged a new city, one that new technologies, attitudes, moralities and political realities shaped urban life in ways that would endure into the next century.

On June 11, 1855, Smithfield market sold livestock for the last time. The *Illustrated London News* marked the occasion with an account of the last market day.

> Mysterious processes seemed going on, and scores of animals and hundreds of pounds of sterling currency changed hands hourly. The immense area was bustling with life. Looking from the quarter nearest to Snow-hill towards Long Lane, almost as far as the eye could reach, it was dotted with blue coats and grey, nicely yet to too strongly relieved by the brownish red of the cattle ... The scarlet coat of the postman, hurrying through the crowd, was too powerful even for the rich deep red of the oxen to harmonize with. Wandering in a dreamy manner from pen to pen, the lowing and bleating might have taken us in memory to green pastures, but for the strange and strong oaths of the drovers, and the peculiar bark of the vulture-headed sheep-dogs. The mind became confused with calculations as to how many millions' worth of human food had here been sold? How many pounds of good English roast beef at Christmas time in the days of 'good Queen Bess'? ... . How many noble men, and even women, have perished not far distant from the Priory Gate? ... . Whose ashes were they which we saw turned up a few years since on the ancient place of execution? ... Dogs yelped and ran over the backs of flocks of sheep. One of the most unpleasant sounds which helped to make the Babel-like confusion was the sharp knocking on the tender part, the horns of the oxen ... Great and beneficial as will be the change effected by the removal of Old Smithfield market – as the time came for the ringing of the last bell – we felt a sort of indescribably regret, something like that occasioned by the necessity which causes us in its old age to change our hack horse for a young one, or of adopting the swift, strong, and wonderful locomotive for the pleasant and sociable stage-coach. This feeling, in different degrees, seemed to be shared by all, but generally in a somewhat jolly manner. The countenances of the drovers had, by numerous potations, become more like the animals who were beside them ... . This, which has been a Fair and market for more than 800 years, was closed without any ceremony – a printed order from the Home Secretary, stuck amongst the notices of dead bodies found etc., on the door of the police station, was all that we saw of an official character.[80]

Not until 1936, would another change in the live cattle market occur. By then, the old Smithfield space would contain a meat market that would continue in its Victorian iron buildings until the twenty-first century.

As one observer stated in *The Farmers' Magazine*,

> ... many a good fat bullock and sheep have exchanged hands in it [Smithfield' – many a sovereign collected and faithfully remitted to the provinces – and now that its requiem is about to be sung, 'the Great Globe itself' has not another field of six acres to

place in the scales with Smithfield. It will be long before so many historical associations surround the new market in Copenhagen Fields as those which arise with the very mention of its name; and it is only when some twelve months have passed over the heads of the bankers, salesmen, butchers, and drovers of the capital, that they themselves will be able to place a proper estimate upon the Herculean task here performed, or to appreciate the benefits which they have gained by the change.[81]

EPILOGUE

Prince Albert, the City and MPs had much to celebrate at the opening of the Metropolitan Cattle Market in Islington that summer day in 1855. The new market, designed by Bunning had room for almost 11,000 cattle, nearly 36,000 sheep and 1,500 calves compared to about 4,000 cattle, 25,000 sheep and 500 calves in Smithfield.[1] The plans indicated separate areas for cattle and sheep, two slaughterhouses, 13,232 feet of rail, 1,749 pens (all lettered and numbered), an elaborate drainage system, bankers' offices, two hotels, public houses and taverns. Roads approached nine entrances to the market and a railroad depot brought animals and traders to the rectangular space.

The new market rested on land that had been raised, lowered and excavated in order to provide the required surfaces for drainage, sanitation and traffic, both bipedal and quadrapedal. Concrete, granite cubes and vitrified bricks provided well-drained surfaces. The vitrification of bricks was in the very early stages of development as a way to pave a surface in a material that would not absorb water.[2] Surfaced with three million Staffordshire blue bricks 'made entirely by machinery', the space nearly glistened with its sanitized appearance. The pavement under the animals sloped to direct manure towards the drainage system. Both liquid and solid manure moved through sluices towards storage tanks so that farmers could utilize it in their fields.[3] Human sanitation was not overlooked; the City had included water closets and urinals at each corner of the market.

Descriptions of the new market were full of the flourishes of enthusiastic reporters, but accounts of how these modern improvements actually functioned during the months that followed are scarce. The accolades surrounding new inventions superseded any doubts about the long-term functioning of the market. Bunning included an impressive utilization of new technologies, 'complete in every detail', with the idea that the market would address any limitations that might arise in the future. He consulted buyers and sellers in order to design a facility suited to their needs while avoiding 'unnecessary torture' in deference to those who objected to animal cruelty in Smithfield and 'obstruction, waste of time, or uproar' to satisfy those who wanted an orderly and rational commercial space.[4] His design yielded such amenities as water troughs (called *abreuvoirs*)

Figure E.2: The Metropolitan Cattle Market, Copenhagen Fields, *Builder*, vol. XII, no. 617 (1854), p. 619.

that overflowed with water delivered through the nearby New River canal and capacious lairages that allowed animals to lie down and rest before the market opened.[5] Leather hoses placed every twenty-seven yards provided plenty of opportunities for cleansing the pavements. Water and hay in all the lairages insured that no animal would be without ample food and water.[6]

The press visited the new market and criticized the City's architect for his design of the columns and railing. The market used both cast and wrought iron construction materials, wrought iron for the columns and cast iron for the ornamentation. Known for his addition of sculpture to his designs, Bunning added cattle, sheep and pig heads as iron ornaments to the railing that traversed the center of the market. Some observers derided this design and saw it as representative of the architectural style, 'Bovine order'.[7] He enlisted John Bell, a sculptor who had just completed 'The Eagle Slayer', on display at the Great Exhibition, to design these rather curious breeds. The iron columns supporting the market buildings encased water drains, an example of what some saw as a forced accommodation of technology with classical architecture.[8]

The proximity of the railroad ensured those in the cattle trade that commerce would proceed unhindered by narrow streets and the associated traffic. These engineered surfaces controlled, contained and facilitated the movement of the animals in and out of the market. Roads and footpaths separated man from animal with railings and pavement designed to lubricate the movement of traffic, making 'the confusion experienced in Smithfield....almost impossible'. Animals, organized in areas so that the space appeared 'very workmanlike and finished' with their heads aligned in pairs, six feet apart, with the innovation of a 'kicking bar' to limit intrusion of the animals upon one another.[9] Descriptions of the market, such as these, met the expectations of those who saw the meat market as a representation of British modernity and identity. With heady memories of the Great Exhibition in 1851, those who visited the new market saw it as another exhibit of imperial greatness, a statement of progress and superiority.

The empire filled the market with cattle from Europe and beyond. Railroads brought thousands of animals into the nearby depot. The promoters of the new market lauded the ability to bring meat to the capital in a matter of days compared to the six weeks required before railways became the preferred mode of stock transport.[10] When the market opened, railways brought cattle to the market both from the north and south of London. Plans existed for additional lines to deliver cattle, sheep and pigs from the south, east and west. Wide thoroughfares, Caledonian Road and Maiden Lane, enabled drovers to bring animals to the market when rail travel proved impractical. While acquiring live animals for the 'great centre of carnivorous consumption', the market shepherded humans into its interior through its huge gates, open to the general public on days when the market was closed.[11]

Greeting the visitor to the market was a clock tower that rose 150 feet above the centre, a totemic representation of the mechanical nature of the new market. The tower contained some of the most technologically advanced telegraph machines that were used by almost a dozen banking houses. Two telegraph companies, including the Electric Telegraph Company, had offices where sales transactions travelled to the City banks on wires laid alongside the railways' right-of-ways. Just ten years earlier, the Electric Telegraph Company had incorporated, possessing the patents to Cooke and Wheatstone's technology.[12] The telegraph companies transmitted market transactions to the City and circulated information about market conditions throughout the country. Electricity for the telegraph machines lit the four thirteen-foot dials on the face of the clock tower that encased a one-ton bell that signaled the opening and closing of the market. Railway companies, the clerk of the market, general supply stores and salesmen's offices also occupied the tower. The scene presented 'a uniform and business-like manner, as cannot fail to have a very imposing appearance when seen from the clock-tower...'.[13]

Gaslights hissing from lanterns provided by the London Gas Light Company, established in June 1833, illuminated the buildings while Arnott's ventilators provided heating with 'smoke consuming fireplaces'. Neil Arnott's ventilators, invented in the 1830s, burnt coal and used a valve to prevent smoke from entering a room.[14] He, like other entrepreneurs and inventors, applied their ideas to solve the litany of problems so familiar to the committees, coffee houses and councils engaged with Smithfield during the first half of the century. Physics, electricity and speed merged to represent the machinery of urban provisioning. A writer in the *Farmer's Magazine* exulted,

> Suffice it to say that machinery is here organized which will collect something like the round sum of £8,000,000 annually from the butchers of the metropolis, and hand it over to the British farmer![15]

The new market exhibited other new and untested, 'mechanical' ideas, such as the combination of previously separate activities. Manufactories in London had long been specialized by trade but the integration of trades within a manufactory was a new concept. The plan envisioned by Bunning was to integrate the long-separated trades in the market, from the buying and selling of stock, to the slaughter of animals, sales of dead meat, hides and skins and manufacturing of leather, glue, violin strings and tallow candles. This new 'principle in the commerce and management of fat stock', included the creating of multi-use space, with the market, lairs and slaughterhouses sharing the same area. Other activities merged within the market, such as manure management, hay and straw storage and cattle sales offices.[16]

Bunning's plans included two public abattoirs, with the capacity of killing 600 animals a week. They were not constructed until some years after the opening of the new market. Six private slaughterhouses provided nearby facilities for the butchers to procure dead meat that the butchers sold through their own private businesses.[17] Bunning had hoped that the construction of a meat market would eliminate the need for butchers to take meat to their own shops near the City. This model for market integration would presage those that later emerged in the markets of Paris, New York and Chicago. While each city had its own geographical considerations, each responded to new technologies and growing urban populations to merge the procurement, processing and distribution of meat during the mid-to-late eighteenth century. The arrival of both specialization and centralization of London's markets during the second half of the nineteenth century would signal the arrival of modern London.

At the opening of the new market, the City, viewed by critics as having been on the sidelines of an unstoppable 'march of progress', turned out in its civic and magnificent regalia. City officers arrived in forty-seven carriages, along with foreign ministers from the United States, Bavaria, Prussia, Belgium, and Sicily. Aristocrats, MPs, and representatives from towns and provinces of the United Kingdom gathered for the celebration. The Lord Mayor of London and aldermen addressed the Prince, thanking him for his presence at the momentous event, a moment 'of deep interest and importance to the great community of the metropolis, and to the country at large'. The coats of arms of foreign countries, along with medallions, plows and sickles, represented not only the national character of the market; it also marked its arrival as the meat victualler to the world, situating the market at the center of the imperial commissariat.

Music played by the Caledonian and Chelsea Asylums and Foundling Hospital entertained the officials as over a thousand celebrants took their places at long tables under the marquée to enjoy a 'substantial and elegant repast'. As if inspired by the rain falling outside, one writer described 'a great storm of music' that filled the air. Raising his glass in one of many toasts that day, Prince Albert, himself a respected cattle breeder, called attention to London's reputation as a 'meat devourer', both a consummate producer and consumer of meat for the metropolis.[18]

The City acknowledged its role in the new market with a broad reference to its 'deference to the suggestions of the National Legislature' through the City's sense of duty to its citizens. With unapologetic magnanimity, the City declared that the new market eliminated all the complaints listed in the minutes of the select committees and thereby provided benefits not only to its people but also to all the businesses engaged in providing food to London'. *The Times* reported this moment of conciliation between the City and private interests, between the public need for food, the private merchants for trade, the City for trading rights, Parliament and its constituents, and the metropolis for public health. The newspaper contended that the competition of interests between the private entities and private interests 'by degree will find its own adjustment'. Seen by some as a 'great national work', the new Metropolitan Cattle Market, also called the Caledonian Cattle Market, accommodated the many individuals who advocated for their interests over the decades. Some signed the memorial commemorating the laying of the first stone for the new market on March 24, 1854.[19] The memorial included familiar names: Henry Lowman Taylor, the City's Chairman of the Committee of Markets and members of the Committee and City Aldermen, all of whom had worked, at various times, either to remove or improve Smithfield.

The Metropolitan Cattle Market would be the largest live cattle market in the world until Chicago took its place in the late 1860s.[20] By then, the City of London had erected a new meat market in the space previously occupied by the cattle market in Smithfield. And so the story of meat in the center of London continues today.

The New Smithfield Metropolitan Meat Market

After the celebrations in Islington, the cattle market operated in much the same way as it did in Smithfield. Drovers and railways delivered cattle to the market, the animals awaited market day while resting in lairs, and the butchers and salesmen convened on market days to provision London with meat. Butchers bought animals and took them to their own slaughterhouses or slaughtered their purchases in Islington. They transported meat to their retail shops using carts and wagons.

After the market closed in Smithfield, the empty space became a favourite location for protestors and vagrants as Londoners awaited the City's decision concerning its building plans. In 1857, the City petitioned Parliament for an act to establish a new meat market in Smithfield.[21] In 1860, Parliament passed an act to close Newgate meat market, long considered too congested and unsanitary. The Markets Improvement Committee (MIC) took charge of the market and began planning for the new meat market in Smithfield. After months of excavations to allow for an underground rail connection, Lowman Taylor laid the first stone in 1867.

The new meat market, (the cattle market remained in Islington), designed by City architect Sir Horace Jones, opened to the great relief of Londoners who welcomed a market located at the convenience of those in the City and that maintained the healthy benefits of large, open urban space. Jones designed an impressive building, with entrances graced by four figures atop the representing England's largest cities, London, Edinburgh, Dublin and Liverpool. These symbols and the Italian and Doric architecture signaled London's place in a national and international market. The banquet celebrating the opening of the market in 1868 filled the market hall with celebrants who dined on boars' heads and barons of beef.[22]

The Smithfield Central Markets, as the meat market is called today, still stands in its historic position in the center of the City, a lasting memorial to London's urban narrative. Arching glass ceilings supported by cast iron columns and gird-ers, enclose the market, still in operation today. Exercising its 'ancient' market rights, the City operates the Central Markets for 'dead meat' to the wholesale trade. It has continuously operated as a private enterprise, although regulated as other businesses in London. Originally, the Metropolitan Railway passed under-neath, collecting meat brought to the railcars by large hydraulic lifts. Every few years, developers approach the City for the purpose of developing the market space, but Londoners manage to keep the meat market in place, its large Victorian iron arches welcoming workers as they pass to and from their offices in the City.

Smithfield in the Twenty-First Century

The Central Markets consist of three large Victorian covered buildings: Two are for meat, the West Market and the East Market, and a third building is the Poultry Market, selling poultry meat. Two of the buildings were demolished by a German VZ rocket bomb in 1945 and rebuilt soon after. The survival of Smith-field as a site for meat is implicit in more than just the Victorian struggle. Within the same walkway, the City has put up a display of the market's history, ending with a group photo of meat salesmen with these words:

> Yesterday, we were here,
> Today, this is where we are,
> Tomorrow, this is where we will be.

Today the Central Markets teem with wholesale customers, porters and meat salesmen from ten at night until about noon the following day. Smithfield brings together the small villages and farms as far away as Ireland, the Western Islands of Scotland, and Wales in a network of roads that brought cattle to the metropo-lis since the days when drovers filled the streets with cattle. On most evenings, large refrigerated trucks roll into Smithfield from Scotland, Ireland and British ports bringing meat from farms in the Scottish highlands and Europe. Large refrigerated trucks bearing names such as J. M. Mackie represent meat wholesal-ers who have operated in this market for generations. Boxes of meat, processed outside London arrive in the City inside refrigerated trucks as whole carcasses. Men ('porters') in white coats and hard hats bustle from truck to wholesale stall, riding electric carts that move fresh meat into the market hall or long hallways used to hang meat. The white coats and hard hats form queues outside the all-night cafes that provide hot tea and meat sandwiches to the trade.

Looking upward, you can hardly take in the full view of the market structure. Through the arched passage walk hundreds of Londoners on their way through Smithfield from the Farringdon tube station to the City, sometimes dodging the early morning meat salesmen still occupied with shifting boxes from trucks to the rows of refrigerators located at the back end of each meat salesmen's stalls. Opposite the Central Markets, St. Bartholomew's Hospital and The Church of St. Bartholomew share the open space and The Worshipful Company of Butchers holds its meetings within the main chapel.

In recent times, the area has become trendy. The all-night club, *Felt*, uses the old underground cold storage rooms of the market for its dance floor. Restaurants such as Fergus Henderson and Trevor Gulliver's *St. John Bar and Restaurant, The Head to Tail Bar, The Butcher's Hoof and Cleaver* remind us that the meat market and eating meat still define this space. The Carthusian Monastery is not five hundred yards away, a hushed space still occupied by vegetarians. The late poet-laureate Sir John Betjeman's flat is on Cloth Fair, opposite the market and above a restaurant called after his namesake and featuring Gloucestershire Old Spots pork entrees that connect animals, meat and urban history. Smithfield provides links to historical memory in still other ways. On the second floor of the Lady's Chapel, part of St. Bartholomew's Church, Benjamin Franklin worked in a printer's shop.

The struggle for a meat market in Smithfield continues today as the SAVE campaign illustrated in 2004. As of 2012, rumors persist about new initiatives to develop the area. In some ways, the voices of protest come from another world, an echo of a centuries-old debate about the cattle market in Smithfield, a debate that began in earnest during the first part of the eighteenth century and that finally ended in 1851.

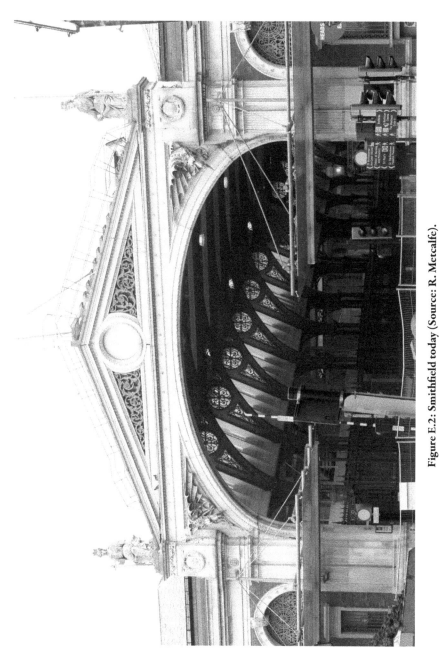

Figure E.2: Smithfield today (Source: R. Metcalfe).

NOTES

Introduction

1. The nomenclature for London's meat market can be confusing. London's live cattle market, the subject of this paper, existed in Smithfield from *c.* 1100–1855. When the market moved to Islington, it was known as the Metropolitan Cattle Market from 1855–1939. In the empty space left by the live cattle market in Smithfield, a dead meat and poultry market appeared in 1868, the Central Markets or Metropolitan Meat and Poultry Market, where it exists to this day. The market complex was renamed the London Central Markets in 1870.
2. 'The Metropolitan Cattle-Market', *Illustrated London News*, 16 June 1855, p. 602.
3. C. Dickens, *Oliver Twist* (New York: Hurd and Houghton, 1866), p. 236.
4. *Report from The Select Committee of Smithfield Market Removal Bill of the Proceedings of the Committee together with the Minutes of Evidence,* The House of Commons, 6 June 1851 (House of Commons Papers Online), p. 62.
5. G. Dodd, *The Food of London* (London: Longman, Brown, Green and Longmans, 1856), p. 2.
6. Ibid., p. 4.
7. 'The Metropolitan Cattle-Market', p. 602.
8. http://www.english-heritage.org.uk/server/show/nav.18051, http://www.english-heritage.org.uk/server/show/ConWebDoc.14257 [accessed 24 January 2009].
9. http://news.bbc.co.uk/2/hi/uk_news/england/london/7547439.stm [accessed 24 January 2009].
10. The evidence for Chapters 4, 5 and 6 comes from testimonies provided by witnesses at Parliamentary committee hearings about impending removal bills in 1828, 1847, 1849, 1850, and 1851. These witnesses included Smithfield inhabitants, local merchants, cattle salesmen, animal welfare reformers, City aldermen, bankers, and doctors. They represented both the private and public interests that struggled to resolve the 'nuisances' in Smithfield. They reveal as much about evidence gathering during this period as they do about attitudes concerning Smithfield.

1 The Smithfield System in the Nineteenth Century: A Grand Complexus

1. Dodd, *The Food of London*, p. 250.
2. A. B. Reach, 'John Bull and his Bullocks', *Douglas Jerrold's Shilling Magazine,* 5 (1847), p. 20.

3. 'Smithfield', *Antiquary*, 2 (September 1880), p. 103. In the sixteenth century, the expression 'Ruffian's Hall' was applied to Smithfield to describe the skirmishes that took place, some replete with swords and bucklers. P. Cunningham, *Handbook for London, Past and Present*, vol. 1 (London, 1850), p. 432–433. See also T. Fielding, *Select Proverbs of all Nations: Illustrated with Notes and Comments: To which is Added, a Summary of Ancient Pastimes, Holidays and Customs: With an Analysis of the Wisdom of the Ancients, etc.* (London: Longman, 1824).

4. In June 1840, Charles Pearson, the City Solicitor, delivered a report to the City's Markets Improvement Committee that made the case for the regulation of Bartholomew's Fair, citing the transfer of ownership of the market rights from the Crown and attorney general, Sir John Rich, during the Dissolution of the Monasteries. Eventually, the City purchased the rights and so held the market rights to both the space for cattle and the Bartholomew Fair. C. Pearson, 'Sketches, History of Bartholomew Fair', *Literary Gazette: Weekly Journal of Literature, Science, and the Fine Arts* (London, 1840), p. 534.

5. 'Smithfield', *Antiquary*, 2 (September 1880), p. 106.

6. Wife selling (a legal way to end a marriage) was practiced in Smithfield, according to various reports in *The Times*, during 1832. (See *The Times*, 25 February 1832.) This practice apparently also occurred at the market in Islington during the 1830s. The practice was later portrayed by Thomas Hardy in *The Mayor of Casterbridge*. A 'Smithfield bargain' was a marriage that defrauded or swindled one of the parties.

7. J. Stow, in his *Survey of London*, written in 1598, and W. Thornbury, in *London Recollected: Its History, Lore and Legend*, written in 1985, both describe these lavish and long tournaments in detail. P. Nightingale argued that knights and other gentry participated in the market economy, particularly the wool trade, during the Middle Ages. These 'urban merchants' suggests that knights both worked and played in Smithfield. (See P. Nightingale, 'Knights and Merchants: Trade, Politics and the Gentry in Late Medieval England', *Past & Present*, 169 (2000), p. 36.) J. Strype's *Survey of the Cities of London and Westminster*, written in 1720, further described the royal tournaments held in the fourteenth century. Stow, J., and J. Strype, *A Survey of the Cities of London and Westminster: Containing the Original, Antiquity, Increase, Modern Estate and Government of those Cities* (London: Printed for A. Churchill, 1720).

8. C. Wriothesley, and W. D. Hamilton, *A Chronicle of England During the Reigns of the Tudors* (Westminster: Printed for the Camden Society, 1875); J. Timbs, *Romance of London: Strange Stories, Scenes and Remarkable Persons of the Great Town* (London: R. Bentley, 1865), p. 732; C. D. Cleveland, *A Compendium of English Literature: Chronologically Arranged from Sir John Mandeville to William Cowper* (Philadelphia, PA: E. C. & J. Biddle, 1857), p. 65.

9. B. Jonson and C. Counsell, *Bartholomew Fair* (London: Nick Hern Books, 1997), pp. v–xvii, 74, 32. Plays with religiously inspired plots appeared in and around Smithfield. In the late 1300s and into the fourteenth century, the Clerkenwell parish clerks acted in plays that were attended by 'nobles and gentles in England'. Stow, *Survey*, p. 36. (See also S. Billington, 'Butchers and Fishmongers: Their Historical Contribution to London's Festivity', *Folklore*, 101 (1990), pp. 97–103.)

10. M. Braddick, 'Popular Politics and Public Policy: The Excise Riot at Smithfield in February 1647 and Its Aftermath', *The Historical Journal*, 34:3 (1991), pp. 597–626; S. Pepys, *Diary of Samuel Pepys*, December 15 1662, ed. G. Smith (London: MacMillan & Co., 1905), p. 166.

11. Several trees that grew by Smithfield Pond, a source of water for horses travelling to and from the City, acquired the name The Elms. The site became known

for executions before the gallows moved to Tyburn. (See J. T. Smith and C. Mackay, *An Antiquarian Ramble in the Streets of London, with Anecdotes of Their More Celebrated Residents* (London: R. Bentley, 1846), p. 305; 'Smithfield', *Antiquary*, 2 (1880), p. 103.) Battles were still fought to settle disputes until the practice was abolished in 1819. (See C. Knight (ed.), *London* (London: H.G. Bohn, 1851), p. 316(. The Proceedings of the Old Bailey, http://www.oldbaileyonline.org/browse. jsp?id=t16741212–2&div=t16741212–2&terms=smithfield#highlight [Accessed 25 February 2009]).

12. 'Endorsed titles and marginal notes, 6 Mar 1327: Markets; infangenthef, etc.; gaol delivery', in London (England) and W. de Gray Birch, *The Historical Charters and Constitutional Documents of the City of London* (London: Whiting, 1887).

13. Ibid., 'Endorsed titles and marginal notes, 18 Oct 1638: Inspeximus', pp. 52–8, 'First charter of Edward III, No. XXIV 6 March, A. D. 1327', pp. 159–200.

14. J. Strype, http://www.hrionline.ac.uk/strype/ TransformServlet?page=book5_351, [accessed 16 January 2009]. (See also William and Mary, 1689, *An Act for Reversing the Judgment in a Quo Warranto against the City of London and for Restoring the City of London to its Ancient Rights and Privileges*, ch. 8, Rot. Parl. Pt. No. 10. http://www. british-history.ac.uk/source.aspx?pubid=352. [accessed 16 January 2009]).

15. City of London, *The Lawes of the Market* (London: Printed by W. Iaggard, printer to the honourable city of London, 1620). Other laws included those that forbid 'nightwalkers', bull and bear baiting, leaving poultry or cats in the street, driving one's cart at a gallop, blowing of horns, and wife beating.

16. Early market laws came from the principles outlined in the Magna Carta. The Magna Carta (1215) codified the workings of government and trader, merchant, and customer within the context of Christianity, individual freedom, and liberty. Markets, established by common law for legal trade, were *markets overts*, operated with minimal interference from the government. The only interference was the Crown's regulation of weights and measures and the City's control over the trading rights of freemen and foreign merchants within the City.

17. 'First Charter of King Charles I', 18 October 1638, No. XLV, London (England) and Birch (ed.), *The Historical Charters*, p. 159.

18. Meat stalls. In Old English, a table or counter for the sale of meat (*Oxford English Dictionary*).

19. Reach, 'John Bull and His Bullocks', p. 121.

20. Dodd, *The Food of London*, p. 228.

21. M. Schlesinger and O. von Wenckstern, *Saunterings In and About London* (London: N. Cooke, 1853).

22. As early as the beginning of the eighteenth century, observers of the metropolis noticed Smithfield's growing reputation as a burgeoning cattle market. Daniel Defoe wrote in a letter in 1738 that Smithfield was 'the greatest in the world; no description can be given of it, no calculation of the numbers of creatures sold there, can be made'. D. Defoe and P. Rogers, *A Tour Through the Whole Island of Great Britain* (Exeter: Webb & Bower, 1989), pp. 108–9.

23. Reach, 'John Bull and His Bullocks', p. 120.

24. A writer for the *Farmer's Magazine* said, 'The modus operandi, under the flickering glare of the lamps, contending with 'November fogs', was 'more easily conceived than described'. One curious observer asked, 'By what complicated wheels does all the machinery move

by which two millions and a half of humans being sit down day by day to their meals as regularly and quietly as though they only formed a snug little party at Lovegrove's (a restaurant that specialized in herring fry) on a summer's afternoon?' *Farmer's Magazine*, 6 (December 1854), p. 474. (London: Rogerson and Tuxford), 'Art. I. Report of the Commissioners Appointed to Make Inquiries Related to Smithfield Market, and the Markets in the City of London for the Sale of Meat', *Quarterly Review*, 95 (1854), p. 272.

25. J. Blackman observes, 'A national market in cattle began to develop at all stages from breeder to butcher' when 'regional markets for store and fat cattle had interposed between the traditional north to south trade for the London market'. Later, regional fatstock markets influenced local breeding practices when railroads began to bring cattle to the London market. (See 'The Cattle Trade and Agrarian Change on the Eve of the Railway Age', *British Agricultural History Society*, 23 (1975), p. 53.)

26. D. Rixson, *The History of Meat Trading* (Nottingham: Nottingham University Press, 2000), pp. 196–7.

27. Ellis (ed.), *Description of Essex* (London: Camden Society, 1840), p. xii.

28. 'Art. I. Report of the Commissioners Appointed to Make Inquiries Related to Smithfield Market, and the Markets in the City of London for the Sale of Meat', *Quarterly Review*, 95/190 (1854), p. 282; A. Wynter, 'The London Commissariat', *Curiosities of Civilization*, 3rd edn (London: R. Hardwicke, 1860), pp. 200–44.

29. Not without controversy, enclosures continued until the nineteenth century. For example, Y. A. Yelling argues that enclosures occurred over such an extended time that they could not have been a significant reason for increases in agricultural productivity. J. A. Yelling, *Common Field and Enclosure in England, 1450–1850* (London: Macmillan, 1977). Chambers and Mingay argue that enclosures provided individual incentives for innovation and productivity, proving Malthus incorrect. J. D. Chambers and G. E. Mingay, *The Agricultural Revolution, 1750–1880* (New York: Schocken Books, 1966); E. L. Jones argues that early industrialization and population growth provided both a demand for agricultural products and a stimulus for economic growth in reciprocal markets. See E. L. Jones, *Agriculture and Economic Growth in England, 1650–1815* (London: Methuen, 1967). See also M. Overton for a view that describes the 'agricultural revolution' as a slow evolution, institutionally driven. M. Overton, *Agricultural Revolution in England: The Transformation of the Agrarian Economy, 1500–1850* (Cambridge and New York: Cambridge University Press, 1996).

30. For a details of turnip feeding and other improved forage practices see T. Hartwell Horne's *The Complete Grazier; or, Farmer and Cattle-Dealer's Assistant* (London: B. Crosby and Co., 1808). Scientific agriculture was often the target of satire, as when F. Moore lampooned improvers such as Arthur Young for sitting upon an 'agricultural divan' while shedding light on methods 'by which animal fat is rendered so excessively nauseous'. F. Moore[pseudo.] and G. Cruikshank, *The Age of Intellect* (London: William Hone, 1819), p. 131.

31. Robert Bakewell's imprint was visible in the animals raised near his Dishley Farm in Leicestershire. Some scholars refute the importance of his contribution to animal husbandry, stating that although Bakewell did much to promote the idea of pedigree, marketing of stock, leasing of rams, and the use of in-and-in breeding to produce large animals, he did not necessarily produce stock well-fattened with the desired marbling characteristics. (See *Farmers Magazine*, 4, (1814), p. 414.) It may also be true that only a relatively small group of farmers actually practiced his system, which may not have been suitable for all breeds. (With tallow prices declining and mutton prices rising, the Leister's propensity for tallow production would have made the breed undesirable in the nineteenth century for meat; the

impact of gas and then electricity precluded any further value for tallow.) For a thorough discussion of British livestock breeds, see H. Ritvo, *The Animal Estate: The English and Other Creatures in the Victorian Age* (Cambridge, MA: Harvard University Press, 1987).

32. Imports of livestock were negligible in the early eighteenth century and but increased dramatically in the late 1840s. In 1842, 1,114 oxen and bulls were imported; by 1848, 17,191 were imported. British Parliamentary Papers, as cited by H. P. R Finberg and J. Thirsk, *The Agrarian History of England and Wales; General Editor, H.P.R. Finberg* (Cambridge: Cambridge University Press, 1967), p. 1022. The import of Irish cattle was made illegal in 1680, an act that was 'found to be beneficial to this Kingdom'. *C. II, c. 2.* It is not clear if Irish stock was of poor quality or if England eschewed competition from Irish farmers.

33. While breeds gathered identity and authenticity through the efforts of Bakewell and other breeders, the Board of Agriculture (1793–1822) developed 'models' for breeds that attempted to develop breed standards in much the same ways as factories develop product specifications. Before the Board dissolved, it published an exquisitely rendered collection of breed 'models', with each breed 'in every point accurately preserved'. These models had been approved by the board and were a representation of the 'ideas of the best judges of the times'. Parliament had copyrighted the models, which had been represented in sculptures 'for all classes'. Although it is not clear that these models had any impact on breeding standards, they hinted at the aspirations of the government to apply principles of science and manufacturing practices to animal husbandry. *Description of Different Varieties of Oxen. An Accompaniment to a Set of Models of the Improved Breeds of Cattle Upon Exact Sale from Nature* (Under the patronage of the Board of Agriculture, J. Smeeton, London), 1800.

34. W. Chambers and R. Chambers, *Chambers Information for the People: A Popular Encyclopædia* (Philadelphia, PA: G.B. Zieber, 1848).

35. 'Account of Smithfield Club, and the Proceedings at the last Christmas Show', *Farmer's Magazine* (May 1807), p. 189.

36. 'Gentlemen farmers' were typically aristocrats, landowners, and entrepreneurs who pursued experimental agricultural practices. The Smithfield Cattle Club was founded by a group of such farmers and improvers. See L. Bull, *History of the Smithfield Club, from 1926 to 1950* (London: Smithfield Club, 1952). The Club, located in Baker Street near Oxford Street, attracted 'groups of smock frocked, raw-boned shepherds ... cutting up deserts [sic] of turnips ... boasting the merit of their respected beasts in every rural dialect of Britain'. 'The Smithfield Cattle Club', *Illustrated London News*, 12 December 1846, p. 375.

37. See M. G. Mulhall, *The Progress of the World in Arts, Agriculture, Commerce, Manufactures, Instruction, Railways, and Public Wealth Since the Beginning of the Nineteenth Century* (London: E. Stanford, 1880). Mulhall cites Bruce Campbell and Scottish political economist John Ramsay McCulloch. According to Mulhall, the number of sheep in the United Kingdom increased from 12 million (Campbell) in 1774 to 27.9 million (McCulloch) in 1855. Cattle increased from 2.8 million (Campbell) in 1774 to 27.9 million (McCulloch) in 1855. The average weight of cattle increased between 1710 and 1775, re-enforcing scholars who think the agricultural revolution and greatest productivity was over by 1770s. Michael Turner provides a general assessment of these increases from 1725 to 1849: average weights for beef cattle were 530.6 pounds during the period 1725–1749 and in the period 1825 to 1849 beef cattle weighed an average of 775.1 pounds. During these same periods, sheep weights increased from 55.6 pounds to 68.8. Porkers (young pigs raised for market) increased in weight from 88.3 pounds to 108.4 pounds. Turner concludes that animal productivity increased 52 percent dur-

ing the first half of the nineteenth century. See M. Turner, Edward, J. V. Beckett, and B. Afton, *Farm Production in England, 1700–1914* (Oxford: Oxford University Press, 2001), pp. 180–200. Charles Knight, a 'statistician' and journalist in the mid-nineteenth century, also provided statistics. In 1732 the Smithfield market sold 76,210 cattle and 514,700 sheep. The cattle weighed an average of 370 pounds and the sheep 28 pounds (an average of sheep and lambs). Knight, *London*, vol. 1, p. 318. Counts by G. King, G. E. Fussell, and Deane and Cole argue for increased weights rather than increased heads of livestock. (See also P. Deane and W. A. Cole, *British Economic Growth, 1688–1959: Trends and Structure* (Cambridge: Cambridge University Press, 1967), G. King, *Natural and Political Observations and Conclusions Upon the State and Condition of England, 1697* (London: J. Stockdale, 1804), G. E. Fussell, *Farms, Farmers and Society: Systems of Food Production and Population Numbers* (Lawrence, KS: Coronado Press, 1976), K. J. Allison, 'Flock Management in the Sixteenth and Seventeenth Centuries', *The Economic History Review*, 11 (1958), pp. 98–112, for a discussion of increases in lambing rates, wool production, and production for London markets).

38. C. Dickens, 'All About Pigs', *Household Words*, 5 (1852), pp. 471–4; T. Tusser, *Five Hundred Points of Good Husbandry: As Well for the Champion or Open Country, as for the Woodland or Several: Together with a Book of Huswifery, Being a Calendar of Rural and Domestic Economy, for Every Month in the Year, and Exhibiting a Picture of the Agriculture, Customs, and Manners of England, in the Sixteenth Century* (London: Lackington, Allen, and Co., 1812), pp. 17, 90. England was essentially a wool-producing country until the eighteenth century, producing enough wool to provide textiles to its own population while sending exports to Europe and beyond. According to Gregory King's estimates, England and Wales had eleven million sheep and most produced fleeces that supplied manufactured textiles. P. Deane, 'The Output of the British Woolen Industry in the Eighteenth Century', *Journal of Economic History*, 17:2 (June 1957), p. 209.

39. Mingay and Thirsk suggest that it is futile to attempt any separation of statistics for farmers and graziers as most accounts are mingled and elusive. (See Mingay and Thirsk (eds), *The Agrarian History of England and Wales*, vol. 6, 1750–1850, and W. H. Heywood, 'Comparative Profits from Making Cheese and Butter from Jersey Milk, and Selling Milk or Grazing', *Journal of the Royal Agricultural Society of England* (1865).

40. W. Youatt, *Sheep, their Breeds, Management and Diseases* (London: Simpkin, Marshall, 1878), p. 549.

41. The Welsh were known for small black cattle. By the early 1800s, both Scotland and Ireland were free of restrictions of their cattle trade and began shipping their cattle to Smithfield. G. E. Mingay and J. Thirsk provide rich narratives of the development of British agriculture throughout the period preceding the Smithfield Removal Act of 1851: G. E. Mingay, *The Agricultural Revolution: Changes in Agriculture, 1650–1880* (London: A. & C. Black, 1977) and J. Thirsk, *The Agrarian History of England and Wales* (Cambridge: Cambridge University Press, 1985).

42. *Quarterly Journal of Agriculture*, 3 (June 1837–March 1838), p. 244.

43. C. A. J. Skeel, 'The Cattle Trade Between Wales and England from the Fifteenth to the Nineteenth Centuries', *Transactions of the Royal Historical Society*, 9 (1926), p. 136. Some farmers who lived near well-traveled roads or local markets might butcher their own animals and sell dead meat directly to the public. Often wives and daughters performed the farm sales. (See Mingay and Thirsk, *The Agrarian History of England and Wales*, pp. 214–15, and Chambers and Chambers, 'Chambers's Edinburgh Journal', pp. 447–8. A. R. B. Haldane, *The Drove Roads of Scotland* (Edinburgh: Edinburgh University Press,

1968), p. 57. F. J. Fisher, 'The Development of the London Food Market, 1540–1640', *Economic History Review*, 5:2 (1935), pp. 46–64.

44. Mr Urban, 'Cattle Not Monopolized by Graziers', *Gentleman's Magazine*, 25 (1755), p. 365. See also J. Thirsk (ed.), *The Agrarian History of England and Wales, Volume VI, 1750–1850* (Cambridge: Cambridge University Press, 1987), pp. 280–1. See also H. P. R. Finberg and J. Thirsk (eds), *The Agrarian History of England and Wales* (Cambridge: Cambridge University Press, 1967).

45. *Select Committee*, 1828, p. 5.

46. Skeel, 'The Cattle Trade', p. 142.

47. Chambers and Chambers, 'Chambers Edinburgh Journal', p. 448. Charles Knight noted that animals during the nineteenth century took only two years to fatten for market instead of the three years previously required. C. Knight, *London* vol. 2, pp. 342, 842.

48. The market affected breeding practices. Responding to an increasing demand for meat in the early nineteenth century, sheep breeders began to select stock for meat production characteristics rather than wool production to benefit from high mutton prices. A. K. Copus, 'Changing Markets and Developments of Sheep Breeds in Southern England, 1750–1900', *American Historical Review*, 37 (1989), p. 45. Far from 'larding up' an animal, a farmer wanted to add fat that marbled the meat, giving meat more tenderness and flavor. If a farmer used the wrong method or forage, his sheep would accumulate layers of fat instead of sinews of fat throughout the flesh. Both the rate of gain improvements and the fat quality increased the prices a farmer could get for his animal and thus his profit.

49. One observer, noted, 'The *mania* of what is called improving the breed of cattle is truly laughable ... the evil is a serious one – Fat Bullocks, Fat Sheep, &c. is all the rage'. J. S. Girdler, *Observations on the Pernicious Consequences of Forestalling, Regrating, and Ingrossing, with a List of the Statutes, &c. Which Have Been Adopted for the Punishment of those offences; ... Thoughts on the Impolicy of the Consolidation of Small Farms; ...* (London, H. Baldwin and Son, 1800), 76. Charles Knight observed that the animals at the Smithfield Club shows were 'fatter than is required for the ordinary market' and were the 'work of supererogation'. Knight, *London*. vol. 2, p. 324. The animals, 'miraculously obese', were displayed in agricultural shows that included the latest agricultural implements, 'garnished with terrific rows of iron fangs'. Sheep appeared as 'mere boxes of wool', and pigs looked like 'blind masses of living lard with no heads. While these farmers preferred pedigrees, most graziers supplying Smithfield sought non-pedigreed, cross-bred animals. 'The Smithfield Cattle Club', *Illustrated London News*, 12 December 1846, p. 375.

50. S. Freeman, *Mutton and Oysters: Victorians and Their Food* (London: V. Gollancz, 1989), p. 53.

51. C. Smith, 'The Wholesale and Retail Markets of London, 1660–1840', *Economic History Review*, 55:1 (2002), p. 43.

52. G. E. Mingay and J. Thirsk provide rich narratives of the development of British agriculture throughout the period preceding the Smithfield Removal Act of 1851. See *The Agricultural Revolution: Changes in Agriculture, 1650–1880* and *The Agrarian History of England and Wales*, p. 216.

53. Girdler, *Observations*, pp. 16, 17. (See also 'Forestalling, Regrating, and Engrossing', *Michigan Law Review* 27 (1929), pp. 365–88, for a discussion of the evolution of the verb 'to forestall'.)

54. Girdler, *Observations*, p. 16; W. Petty, *A Treatise of Taxes & Contributions, shewing the Nature and Measures of Crown Lands, Assessments, Customs, Poll-Money, Lotter-*

ies, Benevolence, Penalties, Monopolies, Offices, Tythes, Raising of Coins, Harth-Money, Excize, etc. (London, Angel, 1662).

55. W. Petty, *Notes and Queries, Volume 7,* 178 (1865), p. 412.

56. From the Middle Ages onward, the government continued to regulate the middlemen that engaged in the cattle trade in Smithfield. During food crises, the City of London attacked high prices and the practices of middlemen. In 1637, The Star Chamber required the butchers of London to refrain from selling cattle under the age of two years, from buying and selling at the same market, from buying fat cattle and selling them alive, and from selling diseased meat. (See Petty, *Notes and Queries,* p. 412.) In 1670, a bill enacted by Parliament enumerated several ways middlemen could be restricted from buying and selling cattle in ways that would prevent 'fair trade' in Smithfield. A 'Jobber, Salesman, or other Broker or Factor' could not buy or sell fatstock (other than pigs or calves) within eight miles of London. The penalty was usually the forfeiture of the cattle or payment for the value of the cattle to the owner. (See *Charles II, 1670 & 1671: An Act to Prevent Fraudes in the Buying and Selling of Cattell in Smithfield and Elsewhere, Statutes of the Realm: Volume 5, 1628–80* (1819), pp. 733–734. In 1708, Parliament enacted a bill to prevent butchers from selling 'any fat Cattle or Sheep either alive or dead' in the City of London or Westminster or within ten miles of the two cities to any other butcher. *States at Large and Statues of the United Kingdom, Volume 4,* p. 340. Chap. VI. 7, p. 64. This would prevent butchers acting as middlemen who would potentially increase the price of meat. In 1764, a plan was presented to the Duke of Bedford and the Lord Mayor, Aldermen, and Common Council of the City for regulating those who interfered with the market in Smithfield. The carcass butchers were 'outbuying' the retail butchers, even buying the cattle on the road before they reached the market, picking only the best cattle and leaving the lesser desirable cattle for the Smithfield. 'G—ge, F., An Abstract of a Plan of Mr. F—G for Reducing the Prices of Butchers Meat, and Regulating Smithfield Markets, Laid Before His Grace the Duke of Bedford, President of His Majesty's Council, and the Right Hon. Sir William Stevenson, Lord Mayor, and the Court of Aldermen and Common Council of the City of London'. *London Magazine, or, Gentleman's Monthly Intelligencer* (1764 December), pp. 661–2. Further debates about forestalling continued into the nineteenth century.

57. R. B. Westerfield, *Middlemen in English Business, Particularly Between 1660 and 1760.* Reprints of economic classics (New York: A.M. Kelley, 1968), p. 127. *Journal of the City Lands Committee, 1760* 52 (1760), p. 236.

58. J. Middleton, *View of the Agriculture of Middlesex; With Observations on the Means of its Improvement, and Several Essays on Agriculture in General. Drawn up for the Consideration of the Board of Agriculture.* (London: B. Macmillan, 1798).

59. *Transactions of the Connecticut Academy of Arts and Sciences.* (New Haven, CT: Connecticut Academy of Arts and Sciences, Yale University, 1915), p. 191.

60. Girdler, *Observations,* p. 76.

61. T. Hardy, *Far From the Madding Crowd* (Modern Library, 2001), p. 360.

62. Dodd, *The Food of London,* p. 218. Agricultural journals instructed farmers in the countryside about ways to send their cattle to market to keep animals in good health and carcasses in high quality for eventual slaughter. To prepare an animal for a drive to London, a farmer should take it off feed for several days, place it in an open area to acclimate it open spaces. Droves should begin slowly, about seven miles per day, and gradually increase speed to twelve or thirteen miles per day. Dogs should work sheep, not worry cattle, and sheep should not become overheated. Pigs were led, not driven, by

placing and removing beans in the desired path. *Quarterly Journal of Agriculture*, 3 (June 1837–March 1838), pp. 261–5. The Scottish drovers began moving large herds of cattle to London in the seventeenth century to the extent that 'England had ... grown to such proportions that Scotland was described as little more than a grazing field for England'. Haldane, *The Drove Roads of Scotland*, p. 18. In areas, such as in Wales, drovers were often farmers, a doubling of occupations unlike Scotland where drovers were in a separate trade. Estimates of the number of drovers in Smithfield are hard to come by. An accurate estimate of the number of drovers would include licensed and unlicensed drovers and drovers who operated both in and outside of Smithfield. Charles Knight and George Dodd estimate that there were at least 1,000 drovers in Smithfield during the 1840s. See 'Smithfield', *Leisure Hour* (March 1854), p. 153, and Dodd, *The Food of London*, p. 236.

63. See K. J. Bonser, *The Drovers: Who They Were and How They Went: An Epic of the Country-side* (London: Macmillan, 1970) and Haldane, *The Drove Roads of Scotland*. Both authors describe the life and business of the drovers who brought beasts, sheep, and pigs to Smithfield. Drovers were part of the country landscape, beginning at least during the period of early pastoralism and transhumance during the Neolithic period when shepherds and farmers moved their animals in search of water and forage. Drovers often bought cattle for Smithfield to Falkirk, a fair and 'tryst' in Scotland; 150,000 cattle marched at two miles an hour from Scotland by the mid-1800s. D. K. Cameron, *The English Fair* (Thrupp: Sutton, 1998), p. 75.

64. *Quarterly Journal of Agriculture*, 3 (June 1837–1838), p. 263; Rixson, *The History of Meat Trading*, p. 201; Bonser, *The Drovers*, p. 24.

65. Not all the stock raised in the provinces went to Smithfield. Local and regional markets also sold stock. Also, graziers often insured animals after purchase from a salesman. London insurance companies insured animals 'against all kinds of diseases'. *Medical Times and Gazette*, 1 (1862), p. 351. If an animal were to become diseased, it became the property of the insurance company that then sent the animal to its own slaughterhouse where the animals was killed and sent to London markets.

66. Cameron, *The English Fair,* p. 82, and Rixson, *The History of Meat Trading*, pp. 197, 198.

67. By the 1850s, droves coming to Smithfield from the south travelled over Blackfriars Bridge on their way to Islington, at the confluence of several rivers and railroad routes. The underground rivers of the Walbook and Fleet converged in Islington along with the New River (1613) and the Regent's Canal (first section opened in 1816). Mostly rural in nature until the beginning of the nineteenth century, Islington was highly regarded for its academic and religious institutions, as well as its spas and healthy air. By 1840, it had several hospitals, orphanages, and a model prison. The Royal Caledonian Asylum (1813) and the Pentonville Model Prison (1842, incorporating the ideas of Jeremy Bentham) occupied the area near the area later occupied by the Metropolitan Cattle Market. J. Richardson, *Islington Past* (London: Historical Publications, 2000); and *Vision of England, Islington, Descriptive Gazetteer* [accessed 9 June 2009].

68. Arthur Young provided anecdotal information about costs, and estimated that droving expenses from Norfolk to Smithfield amounted to 7s 1 1/2d per head during the early 1800s. A. Young, *The Elements and Practice of Agriculture* (London: Unpublished manuscript held by the British Museum, 1810s); Tolls varied but one toll from Paddington Fields into Oxford was 2 pence for 20 cattle and 1 pence for 20 sheep. D. Hughson, *London; Being an Accurate History and Description of the British Metropolis and its Neighbourhood: To Thirty Miles Extent, from an Actual Perambulation* (London: J. Stratford, 1806), p. 599. The Turnpike Act of 1663 required that each animal be accounted for as it passed through a tollgate, often delaying transit. In addition to turnpike tolls, the drover

incurred other expenses. Farmers sometimes charged the drover for grazing rights along the road, blacksmiths earned a fee for shoeing animals, including pigs, and drovers paid for lodgings at inns, about 4d/pence to 6 d/pence. (See Bonser, *The Drovers*.)

69. Bonser, *The Drovers*, p. 69. Also, see Genesis 24:60 (King James Version): 'And they blessed Rebekah, and said unto her, Thou art our sister, be thou the mother of thousands of millions, and let thy seed possess the gate of those which hate them'.

70. Pay for a drover ranged from one shilling per day (about £3.50 British pounds today or $5.75 US) in the early years to three or four shillings in the early nineteenth century. Losses incurred by the loss of animals through diseases or injury became liabilities as drovers had to deduct those expenses from their pay. The cost of a drove was difficult to estimate; veterinarian William Youatt estimated a three-week drove from Scotland to England cost £1 to £4s per head in 1834. Haldane, *The Drove Roads of Scotland*, p. 53; Financial systems, primarily the banking system, emerged out of the practice of drovers buying, selling, and transporting chattel, capital, from one individual to another, even from one government to another. Credit notes, futures, and forestalling were all practices that developed out of the meat trade in Smithfield Market.

71. R. Chambers, *Chambers' Edinburgh Journal*, 'Smithfield', 420 (1832), p. 90.

72. Sir J. Sinclair, *General Report of the Agricultural State and Political Circumstances of Scotland* (Edinburgh, 1844), p. 12.

73. G. Culley, *Observations on Live Stock; Containing Hints for Choosing and Improving the Best Breeds of the Most Useful Kinds of Domestic Animals* (London: Printed for G. Wilkie and J. Robinson 1807), pp. 61–2, and M. Culley, G. Culley, and A. Orde, *Matthew and George Culley: Farming Letters, 1798–1804: Publications of the Surtees Society, v. 210* (Woodbridge: Boydell Press for the Surtees Society, 2006), p. 279.

74. Some drovers were armed, not wanting to part with their stock or cash, and were exempted from laws restricting possession of arms. 'Affray in Smithfield', *Atheneaum* and *Literary Chronicle*, 94 (1829), p. 505.

75. *5–6 Ed. VI, Cap, 14, Sec. 16*. Charles II, 1670 & 1671: 'An Act to prevent Fraudes in the Buying and Selling of Cattell in Smithfield and Elsewhere'. *Statutes of the Realm: Volume 5: 1628–80* (1819), pp. 733–734. https://www.british-history.ac.uk/report.aspx?compid=47441 [accessed: 14 December 2008].

76. Drovers also brought cattle into London on their way to the army and navy victualling offices in East Smithfield. Victualling Commissioners purchased meat for the Navy and had existed since 1654. Drovers had traditionally transported cattle to market for the production of salted meats to satisfy the appetites of the Navy. Haldane, *The Drove Roads of Scotland*, p. 57.

77. 'Smithfield'. *Leisure Hour*, 115 (1854), p. 152. Some drovers sold animals at country markets on the way to Smithfield, including the Barnet market north of London and Southall market ten miles northwest of London, often keeping only highest quality animals to sell in London for the best prices.

78. Laycock owned land in Islington where farmers raised dairy cows. When land was needed to construct the New River in 1821, Laycock provided land from his holdings near Canonbury Square. *Islington: Growth: Canonbury, A History of the County of Middlesex: Volume 8: Islington and Stoke Newington Parishes* (1985), pp. 19–20. Richard Laycock, a dairy farmer, bought up land to provide lairs for cattle in Islington. Built by the 1820s to hold several thousand bullocks and sheep, the lairs were more advantageous than lairage in the open pens used elsewhere along Liverpool Road. Laycock died in

1834 after 40 years in business; both he and Rhodes turned much of their land first to brickmaking, then to building.

79. J. Nelson, *The History and Antiquities of the Parish of Islington in the County of Middlesex: Including Biographical Sketches of the Most Eminent and Remarkable Inhabitants: With Some Account of Several Objects of Interest in the Adjoining Parishes* (London: J. Nelson, 1823), pp. 108–9, 208–13.

80. *Select Committee*, 1828, p. 140.

81. Laycock's lairs complicated the debate about the limitations of Smithfield to contain all the cattle available to the market. The practice of keeping cattle in Laycock's lairs could be seen as a way of forestalling or at least of withholding supply and thereby influencing the prices. If all of the cattle were considered in price setting, including those in off-droves and lairs, then, some critics argued, prices could be set lower, based on a larger supply of cattle. William Collins, a Smithfield cattle salesman, refuted this argument by explaining how 'the buz goes round of what is the quantity', informing the salesmen of the total number of cattle in Smithfield and the surrounding areas. Collins conceded that the system was not perfect and that it was possible that the multiple locations holding out cattle from the market might influence prices. *Select Committee*, 1828, pp. 154–5.

82. Herding pigs to Smithfield caused considerable disruption to London traffic since pigs do not naturally travel in herds as do sheep or cattle. In October 1828, poet Leigh Hunt wrote, 'We beheld a man once, an inferior genius, inducting a pig into the other end of Long Lane, Smithfield. He had got him thus far towards the market. It was much. His airs announced success in nine parts out of ten, and hope for the remainder. It had been a happy morning's work; he had only to look for the termination of it; and he looked (as a critic of an exalted turn of mind would say) in brightness and in joy ... They squeaked and grunted as in ordinary; they sidled, they shuffled, they half stopped; they turned an eye to all the little outlets of escape; but in vain. There they stuck (for their very progress was a sort of sticking), charmed into the centre of his sphere of action, laying their heads together, but to no purpose; looking as if they were shrugging their shoulders and eschewing the tip-end of the whip of office. Much eye had they to their left leg; shrewd backward glances; not a little anticipative squeak, and sudden rush of avoidance. It was a superfluous clutter, and they felt it; but a pig finds it more difficult than any other animal to accommodate himself to circumstances. L. Hunt, 'On the graces and anxieties of pig-driving', *Quotidiana*, ed. P. Madden (1828). http://essays.quotidiana.org/hunt/graces_and_anxieties/ [accessed 9 June 2009].

83. *Letters and Statement to Shew the Practicability of Enlarging Smithfield Market and That No Necessity Exists for Removing It.* Guildhall c45.1, T-1810. CLA/016/AD/02/012.

84. *Select Committee,* 1828, pp. 16, 146.

85. 'Smithfield', *Leisure Hour*, 115 (1854), p. 152. See also 'Art. I. Report of the Commissioners Appointed to Make Inquiries Related to Smithfield Market, and the Markets in the City of London for the Sale of Meat', *Quarterly Review*, 95 (1854), p. 284.

86. Dodd, *The Food of London*, pp. 234–7. A law also stated that 'no salesman, or other broker or factor, who shall be employed to buy or sell any sort of cattle for others, by commission, or for reward to be paid or taken, shall be himself, or any servant or agent, directly or indirectly, on or for his own account, buy and live ox, bull, cow, steer, bullock, heifer, calf, sheep, lamb, or swine, in London or within the said limits of the said Weekly Bills of Mortality, or at any place whilst any such cattle shall be on the road, or be driving, bringing or coming up; to be sold or offered to or for sale in London'. Girdler, *Bills of Mortality*, p. 21. The City acted to protect salesmen by making it difficult for farmers

to sell directly in the market. In 1786, the City licensed salesmen and eliminated the possibility that a butcher or a grazier could act as a salesman. The Clerk of the Market would administer the licenses and provide certificates of sales to account for the numbers of goods entering the market, the sales, and the unsold animals leaving the market to enter toll-free the following day for sale. Farmers resented butchers who acted as salesmen and offered meat at below market prices. Graziers and butchers could not sell the same animal in the market until at least eight market days passed. These regulations sought to eliminate the 'fraud or collusion' in the market and represented a sort of moral economy combined with political economy. *Recommendations Committee of Privileges City of London*, 1786. In 1796, a bill proposed further regulations, including the appointment of salesmen by the City and restrictions of their activity as retail butchers. Other provisions limited engrossing or forestalling by salesmen and attempted to hold drovers more accountable for the numbers of stock they took to the market. 'Monopoly: Price 6d. The Cutting-Cutters Apology to the Legislature upon the High Price of Meat; In which Man of the base Practices of Smithfield Market Are Exposed, and a Remedy Pointed out for the Poor'. *Gentleman's Magazine*, 66:1 (1796), p. 57.

87. The butchers and salesmen passed the tolls on to the grazier who paid them out of the sales of his stock. The quantity of livestock affected the needs for rails, gates, and space. The salesmen informed the Clerk of the numbers of animals sold in order to calculate the tolls owed to the City. If animals failed to sell, or to sell at the salesman's desired price, a drover returned the animals to a lair where the grazier would incur losses from additional expenses related to feed and loss of condition. Many butchers who were graziers brought twenty to thirty 'beasts' to market each week. *Select Committee* 1828, 11, 12, p. 147; F. Sheppard, *London 1808–1870: The Infernal Wen* (Berkeley, 1971), p. 189; *Select Committee*, 1828, 52, 146. B. Andrade, *Trade Truths and Fireside Fancies: Selected from the Miscellaneous Writings of Benjamin Andrade* (London: W. H. & L. Collingridge, 1873), pp. 45–6.

88. Andrade, *Trade Truths and Fireside Fancies*, pp. 45–6.

89. Rixson, *The History of Meat Trading*, pp. 202–3.

90. Dodd, *The Food of London*, p. 236. Other estimates were lower, provided by the witnesses at the select committee hearings in 1828. Charles Merritt, a cattle salesman in Smithfield, explained how there were about 180 salesmen operating in Smithfield, all of whom worked with the country drovers to divide up the animals and to move them with the town drovers into pens. The variance in numbers indicates the ambiguity of Victorian business practices. For example, a salesman might also be a grazier and may not be counted as a salesman. In 1836, Pigot recorded 110 meat salesmen who lived in Newgate, Aldgate, Leadenhall, and a few in Whitechapel. (Four were women.) J. Pigot, *Pigot and Co.'s Classification of London Trades, And Those of The Towns and Principle Villages within Six Miles of St. Paul's*, 1836.

91. Smith, 'The Wholesale and Retail Markets of London, 1660–1840', p. 34.

92. Not all the animals killed by London butchers came into Smithfield. Some bought livestock from nearby country markets. Pigs slaughtered for the dead meat market also bypassed Smithfield since they often came from town pig owners. Some sheep never came to the live market, instead remaining in lairs outside the City until purchased by a butcher.

93. Dodd, *The Food of London*, p. 239; According to *Farmer's Magazine*, 6,000 cattle, 40,000 sheep occupied the space by 1850. These estimates are somewhat ambiguous since some statistics include only animals that sold, while other estimates include all the animals

that came into the market. J. Ridgeway, 'The New Metropolitan Cattle Market', *Farmers' Magazine*, new series, 26 (1854), p. 478.

94. Bonser, *The Drovers*, p. 65.

95. Schlesinger and von Wenckstern, *Saunterings In and About London*, p. 64.

96. *Select Committee* 1828, pp. 361–75. Not all animals came to Smithfield on drove roads. In 1670, over 206 Welsh cattle entered the English market by ship, crossing the sea between the south coast of Wales and the west coast of England. (See Skeel, p. 149.) Cattle traffic on drove roads, particularly from Scotland, began to decline in the 1830s just as railroads were beginning to expand throughout Britain and into the City. Faced with higher costs for arable land, farmers began to charge drovers for grazing rights along the roadside and the increasingly larger stock became more difficult to drive long distances. Steamboats operating between Ireland and Liverpool also began to replace the drovers. R. Perren, *The Meat Trade in Britain, 1840–1914* (London: Routledge, 1978), pp. 14, 17.

97. A. Wynter, 'The London Commissariat', *Quarterly Review*, 190:95 (1854).

98. E. Cockayne, *Hubbub: Filth, Noise & Stench in England 1600–1770* (New Haven, CT: Yale University Press, 2007), pp. 129–30. Cockayne suggests that this 'heightened sensitivity' may have been the increasing density of human occupation that caused 'an acceleration of disquiet caused by the need to acclimatize to a newly formed city'.

99. J. Brewer, 'Commercialization and Politics'. In N. McKendrick, J. Brewer, and J. H. Plumb (eds), *The Birth of a Consumer Society* (Bloomington, IN: Indiana University Press, 1982), p. 205.

100. Bonser, *The Drovers*, pp. 17, 37, 78–9. Also, David Lloyd, a Welsh drover, paid off his employer's bills in London by conveying the required funds; other drovers would convey Ship Money from the countryside to London. R. Colyer, 'Welsh Cattle Drovers in the Nineteenth Century', *National Library of Wales Journal* XVII/4 (Winter 1972).

101. Dodd, *The Food of London*, p. 237.

102. For example, in 1833, the Collector in Smithfield, Thomas Shank, was paid an annual allowance and fee of about £300 pounds and received a residence. The Assistant Collector, at that time Thomas Field, was paid about £60. In all, the City laid out almost £635 in 1833. When added to the total expenses of Smithfield for that year, including repairs and taxes, almost £785 came from the City to support the market in Smithfield. J. Fletcher, 'Statistical Account of the Markets of London: Dues Collected at Smithfield Market, 28 Mar. 1777–31 Dec 1817', *Journal of the Statistical Society of London*, 10:4 (1847), pp. 353–4.

103. *Select Committee,* 1847, p. 378, and Fletcher, 'Statistical Account of the Markets of London', p. 355.

104. *London Saturday Journal*, 1841.

2 The Smithfield System in the Nineteenth Century: The Consumers

1. H. Fielding, 'The Roast Beef of Old England'. According to Fielding expert Martin C. Battestin (*A Henry Fielding Companion*, Greenwood Press, 2000), this famous patriotic song written for the *Grub-Street Opera* (III. iv, Air xlv: *The King's Old Courtier*). While the play was never performed on stage, the song debuted in front of audiences three years later when it was included in the Haymarket production of *Don Quixote in England* (I. vi, Air v). Thereafter, with additional lyrics contributed by Richard Leveridge, it was sung before and after any new play, sometimes even between acts, by audiences throughout the 18th century. The play was published as *The Grub-Street Opera. As it is Acted at the*

Theatre in the Hay-Market. By Scriblerus Secundus. To Which is Added, The Masquerade, a Poem (London: J. Roberts, 1728). William Hogarth took the title of the song as inspiration for his 1748 painting, *The Gate of Calais, or O, the Roast Beef of Old England*.

2. 'On the Preparation of Livestock and Meat in Reference to Their Exportation by Steam-Vessels', *Farmer's Magazine*, 7 (1837), p. 448.

3. *The Experienced Butcher: Shewing the Respectability and Usefulness of his Calling, ... the Laws Relating to It* (London: Darton [etc.], 1816), p. 67.

4. Benjamin Stubbing, Master Butcher in 1828, described the butcher trade as moving away from carcass butchers (50 or more by his county) towards more retail butchers. Since the suburbs had grown, more retail butchers set up their trade and was able to buy a variety of meat products for every type of customers. (See *Select Committee*, 1828.)

5. Often working as butchers, slaughtermen were in between the salesman and butchers. Slaughtermen belonged to a separate group that killed animals but may not have acted as carcass or retail butchers.

6. J. Pigot, *Pigot and Co.'s Classification of London Trades, And Those of The Towns and Principle Villages within Six Miles of St. Paul's* (London: J. Pigot & Co., 1836). Out of 1,640 butchers, ten were women; one female butcher, Maria Pitt, insured her slaughterhouses at 25 Wapping Wall in 1823 for £25 and stock and utensils for £200. (See also D. Barnett, *London, Hub of the Industrial Revolution: A Revisionary History, 1775–1825* (London: Tauris Academic Studies, 1998), p. 141.)

7. T. M. Challis, *Free Trade in Food: Letter to the Right Hon. Lord John Russell ... on the Proposed Removal of Smithfield Market* (London: The City of London Central Markets' Association, 1851), p. 18.

8. Daniel A. Baugh's discussion of British Navy victualling provides useful information on the provisioning of meat for the Navy. The provision of fresh and salted beef through a contracting system included salesmen and butchers from Smithfield. D. A. Baugh, *British Naval Administration in the Age of Walpole* (Princeton, N.J.: Princeton University Press, 1965), Chapter 8.

9. *Select Committee*, 1828, pp. 9, 62, 82.

10. Perren, *The Meat Trade in Britain*, p. 10; Cunningham, *Handbook for London, Past and Present*, pp. 48, 62, 158.

11. C. Dickens, 'The Butcher', *All the Year Round: A Weekly Journal Conducted by Charles Dickens, December 28, 1867* (Oxford: Oxford University Press, 1868), p. 55. Most of those in the poorer classes ate some sort of meat, even it was offal, bacon, and sausage.

12. *Letters, Select Committee*, 1828, p.113. J. Burnett, *Plenty and Want: A Social History of Food in England from 1815 to the Present Day* (London: Routledge, 1989), p. 107.

13. Dickens, 'The Butcher', *All the Year Round*, pp. 54–5.

14. *Select Committee*, 1828, p. 58. In the nineteenth century, sugar refiners used bullock's blood to boil sugar; when boiled, the impurities separated from the sugar, binding to the albumen in the blood. See W. T. Brande, *A Dictionary of Science, Literature, & Art* (London: Longman, Brown, Green, and Longmans, 1842).

15. Dickens, 'The Butcher', *All the Year Round*, p. 54.

16. Girdler, *Observations*, pp. 65, 68, 69.

17. A Philanthropic Butcher, *Monopoly: The Cutting Butchers Appeal to the Legislature Upon the High Price of Meat: in Which Many of the Base Practices of Smithfield Market are Exposed and a Remedy Pointed Out for the Poor* (London: H.D. Symonds, 1795).

18. *British Farmer's Magazine*, 26 (1826, 1854), pp. 197–8.

19. By the beginning of the nineteenth century, the meat trade had grown to such an extent that it adopted a system for weighing cattle that replaced the older method of visually assessing the weight with a table containing a calculated weight based on an animal's measurements. (See *The Experienced Butcher*.)

20. *Select Committee*, 1828, p. 79.

21. Dickens, 'The Butcher', *All the Year Round, pp*. 54–5; *Select Committee*, 1828, pp. 146–55.

22. *Select Committee* 1828, pp. 52, 79–80, 137; A. Ligoe, *A Copy of a Letter, Written to the Lord Mayor of London, and the Gentlemen of the Committee at Guild-Hall Giving Them an Account of the Customary Prices of Cattle, Sheep, &c.... Also the Average Price of Butchers Meat...Likewise Shewing the Various Causes of the Present and Past High Prices of Cattle, Sheep, and Butcher's Meat: Also Describing a Method to Lower the High Prices* (Liverpool: R. Ferguson, 1787); *Honourable House of Commons, to Whom the Petition of the Retail Butchers in London, Westminster, the Borough of Southwark, and the Places Adjacent Thereto, was Referred* (London: Ordered by the House to be printed 29th April, 1796).

23. The British Navy Victualling Board kept track of the amount of salted beef and pork purchased from 1750 through 1870. Canning technology, in use during the second half of the nineteenth century, helped help keep soldiers at sea longer. (See Baugh, *British Naval Administration in the Age of Walpole*.)

24. Rixson, *The History of Meat Trading*, ch. 17. Meat that was unfit for human consumption was called 'cag-mag' and was sold for two pence per pound at Pye Corner in Smithfield. Cag-mag was meat from old animals that were usually thin and boney. *Select Committee*, 1828, p. 17.

25. Rixson, *The History of Meat Trading*, p. 254.

26. Freeman, *Mutton and Oysters*, p. 27.

27. R. Campbell, *The London Tradesman: Being an Historical Account of all the Trades, Professions, Arts, Both Liberal and Mechanic, Now Practiced in the Cities of London and Westminster, Calculated for the Instruction of Youth in their Choice of Business* (London: T. Gardner, 1757), p. 281. The disparagement appeared in laws during the sixteenth century during the right of Edward VI with laws that denied butchers the right to serve on juries, ostensibly because they had a reputation for dishonest pricing of meat. *2 & 3 Edward, VI*, p. 15.

28. P. L. Simmonds, *The Curiosities of Food* (London: Richard Bentley, 1859), p. 2. Both Roy Strong and Sarah Freeman point to the connection between social hierarchy and the consumption of meat. R. Strong, *Feast: A History of Grand Eating*. (London: Pimlico, 2003); Freeman, *Mutton and Oysters*.

29. A. Boorde, 'Compendyous Regyment, or a Dyetary of Health', 1542. Food studies and cultural history scholarship describe the connection between social identity and cuisine. From Claude Lévi-Strauss, Felipe Fernandez-Armesto, and Michel de Certeau provides rich material from the disciplines of food history and cultural studies. B. Rogers, *Beef and Liberty* (London: Chatto & Windus, 2003), provides a scholarship specific to the connections between beef and British identity; See also W. Shakespeare, *The Life of King Henry V*, Act III, Scene 7 ('Give them great meals of beef...').

30. H. Fielding, *The Grub-Street Opera. As it is Acted at the Theatre in the Hay-Market. By Scriblerus Secundus. To Which is Added, The Masquerade, a Poem* (London: J. Roberts, 1728).

31. Rogers, *Beef and Liberty*, p. 80. Until 1867, the members of the club ate beef to mock aristocratic foppishness, promoting their favorite symbol, John Bull.

32. These changes evolved from a longer transformation of ideas about trade and consumption. During the seventeenth century, political economist Nicholas Barbon wrote optimistically about the growth of a consuming 'mentalite' along with a sense of value based on demand. N. Barbon, *A Discourse of Trade* (London: Tho. Milbourn, 1690).

33. Pork, on the other hand, presented multiple problems for many consumers. Associated since Biblical times with impurity and sin, pigs belonged on the table of the London poor. Most of the pork sold in London was grown there or at least very near the periphery of the City. Shepherd's Bush, called 'the pigsty of the metropolis', was one such neighborhood since 'every house has its piggery, and the air is sonorous with the grunting of porkers'. Fewer pigs came to market as Londoners turned to beef and mutton. The aspiring middle class, anxious to leave pork behind, bought only 24,287 pigs in 1852 compared to 250,000 in 1698 when London's population was 550,000. L. Scott, 'The London Commissariat', *The Quarterly Review*, 94–5 (1854), p. 14. Pigs were fattened around the periphery of London and were kept in relationship to starch manufactories and distillers. Pigs consumed the spent malt grains from distillers who often raised pigs for that purpose. Butchers also kept pigs to eat the offal produced by the animals slaughtered in their premises. Most pigs came to London as dead meat, slaughtered in the country, mostly Wiltshire, Berkshire, Essex and even as far away as Ireland. R. Trow-Smith, *A History of British Livestock Husbandry, 1700–1900* (London: Routledge, 2006), p. 220; *Select Committee*, 1828, p. 118.

34. Freeman, *Mutton and Oysters*, p. 53.

35. 'The Prize Show of the Smithfield Cattle Club', *Illustrated London News*, 12 December 1846, p. 375.

36. Simmonds, *The Curiosities of Food*, pp. 2–4.

37. Harriet Ritvo's discussion of meat-eating during the nineteenth century presents further evidence of the connection between British beef and national identity. H. Ritvo, *The Platypus and the Mermaid, and Other Figments of the Classifying Imagination* (Cambridge, MA: Harvard University Press, 1997).

38. During the eighteenth century, London's expanding population also changed in sociological terms. Migration to urban centers increased as manufacturing jobs replaced rural labor. The rising middle classes fueled the growth of the consumer culture as supply increased. H. Perkin, *Origins of Modern English Society* (London: Routledge, 1986), pp. 67, 99.

39. In Smithfield, the cattle market appeared to defy any pretense to elegance or manners. Those who promoted the market removal often complained that wild animals and violent drovers threatened societal decorum and civility. Joseph Fletcher, in his 1847 account of the markets of London, railed against Smithfield for its inelegance. His preference was for a 'noble regular square...for merchants and people of opulence...' Fletcher, 'Statistical Accounts of the Markets of London', p. 357. See also *Select Committee Report*, 1828, p. 119.

40. Mutton was popular with the meat-eating classes, particularly the urban middle classes. Mutton traveled better than beef by rail. There were more prime cuts in a mutton carcass, and the cost of rail travel could be offset by higher revenues. Mutton chops were so popular in London that one could 'Go into any part of the metropolis and look into the windows of the thousand eating-houses and coffee-shops in the great thoroughfares, and in everyone of them there is the invariable blue dish with half-a-dozen juicy, well-trimmed chops, crowned with a spring of parsley'. See 'Art. I. Report of the Commissioners Appointed to Make Inquiries Related to Smithfield Market, and the Markets in the City of London for the Sale of Meat', *Quarterly Review*, 95:190 (1854), p. 289.

41. *Select Committee*, 1828, p. 119.

42. 'A Looking Glass', p. 308.
43. J. C Drummond and A. Wilbraham, *The Englishman's Food: A History of Five Centuries of English Diet* (London: Pimlico, 1970), p. 129.
44. 'A Looking Glass', p. 308.
45. E. Roberts, *Domestic Cookery: A New System of Domestic Cookery Founded Upon Principles of Economy and Adapted to the Use of Private Families* (London: J. Murray, 1840), p. 241.
46. A Lady, *New London Cookery, Adapted to the Use of Private Families* (London: London Cookery, 1836), pp. 11, 12; E. Roberts, *Domestic Cookery*, p. xvi.
47. A Lady, *The Modern Cookery, Written Upon the Most Approved and Economical Principles, and in Which Every Receipt has Stood the Test of Experience, 10th Ed., Greatly Improved and Enlarged, With 165 New Receipts, Including Many for the Sick and the Poor* (London: J. & C. Mozley, 1856), 6; A Lady, *The New London Cookery and Complete Domestic Guide* (London, c1840), pp. 11, 12.
48. Leibig also developed a meat extract from cattle carcasses and eventually founded OXO, the British company that produced beef bullion cubes, in the twentieth century.
49. Peter Earle suggests that by the late eighteenth century the new 'middling' class of the eighteenth century was already expressing its tastes and economic power by increasing the number of days that meat arrived on the tables of many London households, eating meat an average of four out of five days a week. P. Earle, *The Making of the English Middle Class: Business, Society and Family Life in London, 1660–1730* (London: Methuen, 1989), p. 273.
50. 'A Looking Glass', pp. 307–8.
51. 'Sundays and Tuesdays Post, London', *Jackson's Oxford Journal*, 14 November 1840.
52. McKendrick, Brewer and Plumb, *The Birth of a Consumer Society*, p. 24.
53. M. G. Mulhall, *Mulhall's Dictionary of Statistics* (London: Routledge, 1886).
54. Knight, *London*, vol. 1, p. 318. Knight notes that the days of abstinence from meat accounted for some of this dislocation since almost half of all market days fell on days of abstinence when Londoners turned to fish instead of meat for sustenance. This minimized the pressure for Smithfield to expand since the growth of consumption did not match population growth rates; Lord Ernle suggested that English farmers were already unable to keep pace with English demand for beef by the end of the eighteenth century and Deane and Cole argued that England was already reliant upon imports (including Ireland) to feed its growing population. Lord Ernle, *English Farming, Past and Present*, 6th edn (London: Frank Cass & Co, 1961), pp. 316–31; Deane and Cole, *British Economic Growth*, p. 74.
55. N. Gash, *The Life of Robert Peel After 1830* (London: Longman's, 1972), p. 350. W. C. Taylor, 'The Life and Times of Sir Robert Peel', *Westminster Review*, 57 (New York, Leonard Scott, 1852), p. 130.
56. See Perren, *The Meat Trade in Britain*, for a discussion of developments in foreign livestock imports. The percentage of foreign cattle increased by the end of the century, edging up to about 40 per cent of cattle, 50 per cent of sheep, and 80 per cent for pigs. Perren and others concur that these statistics are unreliable, complicated by the inclusion of Irish imports in some cases, conversions of live to dead meat quantities, ad other ambiguities. Also see 'What Our Railways Carry, No. VL, Livestock', *Railway News*, 1 December (London: 1888), p. 891.

57. Dodd, *The Food of London*, pp. 249–50. His estimates are contingent upon animal weights, a much-disputed topic, according to Mulhall and other contemporary statisticians. See M. G. Mulhall, *The Dictionary of Statistics*.

58. Barnett, *London Hub*, p. 140.

59. Author of Random Recollections, 'The Great Metropolis Portraits of Public Character, London Markets', *London Saturday Journal*, 1:10 (March 1841), pp. 111–12.

60. *The Working Man's Friend, and Family Instructor* (London: John Cassell, 1850), p. 290

61. Economic historians continue to assess nineteenth-century market data to determine if product improvements and consumer preferences changed meat consumption patterns during the Victorian period. While some observers state that by the 1880s Londoners spent more on meat than on bread, other historians point out that meat consumption remained static after the early nineteenth century. E. J. Hobsbawm, who analyzed the British standard of living between 1790 and 1850, argued that meat consumption was a useful indicator. He divided economists into optimists and pessimists in terms of estimating whether the nineteenth century experienced overall economic growth and prosperity. Often, the disparity between optimistic and pessimistic accounts resulted from the quality of data available for analysis of meat consumption. Hobsbawm criticized some data because he believed it overestimated the weight of cattle and thus attributed an increase in meat consumption even though the number of animals remained constant while population rose. He argued that real increases in meat consumption occurred before the industrial revolution and remained static after the 1840s, although he warned that no livestock census was available during that period. (See E. J. Hobsbawm, *Industry and Empire: An Economic History of Britain since 1750* (London: Weidenfeld & Nicolson, 1968), and *Laboring Men: Studies in the History of Labor* (New York: Basic Books, 1965), p. 84.

62. R. M. Hartwell, 'The Rising Standard of Living in England, 1800–1850', *Economic History Review*, 13 (1961); *The Industrial Revolution and Economic Growth* (London: Methuen, 1971); A. J. Taylor, *The Standard of Living in Britain in the Industrial Revolution* (London: Methuen, 1975), pp. 113–14.

63. G. Clark, M. Huberman, and P. H. Lindert, 'A British Food Puzzle, 1770–1850', *Economic History Review*, 48:2 (1995), p. 215. See also G. Clark, *A Farewell to Alms: A Brief Economic History of the World* (Princeton, NJ: Princeton University Press, 2007).

64. *British Almanac* (London, 1852): p. 40. See also P. Trippi, *The Great Exhibition of 1851*, The Victoria and Albert Museum, http://www.fathom.com/feature/60964/index.html [accessed 8 September 2009]. A. Foreshaw and T. Bergström, *Smithfield: Past and Present* (London, Heinemann, 1980), p. 54.

3 The Smithfield Battle Begins

1. 'An Unmarketable Market', *Punch*, 22:3 (1852), p. 142.

2. Dodd, *The Food of London*, p. 228.

3. 'Individual Interests – How Affected by Removal of Market', *Farmer's Magazine*, 6 (1854), p. 474.

4. J. Ridgeway, 'The New Metropolitan Cattle Market', *Farmer's Magazine*, new series, 26 (1854), p. 476.

5. 'Smithfield', *Chambers's Edinburgh Journal*, 397 (1851), p. 90.

6. *Hansard*, HC 18 April 1809, vol. 14, cc. 7–5.

7. *A Brief Statement of the Facts Respecting the Existing Nuisance of Smithfield Market*, London (1834), p. 7.

8. P. Johnson, 'Market Discipline', in P. Mandler (ed.), *Liberty and Authority in Victorian Britain* (Oxford: Oxford University Press, 2006), pp. 212–13.
9. *Hansard*, HC Deb 05 June 1828 vol. 19cc pp. 1049–53
10. *Select Committee,* 1828, p. 144.
11. M. J. Daunton and Matthew Hilton discuss the 'client economy' as it developed in the eighteenth to the nineteenth centuries. See *The Politics of Consumption: Material Culture and Citizenship in Europe and America: Leisure, Consumption and Culture* (Oxford: Berg, 2001); J. Brewer, 'Commercialization of Politics', in McKendrick, Brewer and Plumb, *The Birth of a Consumer Society,* pp. 198–9; J. Appleby, 'Ideology and Theory: The Tension Between Political and Economic Liberalism in Seventeenth-Century England', *American Historical Review,* 81:3 (June 1976), pp. 499–515; M. Dintenfass and D. Wahrman, 'Imagining the Middle Class: The Political Representation of Class in Britain, *c.* 1780–1840', *Journal of Social History,* 30:2 (1996), p. 553; Earle, *The Making of the English Middle Class,* p. 273.
12. Recognizing the need for a municipal body to address public safety, Robert Peel instituted a police force that excluded the City. Ensnarled with the rights and privileges of the City, the metropolis and Parliament were unable to envision a police force for all Londoners.
13. F. H. W. Sheppard, *London: A History* (Oxford: Oxford University Press, 1998), p. xviii.
14. The City managed its markets through its City Lands Committees until 1835, when they created the Markets Improvement Committee (intended to both manage the markets and audit their operations, initiating improvements when necessary. Fletcher, 'Statistical Account of the Markets of London', p. 351.) The Committee, which reported to the Court of Common Council and the Lord Mayor, appointed the market collectors, beadles, collectors, and other workers engaged in the markets' operations. The City also provided an inspector for the purpose of inspecting animals for infectious diseases. (*11 & 12 Vict. C 107.*) The City's power to regulate Smithfield was circumscribed within the rights to charge rent and tolls and to set the times and days for the markets' operations (five existed in 1840). The City had also licensed the drovers since the time of King William III. (See *Select Committee,* 1849.) According to John Davis, the problem of London's metropolitan governance was created by the tension between the unity of the economic sphere and the diversity of the social sphere. As Davis pointed out, the 'grey area' between two tiers of governance, local and metropolitan, was vast, and in London during the nineteenth century, it was fluid and contested. The central government, authorized by the monarch and administered through Parliament, represented the municipal public sphere, and the City of London represented one of the localized private spheres. J. Davis, *Reforming London: The London Government Problem, 1855–1900.* (Oxford: Clarendon Press, 1988), pp. 1–9.
15. The City butchers did not always take kindly to the royal interference in their trade. In 1533, butchers' complaints that the graziers' prices were too high resulted in a royal ordinance that reined in graziers' prices. The butchers continued to chafe under restrictions on pricing and weights, sometimes succeeding in getting the Court of Aldermen to appeal to Parliament. In some cases, the butchers controlled prices as they did in the late 1530s but the tug-of-war between the butchers and the government continued and was an example of the negotiated power between private interests and those of centralized government. While Parliament sought ways to affirm its right to statutory regulation, the City – specifically the butchers – resisted most regulations. The government moved to regulate other aspects of the trade, including the practices of flayers, those butchers who skinned sheep. In 1584–5, butchers were leaving bits of skin on mutton to create a more

pleasant appearance to the meat. King James continued to enact ordinances to regulate markets with the aim of eliminating monopolies. But by then it was clear that the King acted both to create monopolies, mitigate them, and to protect existing markets. *Report 1, By Royal Commission on Historical Manuscripts*, 1872, p. 6. (Also see *Parliamentary Papers, Great Britain*. Parliament. House of Commons, Published by HMSO, 1888, Item notes: v. 53 for other regulations of butchers.) In 1666, after the Great Fire, the King Charles II, issued a proclamation 'to secure the said Markets in safety ...', reassuring Londoners that markets such as Smithfield, left unsinged by the Fire, would operate without disturbances. By the King, *A Proclamation for Keeping of Markets to Supply the City of London with Provisions, and also for Prevention of Alarms and Tumults ...* (London: John Bill, and Christopher Barker, Printers to the King, 1666).

16. *Hansard*, HC Deb 05 June 1828, vol. 19 cc. pp. 1049–53.
17. Girdler, *Observations*, p. 21.
18. J. Fletcher, 'The Metropolis: Its Boundaries, Extent, and Divisions for Local Government', *Journal of the Statistical Society of London*, 7 (1844), pp. 69–85, 70–1.
19. Dodd, *The Food of London*, pp. 10–11.
20. R. Perren, *Taste, Trade and Technology: The Development of the International Meat Industry since 1840* (Aldershot, England and Burlington, VT: Ashgate, 2006), p. 398.
21. *Select Committee*, 1828, p. 5.
22. Fletcher, 'The Metropolis', p. 75.
23. *Select Committee*, 1828, pp. 127, 148, 151.
24. Ibid., pp. 19, 26.
25. Ibid., pp. 52, 102.
26. Ibid., pp. 26, 45, 81.
27. R. Perren, 'The Meat and Livestock Trade in Britain, 1850–70', *The Economic History Review*, 2nd series, 27:3 (1975), p. 392.
28. *Select Committee*, 1828, pp. 131, 69–70.
29. Ibid., pp. 4, 67, 145.
30. Ibid., p. 71.
31. Ibid., pp. 17, 18.
32. Ibid., p. 72.
33. T. M. Challis, *Letter to the Right Hon. Lord John Russell, M. P. on the Proposed Removal of Smithfield Market* (London, 1851), p. 13.
34. *Hansard*, House of Commons, HC Deb 17 July 1849 vol. 107 cc. 492–514. A Bude-Light is a bright lamp that was used to light the House of Commons during the nineteenth century, and was named after the town of Bude in Cornwall, England, where the inventor lived.
35. W. A. Mackinnon. *On the Rise, Progress, and Present State of Public Opinion in Great Britain, and Other Parts of the World* (London: Saunders and Otley, 1828), p. 185.
36. *Citizen*, 8, 3 March 1849, p. 65.
37. Traffic congestion was not new in the nineteenth century. In 1791, Horace Walpole observed 'I have twice this spring been going to stop my coach in Piccadilly, to inquire what was the matter, thinking there was a mob; not at all, it was only passengers'. P. 214, D. P. Kidder, *London in Modern Times, or, Sketches of the English Metropolis during the Seventeenth and Eighteenth Centuries* (New York: Lane & Scott, for the Sunday School Union of the Methodist Episcopal Church, 1851).
38. *Hansard*, HC Deb 28 February 1805 vol. 3 c 640; *Hansard*, HC Deb 01 July 1806 vol. 7 cc 871–2

39. *Appendix 14, Select Committee,* 1847, p. 394.
40. *Statement to Shew the Practicability of Enlarging Smithfield Market and That No Necessity Exists for Removing it.* Guildhall c45.1, T-1810.
41. *Removal of Smithfield Market, Case of the Purchasers of Cattle who Petition against the Bill,* April 1809, Street and Woolfe, 1809.
42. *Removal of Smithfield, Case of the Purchasers.*
43. The Board of Trade was a committee appointed to advise the Privy Council on matters of trade and other economic activities of Britain. (Fletcher, 'Statistical Account', p. 358) Also *Appendix to Committee of City Lands Report,* 2 March 1809, pp. 10, 11.
44. *Hansard,* HC Deb 18 April 1809, p. 73.
45. Fletcher, 'Statistical Account', p. 358.
46. 'Smithfield Market', *Morning Chronicle,* 1809, p. 28.
47. *Hansard,* House of Commons, HC Deb 17 July 1849 vol. 107 cc 492–514.
48. *On the Necessity of the Removal of Smithfield Market, and the Advantages the Principal Opposers of that Measure Would Obtain by Such Removal.* 2. CLA/016/AD/01/005. A. Pearce, *The History of the Butchers' Company* (London: Meat Trades' Journal Co., 1929).
49. *A Brief Statement of Facts Respecting the Existing Nuisance of Smithfield Market.* (London: Stirling, 1834), p. 7. See also the petition of *March 25th 1808, and Petition from Butchers to Alter Friday to Thursday market.*
50. Fletcher, 'Statistical Account', pp. 358–9.
51. *Morning Chronicle,* 1809, p. 28.
52. Great Britain. 1812. *Cobbett's Parliamentary Debates During the ... Session of the...Parliament of the United Kingdom of Great Britain and Ireland, and of the Kingdom of Great Britain.* London: [s.n.]. p. 482. *Hansard,* 18 April 1809, hansard.millbanksystems,com/commons/1809/apr/18/smithfield
53. *Hansard,* 18 April 1809, p. 73. House of Commons. After subtracting the space required for adequate thoroughfares, the net amount of space would have been ten acres.
54. Other improvements appeared that related to Smithfield. For example, the Flaying Acts of 1803 and 1808 regulated the butchers until 1824 for the purpose of improving the quality of skins delivered to the curriers (leather finishers) and cordwainers (shoemakers). Butchers had become cavalier about the quality of skins produced as a result of killing the animals and the system of inspections, inspectors, fines, and duties created a galling amount of added record keeping and delays. Finally, after its repeal, the Butchers returned to the issues of Sunday market days and the removal of Smithfield. A. Pearce, *The History of the Butchers' Company* (London: Meat Trades' Journal Co., 1929), pp. 127–34.
55. *Hansard,* 18 April 1809.
56. *Removal of Smithfield Market, Case of the Purchasers of Cattle who Petition against the Bill, April 1809* (London: Street and Woolfe, 1809).
57. Ibid.
58. Ibid.
59. Ibid.
60. *Appendix 14, Report to the Select Committee,* 1847, p. 394.
61. *Smithfield Market, Substance of the Bill now Before Parliament, for Enlarging and Improving the Market-Place with Observations Thereon; also the Objections to the Proposed Measure, and Answers Thereto,* 1813.
62. Ibid. By 1828, however, the City succeeded limiting traffic during market hours despite the ambiguities of traffic control rights. Pearce, *The History of the Butchers' Company,* p. 168.

63. A letter written to the *Monthly Magazine* in 1824 suggested several improvements to the City for consideration. The author proposed that the City build a public slaughterhouse in Smithfield and prohibit private slaughterhouses with four miles of the Post Office and a new arrangement of markets that would specialize in one commodity, scheduled on sequential days. He was resigned to the continuation of the markets for cows and horses, which he saw as ' a partial evil' with 'no remedy'. H., Smithfield; May 11, 1824, 'Projected Improvement of Smithfield Market.' *Monthly Magazine*, 413 (June 1824), pp. 57–396.

64. *Hansard*, HC 12 June 1828 vol. 19 c 1318.

65. *Hansard*, 5 June 1828. Sir H. Parnell, Oxford Dictionary of National Biography, http://www.oxforddnb.com/view/article/21386?docPos=5 [accessed 20 February 2009].

66. A. Robey, 'All asmear with filth and fat and blood and foam: The social and architectural reformation of Smithfield market', *Transactions, Ancient Monuments Society*, 42, 4.

67. *Select Committee*, 1828, pp. 37, 134, 155.

68. *Hansard*, 13 June 1828.

69. *A Brief Statement of Facts Respecting the Existing Nuisance of Smithfield Market.* (London: Stirling, 1834), p. 8.

70. *Select Committee*, 1828, pp. A2, 5.

71. Ibid., 1828, p. 13.

72. Steven Shapin explores the limitations of confirming truth through the experimental process during this period. Reliable knowledge of real physical bodies and processes was to be secured by experimental inquiry not by mathematical speculation. Robert Boyle, he said, saw physical inquiry as often sufficient, though it falls short of a 'mathematical exactness'. S. Shapin, *A Social History of Truth: Civility and Science in Seventeenth-Century England.* (Chicago, IL: University of Chicago Press, 1994), pp. 340–2.

73. *Select Committee*, 1828, pp. 58, 105.

74. Ibid., 1828, pp. 139, 141.

75. Ibid., 1828, p. 141.

76. Ibid., 1828, p. 23; For a more on the history and perception of knowledge during this period, see M. Poovey, *A History of the Modern Fact: Problems of Knowledge in the Sciences of Wealth and Society* (Chicago, IL: University of Chicago Press, 1998); T. M. Porter, *Trust in Numbers: The Pursuit of Objectivity in Science and Public Life* (Princeton, NJ: Princeton University Press, 1995); and B. J. Shapiro, *A Culture of Fact: England, 1550–1720* (Ithaca, NY: Cornell University Press, 2000).

77. *Select Committee*, 1828, p. 140; *Select Committee*, 1828, p. 139.

78. Ibid., 1828, p. 106.

79. Whitechapel was home to many Jews and foreign merchants. It was the setting for *Sweeney Todd*, another carnivorous story. Whitechapel was an imbroglio of dark, narrow streets, crowded even without the addition of distressed animals on their way from Smithfield to a slaughterhouse.

80. *Select Committee*, 1828, pp. 28, 31, 55–6.

81. Ibid., 1828, pp. 36, 41, 132, 133.

82. Ibid., 1828, p. 134.

83. *Brief statement concerning the Facts*, p. 16.

84. A. Briggs, *The Age of Improvement* (London: Longmans, Green, 1999), p. 188.

85. 'March of Intellect'. Etching (G. Humphrey, St. James Street, London, 1828). Artist, P. Pry. *Satire of Acquisition of Knowledge by the Lower Classes*, Science and Society Picture Library, Science Museum Pictorial, London, England.

86. *Select Committee,* 1828, pp. 11, 71, 155.

87. J. Ridgeway, 'Individual Interests – How Affected by Removal of Market', p. 474.

88. *Select Committee* 1828, p. 9.

89. *Morning Chronicle,* Oct. 26, 1828, p. 28.

90. S. Munday, *An Important Improvement in the Supply of London Wholesale Meat Markets, by the ... Abolition of Smithfield Livestock Trade.* (London: Causton, 1832), pp. 4, 12–13.

91. Ibid., p. 12.

92. Ibid., pp. 8, 16, 20, 22.

93. Ibid., pp. 17, 19.

94. 'Projected Improvement of Smithfield Market', *The Monthly Magazine, or British Register,* 57:396 (June 1824), p. 413.

95. See W. Nelson, *A Proposal for a New Cattle Market for the Supply of London to be Erected on the North Bank of the Thames Near Blackwall* (London: Waterloo & Sons, 1851), p. 4.

96. 'South London Market', *The Athenaeum Journal,* January to December 1832 (London, 1832), p. 701.

97. 'London Cattle-Market and Abattoirs, Lower Road, Islington', *The Times,* 12 September 1836. H. Handley, an MP who had been on a select committee to investigate agricultural problems, said that he proposed the Islington market 'for public utility'. He first proposed the bill in 1833 and re-proposed it in 1834. *Hansard,* HC Dev 12 March, 1835, vol. 26, cc pp. 880–4.

98. *The Times,* 21 May 1836. Walter Thornbury calls Perkins a man 'before his age'. See 'Pentonville', *Old and New London: Volume 2* (1878), pp. 279–89. URL: http://www.british-history.ac.uk/report.aspx?compid=45098 [accessed: 19 October 2009].

99. 'General Meeting, Master Butchers Against Removing the Cattle Market from Smithfield', *The Times,* 19 December 1833.

100. Ibid.. C. Pearson, *The Substance of a Speech Delivered Before the Committee of the House of Commons on Wednesday, June 4, 1834... in Supporting the Petition of the Graziers...in Opposition to the...Islington Market Bill* (London: W. Tyler, 1834).

101. 'Smithfield Market', Guildhall Archives, C45.1,T. 1834.

102. *Facts Relating to the Nuisance.* pp. 14–15.

103. Minutes, House of Commons, *Hansard,* HC Deb 18 April 1834, vol. 22, c 938. *London Gazette,* 15 August 1834, p. 1500. Perkins attempted to close Smithfield, and when that failed, he made an unsuccessful attempt to transfer his market to the City.

104. Great Britain, C. Clark, and W. Finnelly, *Reports of Cases Heard and Decided in the House of Lords on Appeals and Writs of Error During the Sessions,* vol. 3, 1834, 1835, & 1836 (London: J. & W.T. Clarke, 1838), pp. 513–523.

105. 'An Account of the Expenses in Prosecuting the Petition to Parliament Against the Islington Market Bill', Guildhall, Chamber of London, 23 March 1847. Fletcher, 'Statistical Account', p. 355; 'Dinner to Celebrate the Defeat of the Islington Market Bill', *The Times,* June 1835.

106. *Islington Market Bill Evidence,* 30 March 1835, vol. 5 HC/CL/PB/2/1/5, Guildhall Archives. *The Act of Parliament to Establish a Market in Ball's Pond in 1835 (6 & 7 William IV, c 68).*

107. 'London Cattle-Market and Abattoirs, Lower-Road, Islington', *Morning Chronicle,* Sept. 13, 1833, Issue 19984.

108. Construction began in 1833 and cost £100,000. 'Domestic Occurrences', *Gentleman's Magazine*, 5 (January–June 1836).
109. 'Islington Cattle Market', 1836. *B'side 30.18*, Guildhall Archive.
110. 'Explosion at the Islington Cattle Market', *The Times*, 23 January 1836, p. 3.
111. 'Supply of Cattle to Smithfield and Islington Markets, Friday, 20 May 1836', *The Times*, 21 May 1836; 'Islington Market', *The Times*, Wednesday, 25 April 1836, p. 6.
112. *Architectural Magazine* (June 1836). Also, *Morning Chronicle* 17 April 1836.
113. 'London Cattle-Market and Abattoirs, Lower-road, Islington', *The Times*, 12 September 1836, W. Pinnock (ed.), 'The Islington New Cattle Market', *The Guide to Knowledge* (London, 1833), p. 700.
114. In 1836, George Jacomb, a retail butcher, complained that the removal would only amplify the existing problems. The destruction of private property would 'be immense' and the public would end up paying for the removal 'without any benefit being derived, or any inconvenience obviated'. G. Jacomb, *Reasons Against the Removal of Smithfield Market to Balls Pond* (London, 1836), p. 1.
115. *Brief Statement of the Facts*, p. 11.
116. Fletcher, 'Statistical Account', p. 359.

4 Smithfield's Urban Landscape: Space in Transition

1. T. Carlyle to A. Carlyle, 14 December 1824, *Carlyle Letters*, C-AC, 14 December Addr: Mainhill, / Ecclefechan, / Dumfries-shire. PM: [DEC] 14 1824. MS: A. Carlyle family, Canada. Pbd: Norton, *EL*, 314–18, inc; Marrs, pp. 181–6. http://carlyleletters.dukejournals.org/cgi/content/full/3/1/lt-18241214–TC-AC-01, [accessed 15 January 2009].
2. Colin Smith offers a broad narrative of London markets from 1660–1840. He places the markets in an 'integrated national market', buttressed by 'provincial eyes' outside London and brought together by a 'price mechanism'. (Smith, 'The Markets of London'). Scholars such as Smith, who study the economic geography of cities, shed light on how maps reveal the nature of urban growth. Henry Rees studied how Northeast London developed during what some historians call 'the Railway Age', looking at how the physical characteristics of the landscape interacted with the human factors to shape the growth of the city. For example, he argues that road transportation drove the location of urban population. H. Rees, *The British Isles: A Regional Geography*, 2nd edn (London: Harrap, 1972), and *The Industries of Britain: A Geography of Manufacture and Power, Together with Farming, Forestry, and Fishing* (London: Harrap, 1970).
3. A. Wynter, 'The London Commissariat', *Quarterly Review*, 95 (1854).
4. See *London Census*, cited in M. Ball, and D. Sunderland, *An Economic History of London, 1800–1914* (London: Routledge, 2001), p. 22. The first official census in 1801 provided the first statistical account of London's population. Before then, anecdotal accounts, tax records, duties, and other official records combined to provide a picture of this historical phenomenon. W. Besant, 'London in the Nineteenth Century (1909)', L. Hollen Lees, (ed.) *The Rise of Urban Britain* (New York, 1985), p. 4.
5. R. Price-Williams, 'The Population of London', 1801–81, *Journal of the Statistical Society of London*, 48:3 (September 1885), pp. 349–440. Population, www.st-andrews.ac.uk/~city.19thvicity/pop.htm/ [accessed 6 March 2009].
6. Challis, *Free Trade in Food*, p. 8.
7. Reach, 'John Bull and His Bullocks', p. 121.
8. 'A Looking Glass', p. 307.

9. The Walbrook, known today as one of London's 'lost' rivers, was covered by silt, disappearing gradually; by the Middle Ages it had completely disappeared. The Fleet River met a similar end, but it disappeared because of building and street improvements during the eighteenth and nineteenth centuries. The Fleet River disappeared in 1737 and the Walbrook by 1300. See N. Barton, *The Lost Rivers of London: A Study of Their Effects Upon London and Londoners, and the Effects of London and Londoners Upon Them* (London: Historical Publications, 1992).

10. Many historians believe that the walls around Roman London were a response to attacks by tribes such as the Iceni, who rebelled against the Roman occupiers in 61 CE and left London in ruins. The sandstone, brick, flint, ragstone (hard rock), clay and rubble filling, covered with mortar, created an impressive bulwark that enclosed almost 330 acres, making London a formidable city already surrounded by its own suburbs. N. Pevsner, *The Buildings of England. 12, 1, London, The Cities of London and Westminster* (Harmondsworth: Penguin, 1957), p. 23.

11. Social anthropologists such as Mary Douglas argue that these boundaries are symbols for separation from the pure and unpure, and the ordered and disordered in society. See M. Douglas, *Purity and Danger: An Analysis of Concepts of Pollution and Taboo* (London: Routledge, 2005).

12. Fletcher, 'The Metropolis', pp. 70, 83–4.

13. J. Ridgeway, 'The New Metropolitan Cattle market', p. 473.

14. For background on the culture of improvement that swept London's landscape during the first half of the nineteenth century, see A. Briggs, *The Age of Improvement* (London: Longmans, Green, 1999).

15. J. Gwynn, *London and Westminster Improved, Illustrated by Plans to Which is Prefixed, A Discourse on Publick Magnificence; with Observations on the State of Arts and Artists* (London, 1766), pp. 18, 19.

16. *The Facts Concerning the Nuisance*, p. 14

17. 'From a Correspondent', *British Farmer's Magazine* (London: Rogerson and Tuxford, 1848), p. 446.

18. *Builder*, 8:408, 30 November 1850, p. 571. The numer and scale of improvement projects during this period was overwhelming. The Holborn Viaduct carried the London, Chatham, and Dover Railway (LCDR) from Ludgate Hill to the Metropolitan Railway under Smithfield market, a line that opened in 1866. The LCDR, a north-south railway, is not in use today. The Viaduct project was managed by the Holborn Valley Improvement Committee of the Corporation of London. The Holborn Viaduct was a massive project undertaken between 1867 and 1869. The City chose the design of William Haywood (Engineer to the Commission of Sewers in the City of London) in 1863. Opened by Queen Victoria in 1869, the project used corrugated iron plating and girders for the bridge structure. See G. Stamp, *The Changing Metropolis: Earliest Photographs of London, 1839–1879* (Harmondsworth, Middlesex, England: Viking, 1984). Also see J. H. Winter, *London's Teeming Streets: 1830–1914* (London: Routledge, 1993). A re-built Blackfriars Bridge was opened on the same day as the Viaduct (note later placement of statues representing Commerce, Agriculture, Science, and Fine Art). Farringdon fish market later occupied space around the ridge of the Viaduct. The new streets, such as the northward extension of Farringdon Street, were integral to slum clearances that occurred between 1845 and 1856 and were City improvement projects. (Fleet Market became Farrington Market in the process of removing old buildings.)

19. P. Temple, *South and East Clerkenwell* (New Haven, CT: Published for English Heritage by Yale University Press, 2008), p. 360.
20. Some of these improvements came to a halt as the City anticipated the arrival of the railways. Parliament passed Metropolitan Railway Act in 1854 and the railway company began to purchase the land surrounding the proposed line directly adjacent to Smithfield. The Holborn Viaduct, built between 1867 and 1869 to bridge the Holborn Valley near Smithfield, cleared slums and was directed by the City to improve the area. The project provided a thoroughfare for railways and used iron construction just as did the new Blackfriar's Bridge.
21. See Smith, 'The Wholesale and Retail Markets of London, 1660–1840', pp. 44–7. Also, *Builder,* 2 November 1867.
22. J. Schmiechen and K. Carls, *The British Market Hall: A Social and Architectural History* (New Haven, CT: Yale University Press, 1999), pp. 149, 151–2. Schmiechen and Carls focus their research on markets outside London, but their research points to developments in market design and response to reforms in other areas and increasing pressure of demand for market capacity.
23. The ground surface material in the market became a target of criticism and an opportunity for improvement. The Westminster Pavement Act in 1762 improved the street pavement with 'squares of Scotch granite laid in gravel' and the posts lining the footpaths were removed. At the same time, the streets acquired curbs and gutters, improving drainage throughout London and Westminster. Some witnesses in the select committee hearings had mentioned that the pavement stones were round and that the space was not flat. Some recommended smooth stones similar to the 12–inch-square pavement in Lincoln's Inn Fields. Walter Besant described the pavement for 'foot passengers protected with rows of posts at intervals of four or five feet', and 'small uneven paving stones'. The pavement for horses and carriages was made of round stones, uneven and often unstable. W. Besant, *London* (New York: Harper & Brothers, 1892), pp. 444–6.
24. *Select Committee,* 1828, p. 110.
25. W. Pittman, *On London Improvements, On the Necessity for Making More Markets,* 1826, Guildhall, MS p. 496.
26. *Select Committee* 1828, p. 44.
27. Gareth Shaw and M. T. Wild's study of Victorian retail markets provides rich detail about the reorganization of London markets during the nineteenth century. They argue that the increasing pressure on urban markets created a symbiotic relationship between urbanization and retail markets, each one stimulating growth of the other. The pressure on markets yielded the sharp increase in market acts between 1831 and 1870. See 'Retail Patterns in the Victorian City', *Transactions of the Institute of British Geographers,* new series, 4:2, *The Victorian City* (1979), pp. 278–91.
28. Schmiechen and Carls, 'The Grand Age of the Market Hall', *The British Market Hall.*
29. For more on the changes in the consumer culture, see E. D. Rappaport, *Shopping for Pleasure: Women in the Making of London's West End* (Princeton, NJ: Princeton University Press, 2000). Iron technology and design developed through bridge construction in the eighteenth century as iron became a useful material for a broad range of buildings during the nineteenth century. Samuel Johnson was captivated by iron as a construction material but others, more critical of iron's architectural use, saw iron designs that contradicted the contemporary preference for truthfulness in construction. Its use for engineers was often at cross-purposes with its use for architects, who used iron to decorate rather than support buildings. Art critics saw buildings such as the Crystal Palace,

constructed for the 1851 Exhibition, as an example of how far a design could belie its structural use. By mid-century, iron became part of the architectural vernacular, particularly for public buildings that wanted to enclose large spaces. Both the new cattle market and the new meat market in Smithfield used iron throughout their designs. See S. Muthesius, 'The Iron Problem', *Architectural History*, 13 (1970), pp. 58–131.

30. *Select Committee, 1828*, p. 6.
31. W. Pittman, *On London Improvements.*
32. *Select Committee, 1828*, p. 78.
33. Ibid., 1828, pp. 111, 158.
34. Ibid., 1828, pp. 110–1.
35. At least four types of cattle came during this time: Lincoln, Scots, Devon, and Sussex. The 'breeds different from north to south'; for example, the quality and type of animal varied according to regional and seasonal climatic conditions. Since different types of cattle came to the market from different locations, buyers such as butchers would want to have access to all types at one time, requiring a single market that would accommodate all the cattle available at any given time. *Select Committee, 1828*, p. 98.
36. Moving the market farther away also impeded such activities as the sale of offal, which required special treatment after slaughter and was dependent upon quick removal and cleaning. *Select Committee, 1828*, pp. 45, 46, 73–5, 116.
37. *Select Committee 1828*, p 63.
38. Ibid., 1828, pp. 19, 95, 111.
39. Ibid., 1828, pp. 110, 111, 115.
40. The select committee in 1849 found that salesmen had the habit of renting spaces in the market that were larger than required, just to protect their animals from the pressing hordes of others in order to gain 'proper room'. *Select Committee, 1828*, p. 137.
41. 'A Plan of the Ground Situated in Aldersgate and Long Lane in the City of London, Belonging to the Corporation of Rochester' (Stroud: Medway Archives).
42. *Select Committee, 1828*, p. 47.
43. Ibid., 1828, p. 121.
44. Ibid., 1847, pp. 383, 394–5.
45. *Hansard*, 18 April 1809, p. 73. House of Commons.
46. B. R Mitchell, *British Historical Statistics* (Cambridge: Cambridge University Press, 1988), p. 708.
47. *Select Committee, 1828*, p. 143.
48. 'Cattle and Corporation', *Punch*, 16 (January–June 1849), p. 22.
49. *Select Committee, 1828*, p. 94.
50. *A Brief Statement of Facts*, p. 3.
51. After 1832, Parliament passed an act to limit hackney control of short-stage traffic, allowing omnibuses to pick up passengers within the city. Two-wheeled carriages (cabriolets) appeared in the streets around 1823, adding to the existing hackney traffic. Shillibeer's omnibus appeared in the metropolis in 1823 and by 1834 hundreds of cabs traveled along High Holborn and the New Road, crossing the paths of drovers and their livestock. See T. C. Barker and M. Robbins. *A History of London Transport: The Nineteenth Century* (London: Routledge, 2007), pp. 14, 25, 26.
52. Traffic problems were considered common in the Smithfield area long before the nineteenth century. On 8 April 1669, Samuel Pepys saw a coach run over young girl in Smithfield, an occurrence more frequently noted as the congestion in the City alarmed Londoners. *Samuel Pepys Diary 1669*, Extracts, 1 January 1669. http://www.pepys.info/1669/1669.html, [accessed 19 January 2009]. As London rebuilt after the Great Fire, new markets appeared,

networking the national market to its nexus in London, benefitting from the turnpike system and 'fly wagons', vans that carried commercial goods only at a speed of about 5–6 miles per hour. See W. T. Jackman, *The Development of Transportation in Modern England. Vol. 2* (Cambridge: Cambridge University Press, 1916), pp. 33, 347.

53. *Select Committee*, 1828, p. 73.
54. Ibid., p. 146, G. M. 'The Smithfield Nuisance', To the Editor of the Times, *The Times*, 26 November 1846, p. 5.
55. *A Brief Statement of the Facts*, pp. 3–4.
56. *Select Committee*, 1828, pp. 68–9.
57. Ibid., 1828, p. 130.
58. *Select Committee*, 1847, 381; *Select Committee*, 1828, p. 119.
59. *Select Committee*, 1828, 83. On some occasions, coach drivers even raced each other. In 1820, two drivers, Butler and Perdy, were found guilty of manslaughter after flogging their horses in a race between each other's mail carriage; William Hart, a passenger in one of the carriages died, and his servant was severely injured. A. Maudslay, *Highways and Horses* (London: Gardners Books, 2007), pp. 159–60.
60. Ibid., 1828, p. 82.
61. Ibid., 1828, pp. 43, 46, 110. A dray is a slow but sturdy cart with removable sides that is used for moving bulky or heavy objects.
62. Over a decade after Robert Trevithick built the first locomotive in 1804, George Stevenson built upon Trevithick's locomotive technology to develop the now 'standard gauge' (4 feet 8 ½ inches) for railways and used the more reliable wrought iron rails, not cast iron. His experience with building both the Stockton and Darlington and Liverpool and Manchester railways contributed needed expertise to the investors of the Metropolitan Railway, the railway that eventually pierced through Smithfield's landscape. Isambard Kingdom Brunel, engineer for the Thames Tunnel (opened in 1843), an underground tunnel crossing the Thames, contributed experience and technology (shield technology) for underground tunnel construction. These technologies consisted of ventilation systems and methods of restraining, draining, lighting, and supporting the tunnel during construction. The construction of the Metropolitan Railway was dependent upon the development of these preceding technologies.
63. The arrival of rail transport for cattle did not eliminate transport by sea. On the contrary, the two modes of transport co-existed, carrying relatively equal percentages of the overall traffic in cattle. See Perren, *The Meat Trade in Britain*.
64. Mutton was a fragile meat compared to beef and pork and so benefitted more from rail transport.
65. The statement 'Time is money' is attributed to Benjamin Franklin, in *Advice to a Young Tradesman* (Philadelphia, PA: Printed by Daniel Humphreys, at the new printing-office, in Spruce Street, near the drawbridge, 1785). Dodd had good reason to worry about weights and distances since British livestock were larger and fatter than their pre-nineteenth century predecessors. The longer an animal took to reach a market weight, the more costs went in to producing the animal and the less profit resulted from its sale. Dodd, *The Food of London*, pp. 101–23.
66. D. Lardner, *Railway Economy a Treatise on the New Art of Transport, Its Management, Prospects and Relations* (New York: Harper, 1855), pp. 8–10.
67. *Second Report from the Select Committee on the State of Smithfield market*, Ordered by the House of Commons, 19 July 1828, pp. 52, 57, 97.

68. Lardner, *Railway Economy*, p. 10.
69. Dodd, *The Food of London*, p. 219. Imports from Australia and North America began after Smithfield's relocation.
70. Dodd's reference to 'annular belts' around London, separating agricultural production activities in varying distances from the market, may have been inspired by the work of Johann Heinrich von Thünen. A German economist, von Thünen developed the theory of the 'Isolated State' in 1826, a theory that included four zones around an urban center. Each zone defined land use by the cost of transport, the land rent, and the perishable nature of an agricultural product. J. H. von Thünen and P. G. Hall, *Isolated State: An English Edition of Der isolierte Staat* (Oxford: Pergamon Press, 1966).
71. W. Harding, 'Facts Bearing on the Progress of the Railway System', *Journal of the Statistical Society of London*, 11:4 (November 1848), pp. 322–42, on p. 341. Most of the animals came on the Eastern Counties Railway, followed by the London and North Western and the Great Northern and Great Western, Brunel's wide-gauge creation.
72. Foreshaw and Bergstrom, *Smithfield Past and Present*, p. 60; Dodd, *The Food of London*, p. 242; Perren, *The Meat Trade in Britain*, pp. 41–5.
73. Great Britain, *Report of the Royal commission appointed to inquire into and report upon the means of locomotion and transport in London* (London: Government, 1905), p. 96.
74. In 1845, 19 bills went to Parliament to authorize the construction of new rail lines. Still, Parliament was wary of any line that wanted to cross over roads, worrying that the bridge would confuse or obstruct pedestrian traffic. *Minutes and Proceedings of the Institute of Civil Engineers*, ed. J. Forrest, vol. 81 (London: ICE, 1885). As interest rates lowered and the wealth of a rising middle class increased, investors saw railway companies as a way to profit from a relatively unregulated market economy. New train terminals appeared. Work began on King's Cross Station in 1859 with the assistance of John Jay, a builder who was later involved in the construction of the Metropolitan Railway, a line that ran eventually ran directly underneath Smithfield. Stamp, *The Changing Metropolis*, p. 214.
75. At the same time Brunel was working on the Great Western Railway Company (1835), building a line from Paddington to Kings Cross with his wide gauge railway. The Great Northern Railway, established in 1846 and originating from the north of London through Islington, ended at King's Cross Station. This major railway terminus, designed by architect Lewis Cubitt, opened in 1852. But the 'gauge war' that ensued between Brunel's wide gauge and Stevenson's standard gauge delayed cooperation between these two lines to extend the railway from Farringdon to Moorgate. W. Pinks, *The History of Clerkenwell*, 2nd edn (London: Charles Herbert, 1881), p. 357.
76. Barker and Robbins, *A History of London Transport*, p. 54.
77. Pinks, *The History of Clerkenwell*, p. 358.
78. 'Proposed Central Terminus in the City', *Railway Times*, November 1851, p. 1154.
79. C. Pearson, *A Twenty Minutes' Letter to the Citizens of London, in Favor of the Metropolitan Railway and City Station*, 1859; C. Wolmar, *The Subterranean Railway: How the London Underground Was Built and How It Changed the City Forever* (London: Atlantic Books, 2004).
80. See L. Picard, *Victorian London: The Life of a City, 1840–1870* (New York: St. Martin's Press, 2006), Chapter 4: 'The Railways', for a discussion of railway speed.
81. 'Art. I. Report of the Commissioners Appointed to Make Inquiries Related to Smithfield Market, and the Markets in the City of London for the Sale of Meat', *Quarterly Review*, 95:190 (1854, September), p. 283.
82. Pittman, *On London Improvements*.

83. Wolfgang Schivelbusch discusses the development and meanings of lighting in nineteenth-century England in *Disenchanted Night*. Lynda Nead's analysis of the uses of gaslight at Cremorne Gardens offers some insights into the impact of lighting on Smithfield. Chris Otter about the visual and illuminated experience in London, including understandings of eyes and the technologies that produced an array of lighting practices in Victorian Britain. C. Otter, *The Victorian Eye: a Political History of Light and Vision in Britain, 1800–1910* (Chicago, IL: University of Chicago Press, 2008); W. Schivelbusch, *Disenchanted Night: The Industrialization of Light in the Nineteenth Century* (Berkeley, CA: University of California Press, 1988); L. Nead, *Victorian Babylon: People, Streets and Images in Nineteenth-Century London* (New Haven, CT: Yale University Press, 2000). Gas for lighting was produced by distilling coal and so was called 'coal gas'. The first public use of coal gas was the lighting of Pall Mall in 1807; Westminster Bridge was lit with gas in 1813.

84. J. S. Gamgee, 'The Cattle Plague and Diseased Meat, A Second Letter to Sir George Grey', London, 1857. J. Johnson, *Medico-Chirurgical Review (London, England)* (London: Burgess & Hill, 1824), p. 90.

85. D. Hughson, *Walks through London Including the Suburbs* (London, 1817).

86. Nead, *Victorian Babylon*, pp. 85–8.

87. J.-B. Fressoz, 'The Gas Lighting Controversy: Technological Risk, Expertise, and Regulation in Nineteenth-Century Paris and London', *Journal of Urban History,* 33 (2007), p. 735.

88. *Select Committee*, 1828, p. 76.

5 'A Grateful Odor Runneth Round': Public Health and Smithfield

1. J. Swift, 'A Description of a City Shower', *Tatler,* 238 (17 October 1710).

2. See E. L. Sabine, 'Butchering in Medieval London', *Speculum,* 8:3 (July 1933), pp. 335–53 for a discussion of ways that medieval Londoners perceived the connection between animal slaughter and disease. King Richard II responded to the residents of Smithfield and Holborn who were complaining about the butchers who were 'casting entrails into the ditches'. He forbad butchers from dumping their garbage into ditches and rivers and from slaughtering within the City of London. *Petition in Parliament 3 Richard, II, 12th Rich. 11 c 13*m and *Rot. Parliament 16 Rich 11, 'Early State of the Law for the Protection of Public Health',* Great Britain, and E. Chadwick, *Report to Her Majesty's Principal Secretary of State for the Home Department, on an Inquiry into the Sanitary Condition of the Laboring Population of Great Britain; With Appendices* (London: Clowes, 1842). The Thames and Fleet rivers became conveyances of the effluvium from the butchers' slaughterhouses. One observer in 1736 said, 'A fatter boar was hardly ever seen than one taken up this day coming out of Fleet Ditch into the Thames. It proved to be a butcher's, near Smithfield Bars, who had missed him five months, all which time he had been in the common sewer, and was improved in price from ten shillings to two guineas'. Thornbury and Walford, 'The Fleet River', *London Recollected.* Also the Fleet Market, a dead meat market, opened near the river in 1737. The City was responsible for maintaining the river and for providing drains.

3. See F. Driver, 'Moral Geographies: Social Science and the Urban Environment in Mid-Nineteenth Century England', *Transactions of the Institute of British Geographers,* new series, 13:1 (1988), pp. 275–87, for a discussion of the ways social behaviour interacts

with the environment. He argues that Victorians sanitized their landscape, projecting their ideas about moral landscapes and spatial orientation.

4. H. Mayhew's *London Labor and the London Poor*, first published in 1851, described the street vendors and should be included in a consideration of the entire marketplace of London. These itinerant laborers were micro-entrepreneurs that created a market for those goods and services left outside the formal market spaces of London.

5. *A Country Meat Salesman, An Important Improvement in the Supply of London Wholesale Meat Markets, by the Total Abolition of Smithfield Live Stock Trade and London Slaughter-houses* (London, 1832), p. 7.

6. S. Bushnan, *The Moral and Sanitary Aspects of the New Central Cattle Market as Proposed by the Corporation of the City of London, with Plans* (London: W. Orr, 1851), pp. 12–14.

7. K. Clafin and D. Brantz have both explored urban slaughterhouses during the nineteenth century and offer insights concerning the relationship between sanitation reform and animal slaughter. C. Otter, R. Perren, and I. MacLachlan have produced fresh scholarship about British slaughterhouse reform in P. Y. Lee (ed.) *Meat, Modernity, and the Rise of the Slaughterhouse* (Durham, NH: University Press of New England, 2008). Some scholars view the design and placement of slaughter in terms of political and social contexts. Others see the subject as a lens for viewing animals and their place in the urban environment.

8. *Robson's London Directory, Street Key, Classification of Trades, and Royal Court Guide and Peerage: Particularizing the Residences of 70,000 Establishments in London and Its Environs, and Fifteen Thousand of the Nobility and Gentry, also an Extensive Conveyance List, Alphabetical List of Public Carriers, Together with the Street Guide* (London: Robson, 1842). Violin strings were made from 'small muscular intestines [of small sheep] fed upon dry, mountainous pasture'. P. Davidson, *The Violin: Its Construction Theoretically and Practically Treated: Including an Epitome of the Lives of the Most Eminent Artists, a Dictionary of Violin Makers and Lists of Violin Sales* (London: F. Pitman, 1881).

9. 'A Looking Glass', p. 307.

10. *Robson's London Directory*.

11. See W. J. Gordon, *The Horse-World of London* (London: The religious tract society, for a discussion, from an animal welfare perspective, of horse slaughter in Victorian London, 1893).

12. R. Grantham, *A Treatise on Public Slaughter-Houses, Considered in Connection with the Sanitary Question. Describing the Practice of Slaughtering in France and England, with an Historical and Statistical Account of the Abattoirs of Paris, and Accompanied by Plans, with the View to the Introduction of Similar Establishments into England* (London: J. Weale, Architectural Library, 1848), pp. 4–13.

13. Cholera deaths: 1831–2: 6,536, 1848–9: 14,137, 1853–4: 10,738, 1866: 5,596. C. Creighton, *A History of Epidemics in Britain* (Cambridge: Cambridge University Press, 1894), p. 858; *Cholera Epidemics in 19th Century Britain*, Institute of Biomedical Science, http://www.ibms.org/index.cfm?method=science.history_zone&subpage=history_cholera [accessed 11 September 2008].

14. 'The Fleet River and Fleet Ditch', *Old and New London: Volume 2* (1878), pp. 416–26. http://www.british-history.ac.uk/report.aspx?compid=45112 [accessed 30 June 2009].

15. 'The General Nuisance of the Great Metropolis', *Lloyd's Weekly Newspaper*, Jan. 14, 1849, Issue 321.

16. E. Chadwick, D. Gladstone and S. E. Finer, *Edwin Chadwick: Nineteenth-Century Social Reform* (London: Routledge, 1997), pp. 1–2, 4.

17. S. E. Finer, *The Life and Times of Sir Edwin Chadwick* (London: Methuen, 1952), p. 4.

18. An even earlier report on the sanitation of the metropolis was prepared in 1833 by Neil Arnott, inventor of the coal heaters used at the Metropolitan Cattle Market in Islington in 1855. See Chadwick, E., and M.W. Flinn, *Report on the Sanitary Condition of the Labouring Population of Great Britain* (Edinburgh: Edinburgh University Press, 1965). Robert Owen, professor of natural science, was also on the Smithfield Select Committee in 1850 and on this Commission of Inquiry in 1847, thought to be progressive and in favor of sanitation reform.

19. R. A. Lewis, *Edwin Chadwick and the public health movement, 1832–1854* (London: Longmans, Green, 1952), pp. 134–5.

20. See P. Dobraszczyk, 'Mapping Sewer Spaces in Mid-Victorian London', in B. Campkin and R. Cox's *Dirt, New Geographies of Cleanliness and Contamination* (London: I. B. Tauris, 2007) for a discussion of the maps that Chadwick produced of London's sewage system.

21. 'Sanitary Reform', *Mechanic's Magazine, Museum, Register, Journal, and Gazette*, 1279, 12 February 1848, p. 149. In reference to agriculture, he said that 'All smell of decomposing matter may be said to indicate the loss of money'. See F. Coxworthy, *Pollution of the Atmosphere by the Ventilation of the Sewers, How It May Be Remedied* (London: George Pierce, 1848).

22. *The Proposed Central Live and Dead Meat Market for the Metropolis. The Opinions of and Extracts from the Public Journals* (London: Effingham, Wilson, 1851), p. 5.

23. E. Coltman, *Cursory Remarks on the Evil Tendency of Unrestrained Cruelty: Particularly on That Practised in Smithfield Market* (London: printed for Harvey and Darton, 1823).

24. *Select Committee*, 1828, pp. 22, 23.

25. Miasma was believed to be poisonous gases produced from rotting animal or vegetal mater. The miasma theory, which held that these gases or 'bad air' entered the body and caused disease, was discredited when Louis Pasteur and Robert Koch developed germ theory during the 1860s and 1870s. See 'Of the Contagious or Non-Contagious Nature of the Plague', *The Lancet*, ed. Thomas Wakley, MDCCCXXXIX-XL, 1840, p. 418. One writer, revealing the general consternation felt by physicians at that time about the cause of cholera, stated that either the theory that single individuals are predisposed to contagion 'must be adopted, or the doctrine of the transference of the disease through the air, or of its evolution in a subtle form by miasma from the earth, must be abandoned'. *London Medical Gazette*, 7 January 1848, new series, 6 (London: Longman, Brown, Green & Longmans, 1848), pp. 21, 22.

26. Reach, 'John Bull and His Bullocks', p. 121; Cunningham, *Handbook for London, Past and Present*, p. xxviii.

27. While Chadwick argued for a centralized metropolitan response to ameliorate London's sanitation problems during the 1840s, William Farr, a medical statistician, gathered information about deaths and disease in London, providing information that would support the development of another theory for the transmission of cholera. He observed that deaths caused by cholera were more frequent in relation to their relationship to the height of the Thames River. His *Weekly Returns* gave John Snow, a physician and later proponent of chloroform as anesthesia, the evidence he needed to credibly argue that miasma was not the reason cholera passed from one Londoner to another. Snow wrote in 1854 about his observations of a water pump in Broad Street in the *Medical Times and Gazette* where he gathered to empirical evidence to support his new theory that cholera passed through water into human intestines. These sanitary reformers, Chadwick, Farr, and Snow, contributed to a debate about the causes of

cholera, a debate that influenced the witnesses called to testify at the Select Committee sessions from 1840 through 1850. Their ideas pushed sanitation reform in multiple directions as they looked at Smithfield as a potential culprit. See S. Johnson, *The Ghost Map: The Story of London's Most Terrifying Epidemic—And How It Changed Science, Cities, and the Modern World* (New York: Riverhead Books, 2006), pp. 100–1. Also see Farr's writings in W. Farr and N. A. Humphreys, *Memorial Volume of Selections from the Reports and Writings of William Farr* (London: The Sanitary Institute of Great Britain, 1885).

28. 'Individual Interests—How Affected by Removal of Market', p. 475.

29. *Hansard, House of Lords,* Deb. 31 July 1906, vol. 162, cc603–8. Public Slaughterhouses Bill. See the acts passed as early as the Middle Ages that controlled the activities of butchers who polluted streets and rivers with byproducts of their slaughterhouses.

30. G. Eyre and A. Spottiswoode, *A Collection of the Public General Statutes* (London: Steven Richards, 1844), p. 573. *Metropolitan Buildings Act, 7th and 8th, Vict. Cap. 84, with Notes* (London: Weal, 1844), pp. 70–1; 'Metropolitan Slaughterhouses', *The Lancet,* Sept. 20, 1873, pp. 425–6.

31. *London Gazette,* Tuesday, Oct. 9, 1832, p. 5. *An Appeal to the British Public on the Abuses and Advantages of a Central Cattle Market Fairly Considered* (London: Effingham Wilson, c1850), p. 7. Stevenson Bushnan M. D. *The Moral and Sanitary Aspects of the New Central Cattle Market, as proposed by the Corporation of the City of London with Plans* (London: William S. Orr & Co, 1851), p. 10.

32. *An Appeal to the British Public,* pp. 8, 9.

33. *Select Committee,* 1828, pp. 63, 108.

34. *Select Committee* 1847, pp. 30, 38.

35. *Select Committee* 1828, pp. 107–8, 156–7.

36. *10 & 11 Vic. C 34.* 'Provided for the registration, licensing and management of private slaughterhouses'.

37. The Public Health Act of 1848 restricted private slaughterhouses outside London. Even by 1903, there was only one public abattoir in London, Deptford, built to handle foreign cattle. (See *Hansard,* Debate in the House of Lords on the Public Slaughter Houses Bill. HL Deb 31, July 1906, vol. 162 cc. pp. 603–8.

38. In the nineteenth century, meat was described as 'unwholesome', a term used to describe food that was injurious to health. *1849 Report* (85) 1679, or Great Britain, and J. Daw, *The City of London Sewers Act[S], 1848 … 1851* (London: printed by Lownds, 1858).

39. *Select Committee,* 1847, p. 67.

40. *Select Committee ,* 1847, pp. 84–290. *Minutes of the London Gas Light Company,* LMA. Papers read at the Royal Institute of British Architects, Session 1862–3 (London: RIBA, 1863), p. 136. Also, N. Arnott, *On the Smokeless Fire-place, Chimney-valves, and Other Means, Old and New, of Obtaining Healthful Warmth and Ventilation: And Other Means, Old and New, of Obtaining Healthful Warmth and Ventilation.*

41. J. Hakewill, *Plan, Sections, and Elevations, of the Abattoirs of Paris, with Considerations for Their Adoption in London: Most Respectfully Recommended to the Attention of His Majesty's Government, the Right Honourable the Lord Mayor and Aldermen of the City, and the Magistrates of London and its Environs* (London: Printed by W. Foat, for Carpenter and Son, 1828), pp. 6–11.

42. S. Munday, *An Important Improvement,* p. 7.

43. R. Grantham, PC 1/2453, 'Proposition for Establishing Public Slaughter-Houses in the Principal Towns of England', 1849.

44. R. Grantham, *A Treatise on Public Slaughter-Houses, Considered in Connection with the Sanitary Question. Describing the Practice of Slaughtering in France and England, with an Historical and Statistical Account of the Abattoirs of Paris, and Accompanied by Plans, with the View to the Introduction of Similar Establishments into England* (London: J. Weale, Architectural Library, 1848), p. vi.

45. *Select Committee*, 1847, pp. 10–20.

46. Preceeding Bazalgette and his grand project for London drainage, John Snow and William Farr plunged into the currents of conflicting theories about the cause of cholera. Unconvinced that miasma was the cause of cholera, Snow joined the few who began to think that water was the carrier for the disease. Snow, a methodical and hardworking Yorkshire man, focused on a water pump on Broad Street and eventually determined that those who drank from its polluted well became ill. After he removed the pump handle, cases of cholera dramatically declined, leading to his theory that the disease was water borne. His colleague, William Farr, gathered the statistical evidence to support Snow's work, leading to eventual public acceptance of the theory and providing the foundation for germ theory. See S. Halliday, *The Great Stink of London* (Thrupp, Stroud, Gloucestershire: Sutton Publishing, 1999).

47. *Hansard*, HC Deb 05 June 1828, vol. 19 cc. pp. 1049–53.

48. *An Appeal to the British Public...* p. 11.

49. Chris Otter argues in *The Vital City* that public slaughterhouses would reverse centuries of private ownership of slaughterhouses and would 'open [slaughter] to municipal vision while concealing it from the eyes of polite society'. 'The Vital City: Public Analysis, Dairies and Slaughterhouses in Nineteenth-Century Britain'. *Cultural Geographies* 13, No. 4 (2006), pp. 517–537.

50. *Select Committee*, 1828, p. 122.

51. 'Smithfield and Its Environs, *Northern Star and National Trades Journal*, 23:586 (13 January 1847), p. 2.

52. *Second Report, Select Committee*, 1828, pp. 13, 14.

53. *Select Committee*, 1828, pp. 123, 128.

54. *Select Committee*, 1828. p. 77.

55. The first British abattoir was in Edinburgh in 1851. (Otter, *The Victorian Eye*, 50.)

56. *Medical Times and Gazette*, new series, 5 (1 July–30 December 1854), p. 352.

57. 'The Smithfield Cattle Market', *Farmer's Magazine*, 19 (1849), p. 142.

58. *British Farmer's Magazine*, new series, 15 (London: Henry Wright, 1849), pp. 142–4.

59. *Medical Times and Gazette*, p. 352.

60. *Select Committee*, 1828, p. 60.

61. One of the more dissident observations shared by Mr. Whitlaw of the effects of the increase of diseased meat in Smithfield concerned musical instruments. According to Whitlaw, an Italian craftsman came to London to make fiddle strings in Whitechapel but soon resigned, citing the 'diseased state' of the animal intestines that made it impossible for the strings to 'come to the concert pitch' without breaking. Further, the bladders used to make footballs were 'hardly fit to cover a jelly pot.'; *Select Committee*, 1828, pp. 88–91.

62. 'The Smithfield Cattle Market', *Farmer's Magazine*, 19 (1849), p. 143. Polonics and saveloys are dry, cooked sausages. *Select Committee* (1828), pp. 84–92.

63. 'Case of Glanders in the Human Subject, To the Editor of The Lancet Charles Clark', *Lancet*, 2 (15 May 1841), p. 361. The congestion in Smithfield appeared to only encour-

age the transference of disease as human to non-human contact intensified. *A*mong the culprits were urban cowsheds, locations that were too crowded and 'ill-ventilated'. Food adulteration had been evident since the Middle Ages.
64. 'Removal of Smithfield Market' (*Punch*), *Era*, 545 (4 March 1849).

6 Necessarily Cruel? Beef, Brutes and Women in Smithfield

1. C. Dickens, 'The Heart of Mid-London', *Household Words*, 4 May 1850, p. 123.
2. 'The General Nuisance of the Great Metropolis', *Lloyd's Weekly Newspaper*, 14 January, 1849, Issue 321.
3. See Gertrude Himmlefarb's *Victorian Minds* for a discussion of the contradictions in what she called a 'conservative revolution' of morals during the Victorian period. G. Himmelfarb, *Victorian Minds* (New York: Knopf, 1968).
4. *A Brief Statement of Facts Respecting the Existing Nuisance of Smithfield Market* (London: printed by Stirling, 1984), p. 4.
5. H. Ritvo, *The Animal Estate* (Cambridge, MA: Harvard University Press, 1987), p. 126. Ritvo writes about Victorian attitudes about animals in her chapter, 'A Measure of Compassion', which reveals the conflicts within the Victorian ethos concerning animal welfare. Her work focuses on the connection between morals and the treatment of animals. In her book, *Animal Rights,* Hilda Kean discusses the social meanings of institutions that developed during this period to ameliorate the treatment of animals in such places as Smithfield. H. Kean, *Animal Rights: Political and Social Change in Britain Since 1800* (London: Reaktion Books, 1998). Diana Donald approaches this topic from a visual perspective in *Picturing Animals in Britain*, with a discussion of the spectacle of animals in Smithfield. D. Donald, *Picturing Animals in Britain, 1750–1850* (New Haven, CT: Yale University Press [for] The Paul Mellon Centre for Studies in British Art, 2007). Ian MacLachlan provides a useful discussion of animals and slaughter in Britain during the nineteenth century in *Coup De Grâce: Humane Slaughter in Nineteenth Century Britain*, Brepols Arts and Science Geography (Alberta: University of Lethbridge, 2007).
6. '*Petition of the Inquest Jury of the Parish of St. Sepulchre London with order of reference thereon*'. To improve public safety, the City decided to require that an animal, known to be 'wild', should be slaughtered by the butcher in the market before going to the butcher's slaughterhouse. The determination of 'wildness' was to be made by a drover or salesman who knew 'the Beasts that are wild as easily as [they] distinguish the Faces of each other'; CLA/06/AD/02/008, 3 March 1774.
7. Ibid.
8. 'A Bill to Prevent the Mischiefs that arise from driving Cattle, within the Cities of London and Westminster, and the Bills of Mortality'. Thirteenth Parliament of Great Britain; Seventh Session (13 January 1774–22; June 1774, Cambridge University.)
9. *Extracts of the Proceedings of the Court of Aldermen, and a Report of the Committee for Letting the City's Lands, Relative to Smithfield Market*, January 1777.
10. *Hansard*,   http://hansard.millbanksystems.com/lords/1809/may/15/cruelty-to-animals-bill.
11. Ibid.
12. Burn, R., and G. Chetwynd, 'The Justice of the Peace, and Parish Officer' (London: Printed by A. Strahan for T. Cadell and W. Davies).

13. D. Ricardo, *The Works and Correspondence of David Ricardo*, ed. P. Sraffa with the Collaboration of M. H. Dobb (Indianapolis, IN: Liberty Fund, 2005), vol. 5 Speeches and Evidence 1815–23. Chapter: Ill-Treatment of Horses Bill, 1 June, 1821, Public General Act, 3 George IV, c. 71. Parliamentary Archives. By 1835, the Act included other domestic animals and activities such as bear-baiting. Martin's Act required testimony of an observer within ten days after the offense of 'wanton' and 'cruel' treatment of the animals for the exaction of a five-pound penalty from the perpetrator. http://oll.libertyfund.org/title/206/38795 [accessed on 12 December 2009]. *Select Committee*, 1828, pp. 45, 181.

14. Some witnesses stated that Martin's Act had appreciably improved the treatment of animals in Smithfield, eliminating much of the unnecessary cruelty. Michael Scales, an owner of a slaughterhouse, argued that since Martin's Act, 'the drovers are under much more restraint; they pay attention when you speak to them and instantly desist'. *Select Committee*, 1828, pp. 44–6, 147.

15. 'Smithfield', *Chamber's Edinburgh Journal*, 397 (August 1851), p. 90.

16. *Select Committee* 1828, pp. 11, 15. December and January were the two months when the market was most congested. During these months, most cattle and sheep were reaching market weights and the Christmas holidays signaled a rise in meat consumption for the holidays.

17. Ibid., 1828, p. 40.

18. Ibid., 1828, pp. 84, 151.

19. J. Plumptre and T. Lantaffe, 'The Experienced Butcher' (London, 1816).

20. *Select Committee* 1828, p. 102.

21. Some witnesses stated that Martin's Act had appreciably improved the treatment of animals in Smithfield, eliminating much of the unnecessary cruelty. Michael Scales, an owner of a slaughterhouse, argued that since Martin's Act, 'the drovers are under much more restraint; they pay attention when you speak to them and instantly desist'. *Select Committee*, 1828, p. 147.

22. *Select Committee*, 1828, p. 59.

23. Great Britain. 1828. Second report from the select committee on the state of Smithfield market. 15.

24. *Select Committee*, 1828, 16.

25. Ibid., 1828, pp. 66–7.

26. Ibid., 1828, p. 23.

27. The meat that failed to pass Jewish inspections was sold to Christians. *Select Committee*, 1828, p. 67.

28. *Select Committee*, 1828, p. 64.

29. *A Brief Statement of Facts Respecting the Existing Nuisance of Smithfield Market*. (London: printed by Stirling, 1834), p. 9.

30. *Select Committee*, 1828, p. 131.

31. Ibid., 1828, p. 93.

32. Ibid., 1828, p. 112.

33. Ibid., 1828, p. 126. Pearce, *The History of the Butchers' Company*, p. 136. Some critics felt that the darkness of the early morning hours, when the cattle came into Smithfield, obscured the cruelty of inflicted upon the animals by the drovers.

34. *Select Committee*, 1828, pp. 254–5.

35. A Quaker meeting house was located on St. John Street near the entrance to the market.

36. *Select Committee*, 1828, p. 13.

37. Ibid., p. 42. The actual number of cattle accommodated in Smithfield and in the off-droves was closer to twice that by the 1840s.

38. Ibid., 1828, p. 32.

39. *The Working Man's Friend, and Family Instructor* (London: John Cassell, 1850), pp. 289–90.

40. *Select Committee*, 1828, p. 33. The availability of feed and water remained a concern of the animal welfare reformers and led to the capacious troughs and lairs at the Metropolitan Cattle Market in Islington. Some medical doctors argued that cruel treatment of animals in the market 'poisoned' the meat and therefore caused diseases in humans. A surgeon, Charles Harris, was convinced that the beating and prodding of animals made their meat 'febrile', a condition, he argued, that was the cause of diseases in humans, such as yellow fever. Charles Whitlaw, a botanist, argued that cruel treatment of animals before slaughter was a cause of diseases in humans, not the 'filth and smell' associated with Smithfield. *Select Committee*, 1828, pp. 84–92.

41. See *The Experienced Butcher* and Rixon's *History of the Meat Trade*, p. 230.

42. *Select Committee*, 1828, pp. 97–8, 100. One sensational story appeared in *The Times* described short-horned Devonshire ox that escaped from a drover and 'fixed his eye upon a poor man, who, in order to avoid the attack of so formidable an antagonist, wheeled round one of the posts which stood near the fountain in the centre on the square'. According to the florid account, the ox 'with both horns threw him at least twelve feet in the air', causing the body of the man to be 'taken up motionless, blood flowing profusely'. *The Times* reported that the drover was not at fault since the animal's reckless behaviour was the result of 'the want of water'. *A Brief Statement of Facts Respecting the Existing Nuisance of Smithfield Market*, p. 5.

43. *Select Committee*, 1828, pp. 19, 38, 44.

44. 'To Graziers and Agriculturalists', Broadside 30.9 (Northcroft & Co, Printers, 1835).

45. Brian Harrison's study of the association of reforming institutions and religion makes a cogent case for evangelical nature of three organizations, the Lord's Day Observance Society (LDOS), the RSPCA and the temperance movement. All three had their origins during the Smithfield debate and reflected growing association between secular self-improvement and religion. These improvement institutions did have class identities as the RSCPA tended to attract more interest from the aristocratic classes and the LDOS drew upon middle class merchants. See B. Harrison, 'Religion and Recreation in Nineteenth-Century England', *Past & Present*, no. 38 (December 1967), pp. 98–125, for a discussion of these three groups and their association with religion and secular entertainment.

46. *Select Committee*, 1849, Appendix, p. 404.

47. *Select Committee*, 1828, p. 49.

48. Ibid., 1828, pp. 47, 49.

49. Ibid., 1828, p. 7; Schlesinger and von Wenckstern, *Saunterings In and About London*, p. 64.

50. The horse market took particular heat for attracting especially low-grade individuals, 'the most lawless set'. One City officer described the horse market as a place that 'brings together all the thieves and rogues within ten miles of London'. The idea of moving the horse market to another site was met with the resistance of tradition and concern that the public houses would lose customers. In addition to horses in the market on Fridays, goats, dogs, and donkeys sold in what was called 'an inferior traffic' compared to the 'rogues' that frequented the horse market. 'Some Fact about Smithfield', *Working Man's Friend*, 3:71 (5 February 1853), p. 290.

51. *Select Committee*, 1828, pp. 4, 24.
52. Ibid., p. 79.
53. 'Court of Common Council, The Removal of Smithfield Market', *Morning Chronicle*, Feb. 24, 1837, Issue 2096.
54. Public concern over the welfare of drovers motivated the founding of the Drovers' Benevolent Association in 1844. Later in the nineteenth century, the institution collected alms for drovers and eventually merged with the London Meat Trades Association. See *Working Man's Friend*, p. 290.
55. *Select Committee*, 1828, pp. 20, 35.
56. J. Baylee, *History of the Sabbath, or, Day of Holy Rest* (London: C.F. Hodgson, 1857), pp. 252–3. A. Rees, *The Cyclopedia; or, Universal Dictionary of Arts, Sciences, and Literature* (London: Longman, Hurst, Rees, Orme & Browne. [etc.], 1820).
57. See J. Brewer's, *The Pleasures of the Imagination: English Culture in the Eighteenth Century* (New York: Farrar Straus Giroux, 1997), for a discussion of the emerging consumer revolution and Rappaport, *Shopping for Pleasure*, for a study of West End shopping in the late nineteenth century.
58. L. Nead, *Victorian Babylon*, p. 108; A. Wynter, 'The London Commissariat', *Quarterly Review*, 95 (1854), p. 283.
59. Schlesinger and von Wenckstern, *Saunterings In and About London*, p. 64.
60. *Select Committee*, 1828, pp. 24, 39, 93, 145.
61. Ibid., pp. 71, 72.

7 The Final Act: 1840–55

1. When the Great Exhibition opened in 1851, the public was astounded at the technology exhibited in the Crystal Palace. Much of it testified to British innovation in the industrialization of the economy and displayed technologies evident in the new designs of British urban markets. J. A. Auerbach, *The Great Exhibition of 1851: A Nation on Display* (New Haven, CT: Yale University Press, 1999).
2. *A Brief Statement of the Facts*, p. 4.
3. J. Fletcher, 'Statistical Account', p. 356. Pearson argued for increased vigilance over the fair since trade there was minimal and bizarre amusements were commonplace. Subsequent to his argument, critics of the City's effort to remove the more disruptive entertainment from the fair accused the City of depriving the lower classes of entertainment. They thought the City acted 'improperly to interfere with the recreations of the humbler classes'. C. Pearson, 'Sketches, History of Bartholomew Fair', *Literary Gazette, Weekly Journal of Literature, Science, and the Fine Arts* (London, 1840), p. 534.
4. C. Pearson, *The Substance of an Address; Delivered by Charles Pearson, at a Public Meeting, on the 11th, 12th, and 18th of Dec. 1843 ... Containing a Brief History of the Corporation of London as the Asylum of English Freedom in Past Ages, with a Statement of its Public Services in More Modern Times* (London: P. Richardson, 1844), pp. 31–4.
5. R. Cavendish, 'London's Last Bartholomew's Fair, September 3rd, 1855', *History Today*, 55:9 (September 2005), p. 52; Hillman's Hyperlink, *Chamber's Book of Days*, 1869, http:thebookofdays.com [accessed 16 September 2009]. The Every-Day Book, Sept. 6, 1750 (Oxford: William Tegg, 1825), p. 1252. (It was not until 1855 that the fair finally folded its tents and departed from the City.)

6. King's Cross Station would open in 1852 and Paddington Station was modernized in 1854. C. Pearson, *The Substance of an Address*, pp. 31–4.

7. 'Corporation Affairs, Court of Common Council', *Citizen*, 8 (3 March 1849), p. 71.

8. *British Farmer's Magazine*, new series, 15 (London: Henry Wright, 1849), pp. 142–4.

9. 'Smithfield Market', *Citizen*, 8 (3 March 1849), pp. 65–74.

10. Challis, *Free Trade in Food*, p. 10.

11. Hansard, HC/Deb 18 March 1847 vol. 91 ccl, pp. 86–8.

12. *Select Committee*, 1847, p. iv.

13. Ibid., 1847, pp. iii, x.

14. *British Farmer's Magazine*, new series, 15 (London: Henry Wright, 1849), pp. 142–4.

15. W. Howitt, 'Visits to Remarkable Places, The New Market at Islington', *Howitt's Journal*, 1 (London, 1847), pp. 72–4.

16. 'One Pound Shares', *British Farmers Magazine*, 20 (London: Henry Wright, 1849), p. 238.

17. The new company was first registered in November 1847 and changed ownership from Perkins to the 'Company'. With about three new shareholders, the Company petitioned Parliament for another bill, the Islington Market Bill, that would enable them to expand the market, adding a meat market, more land, and abattoirs. Concerns remained about adequate drainage of the site. *Select Committee on the Islington Market Bill*, 6 June 1851, vol. 47, Evidence 1851, Committee Office. 'The Islington Cattle-market and Abattoir Company, Notice', *Era*, 566 (29 July 1849), p. 16. The company never sold enough shares to finance the venture. Further, disputes arose between the Company and the Perkins family concerning the terms of sale of the property and assets. The market opened for a brief time in 1849. 'Opening of the Cattle Market at Islington', *Lloyd's Weekly Newspaper*, 321 (14 January 14 1849). In 1853, Richard Westbrook, the Deputy Chairman of the venture was in the Court of Bankruptcy. The Company never operated again and the site was used only for hay sales and lairage for cattle on the way to Smithfield. 'Court of Bankruptcy', *Morning Chronicle*, issue 27090, 20 October 1853. Other officers also declared bankruptcy.

18. 'Corporation Affairs, Court of Common Council', *Citizen*, 8 (3 March 1849), pp. 71–4.

19. William Miles was removed at Charles Pearson's request and replaced with Sir De Lacy Evans, a reformist military officer. *Select Committee*, 1849.

20. *Select Committee*, 1849, pp. xiii–xix.

21. *Select Committee*, 1847, pp. xi–xii.

22. The Royal Commission 'To Consider the Bill for the Removal of Smithfield', begins 11 December1849. The seven commissioners included Lewis, Duke, Verney, Miles, Owen, Byng and Wood.

23. G. Cornewall Lewis, http://www.oxforddnb.com/view/article/16585, [accessed 16 January 2009].

24. E. Hertslet, *Recollections of the Old Foreign Office* (London: J. Murray, 1901), pp. 139–40.

25. *Oxford Dictionary of National Biography*, Online Edition for all references to Matthew Wood, and Harry Verney, http://www.osforddnb.com [accessed 16 January 2009]. Later, in 1888, Verney helped found the Royal Agricultural Society.

26. Ibid.

27. 'Brooks's Club, London', *Memorials of Brooks's* (London: Ballantyne, 1907), pp. 258–9.

28. *Hansard*, House of Commons, HC Deb 17 July 1849, vol. 107, cc. pp. 492–514.

29. 'Smithfield Market', *The Theatrical Journal*, 13 December, 1849, 10:522, p. 392; 'To the Editor of the Theatrical Journal, April 28ᵗʰ 1850, Smithfield Market', *The Theatrical Journal*, May 1850, 11:542, p. 142.

30. Discussions about centrality of Smithfield and its proximity to buyers lingered on after the removal of the cattle market to Islington. Separating the live from the 'dead' meat became a major sticking point for the decision to remove the market and for the use of the empty Smithfield site after 1855 when the cattle left for Islington.

31. Great Britain, *Report of the Commissioners Appointed to Make Inquiries Relating to Smithfield Market and the Markets in the City of London for the Sale of Meat* (London: H.M. Sta. Off., 1850).

32. *Markets Improvement Committee Minutes*, 1849 to 1855. Court of Common Council: Minutes, Court of Common Council. This citation is for all references to activities of the MIC from 1849 to 1855.

33. James Bunning was the son of a surveyor and became the City architect in 1847. *Oxford Dictionary of National Biography*, Online Edition. Note that surveyors were called architects beginning in the 1830s when the practice of designing buildings, spaces, and streets became professionalized. Although references to 'architects' appear as early as the sixteenth century, the term usually refers to a builder rather than a designer.) Later, Bunning made innovative use of iron in his designs, especially in his design for the Coal Exchange (1847). Other works included the Thames Tunnel, the Royal Humane Society receiving house in Hyde, and the City of London School in Cheapside. Some of his critics thought that his designs displayed vulgar taste, perhaps a result of pandering to his patrons. Italian design motifs appeared in many of his designs; his wife was Italian but that did not excuse him from his critics who thought the use of Italian themes as affected. Obituary, J. B. Bunning, Esq., F. S. A., *Gentleman's Quarterly and Historical Review*, July 1863, S. Urban 1863, 799–800. Bunning's design for the Metropolitan Cattle market was on display at the Paris Universal Exhibition in 1855. 'List of Exhibitors', *Board of Trade, Department of Science and Art* (Marlborough House: London, 12 February 1855), p. 612.

34. Clearly underrepresented in this debate, pigs were not in the least considered important to the petitioners. No pig salesman appeared to defend his interest and the petitioners wanted the pig market removed to another location.

35. Challis, *Free Trade in Food*, p. 23. As part of his continuing campaign to defeat the removal bill, Challis wrote a response to the MP Frederick Byng who had become an ardent proponent of the bill to relocate Smithfield. Challis attacked Byng for his disingenuous representation of his objectivity by pointing out that Byng and others (such as Cornewall and Owen) on the Royal Commission had provided evidence against the Smithfield market in the select committee sessions of 1849. He accused the committee of not revealing these conflicts of interests by redacting their testimonies in the commission report. Because these commissioners appeared prejudiced against the market in Smithfield, Challis felt that they ignored the 'practical men' (butchers) who were almost entirely against a removal of the market. Challis challenged MP Byng for allegedly making gross errors and exaggerations concerning the 'facts' about Smithfield. He reprimanded Byng for not recognizing that the City had already made improvements to address sanitation, space, and congestion. Point by point, Challis challenged not only Byng, but also the government's main arguments for removing the market. Key among Challis's objections was Byng's insistence that the removal of the market to Islington would alleviate the driving of cattle through the City. This, Challis argued, was impossible since cattle traveling from the south of England would arrive over Blackfriars Bridge

and move through the City on their way to Islington. T. M. Challis and F. Byng, *Smith-field and Newgate Markets as They Should and Might Be: An Answer to the Hon. Frederick Byng* (London: J. Ridgway, 1851)

36. 'Metropolitan Cattle market', *London Gazette*, 26 November 1850, p. 3212.

37. 'Smithfield Enlargement', *London Gazette*, 26 November 1850, p. 3141; G. Jacomb, *An Appeal to the British Public, or, The Abuses of Smithfield Market and the Advantages of a New Central Cattle Market Fairly Considered* (London: E. Wilson, 1850), pp. 3, 7, 9.

38. Challis, *Free Trade in Food*. Challis held liberal political views, was a member of The Butchers' Company, and would become Lord Mayor from 1852–3.

39. T. M. Challis, *M. Letter to the Right Hon. Lord John Russell*, pp. 4–8.

40. Ibid., pp. 4, 6, 13. Challis requested that the City provide rooms near the market where those working in the market could meet to discuss trade and sales; in addition, his members were not all that keen to learn about the graduated scale for market tolls, a discouraging prospect for cattle buyers. Further, Challis delivered more concerns: the tolls for hay and straw were too high. The Markets Improvement Committee argued that the toll was for regulating market traffic, not for the purpose of raising revenues. The committee continued to calculate the new toll schedule and decided to raise the payback period from 30 to 45 years while lowering their proposed toll increases and changing the hour for the graduated tolls from 7 to 9 in the morning.

41. G. Jacomb, *An Appeal to the British Public of the Abuses of Smithfield Market and the Advantages of a New Central Cattle Market Fairly Considered of 1850* (London: Effing-ham, 1850), p. 1.

42. Ibid., p. 2.

43. 'The Smithfield Nuisance', *The Times*, 30 January 1851, p. 2.

44. C. Dickens, 'Parliament and Politics', *Household Narrative of Current Events* (London, 1851).

45. 'The Smithfield Nuisance', *The Times*, 21 March 1851, p. 5.

46. *The Times*, 17 January 1851, p. 8.

47. Challis, *Free Trade in Food*, p. 19.

48. J. Stevenson Bushnan, *The Moral and Sanitary Aspects of the New Central Cattle Market, as Proposed by the Corporation of the City of London*, 1851.

49. Parliament began discussions of a bill that would establish a new cattle market 'in lieu' of the Smithfield market that would be authorized and maintained by the government. Further, the bill required that Smithfield market be closed and that no other market would be opened up within five miles of St. Paul's cathedral. No mention of Isling-ton appeared in the notice of the arrival of the bill in Parliament. 'Smithfield Market Removal Bill', *London Gazette*, 18 March 1851, p. 768. Critics of the government bill cited the 'broad discretionary powers' given to the government and the potential for 'wholesale interference with public charters and private property'. C. Dickens, 'Parliament and Politics', .

50. 'Smithfield Cattle Market Removal Bill', *The Times*, 5 June 1851, p. 2.

51. *Hansard*, HC Deb 9 April 1851, vol. 115 cc. pp. 1335–49.

52. William Johnson was a 'licensed victualler' and wine merchant in Smithfield who even-tually went to work at the Metropolitan Cattle market. He filed for bankruptcy in 1856. Johnson had written a petition to the City's Common Council, objecting to the City's plan on the basis of the destruction of existing buildings, damage done to the trade sur-rounding the market, the high tolls required implementation of the City's plan, and the failure of the Islington market in the 1830s. *Reasons for Objections and Respectfully*

Adduced as a Protest Against the Plan and Scheme of the Above Corporation as Embodied in their Bill Now Before Parliament in Relation to Smithfield Market (London: William Johnson, 1851).

53. Great Britain, *Committee on Smithfield Market Removal Bill: Minutes of Proceedings,* 23rd May, 1851 (London: William Johnson, 1851), p. 5.

54. *Select Committee,* 1851, pp. 8–12.

55. 'Historical Chronicle, Proceedings in Parliament', *Gentleman's Quarterly,* 36 (July–December 1851), p. 181.

56. In the fall, the committee paid those who had provided services for the effort to promote the City's improvement bill and sent copies of the removal act to members of the Court of Common Council and others in the City government. The City spent £310,000 to promote its own improvement plan and £3,132 to defeat the removal bill. Interesting that the City spent less to promote its own plan.

57. When the Act passed in 1851, the House of Lords protested on several counts. It was inconceivable to them that a new market could be erected without affecting the rights and privileges of the owners of Smithfield, the City. The Lords argued that a new market could only be granted to accommodate the additional capacity required to address the objections and requirements for traffic and animals. If Smithfield needed ten more acres, the Crown could only create a market for the ten acres, not the entire market. They viewed the rights of individual citizens separately, and felt that their rights to a market would be overridden by the creation of a new market in Islington. It did not make financial sense to them, and they expressed their distaste for the removal of the market to Islington a by calling the move 'a dangerous speculation'. The Lords also protested the inadequate compensation given to the City for the removal, an amount already determined through the negotiations in 1835 when the Islington market Bill passed. Great Britain, and J. E. Thorold Rogers, *A Complete Collection of the Protests of the Lords, with Historical Introductions* (Oxford: Clarendon Press, 1875), pp. 376–7.

58. By a lawyer, 'On the Government of London', *Fraser's Magazine,* 12 (London, 1876), p. 776. In 1854, a royal commission called the City officials to Parliament for an examination of City governance, a moment of political reckoning for the Aldermen and Common Councilors.

59. 'The Siege of Smithfield', *Tait's Edinburgh Magazine,* January–December 1851, pp. 245–6.

60. David Owen's study of London's governance argues that the City was 'institutionally and spiritually...at variance with the new Victorian zeitgeist. The world no longer held with monopolies, special privileges, and ancient and prescriptive rights'. D. E. Owen and R. M. MacLeod, *The Government of Victorian London, 1855–1889: The Metropolitan Board of Works, the Vestries, and the City Corporation* (Cambridge, Mass: Belknap Press of Harvard University Press, 1982).

61. Some observers suggested that the City simply move the market to the existing Islington market. The Islington site would require the addition of more land and would re-engage the familiar arguments of ownership and monopoly. Would the company who owned the market sell the market to the City? Or, would the private company insist on its right to operate the market? Mr Tyrrell, a solicitor who promoted the Islington bill in Parliament, indicated to the committee that the proprietor of the Islington market was interested in selling his interest to the City. By then, representatives of those who favored

the Islington expansion appeared at the committee to offer to insert clauses favorable to the City to protect the interest of the City in the Islington site. But the City decided that it was 'inexpedient' to attempt any negotiations at that time.

62. When planning the Metropolitan Cattle market, the City provided a map. *'The Principal Streets in London, Showing their Relative Distance from Smithfield Market'.* The map featured rings around both the Islington market location and Smithfield with indications of the butcher shops to illustrate the distribution of shops relative to each market. Guildhall Archives, c 1851.

63. C. Dickens, *Household Words* (London: Bradley and Evans, 1852), V. 5, pp. 422–3.

64. 'The Metropolitan Markets Question', *Builder*, 11September 1852, pp. 582–3.

65. 'An Unmarketable Market', *Punch*, p. 142.

66. Copenhagen House, located in Copenhagen Fields, Islington, may have belonged to a Danish Prince in the seventeenth century; by the nineteenth century, it had become a teahouse. See P. Zwart, *Islington: A History and Guide* (London: Sidgwick and Jackson, 1973), p. 158.

67. In 1857 Parliament enacted another bill that repealed the Act of 1851, officially giving the rights of the Metropolitan Cattle market to the City, 'to maintain and uphold' the market and related buildings. A.D. 1865, 28 and 29 Victoriae, c.ccviii, *The Metropolitan Market Act*, 1865 (5 July 1865), Recites Act of 1857, 559, 560; 'Metropolitan Market Act, 1851, Notice', *London Gazette*, 1 June 1855, p. 2114; *Illustrated London News*, 16 June 1855, p. 602.

68. In practice, many butchers lived in the suburbs and had to travel at least three miles to the market. *Select Committee*, 1851, p. 42.

69. 'Individual Interests – How Affected by Removal of Market', *British Farmer's Magazine*, new series (1854), p. 474.

70. *Select Committee,* 1828, p. 78.

71. Science also entered the landscape through a greater public knowledge of the 'chemistry of animal food' that informed consumers with new expectations of wholesome, fresh meat. 'Individual Interests', pp. 474–9.

72. Ibid.

73. Ibid., pp. 474–9.

74. Ibid.

75. *Chamber's Edinburgh Journal* (August 1851), pp. 92, 93.

76. 'Cruelty to Animals', *Leader*, 7:334 (16 August 1856), p. 773.

77. 'New Metropolitan Cattle Market', *Daily News,* 27 September 1856.

78. Schlesinger and von Wenckstern, *Saunterings In and About London*, p. 64.

79. 'The Metropolitan Cattle-Market', p. 602; 'Smithfield', *Chambers's Edinburgh Journal*, 397 (August 1851), p. 90.

80. *Illustrated London News* (16 June 1855), p. 599.

81. 'The New Metropolitan Cattle Market'.

Epilogue

1. Contractors were John Willson of Southwark and John Jay. Kennard provided the iron-work. Chadwick was the contractor for roads, paving. Construction Supervisor was H. Lowman Taylor, Chairman of the Market Committee. (City) Clerk of the Works, Lau-

rie. Projected costs were £300,000; Mondays and Thursdays cattle, sheep, and pigs were sold. Horses, donkeys and goats, were sold on Fridays.

1855	7,000
1863	10,300

At the first Christmas market at Copenhagen Fields, the number of beasts offered for sale was 7,000; in 1863, as many as 10,300 were shown, which was almost double the number brought to market in 1868. Since the latter year the numbers have ranged from 6,300 to 7,600, W. Thornbury and E. Walford, 'The Northern Suburbs', *in Old and New London: A Narrative of its History, its People, and its Places* (London and New York: Cassell, Petter & Galpin, 1880), vol. 5, pp. 373–88.

2. See G. W. Tillson, *Street Pavements and Paving Materials a Manual of City Pavements; The Methods and Materials of their Construction* (London: Wiley, 1912). He suggests that the use of vitrified bricks became accepted practice by about 1870, at least fifteen years after installation at the new cattle market.

3. *Illustrated London News*, 16 June 1855, p. 602; Vitrification of bricks: http://www. thepotteries.org/focus/006.htm [accessed 11 May 2009]. The Staffordshire bricks were particularly hardened pavers made by heating the red clay of Staffordshire at a high temperature in a low-oxygen-reducing atmosphere. 'The New Metropolitan Cattle Market', *Farmer's Magazine*, new series, 26 (1854), pp. 468–80.

4. 'The Metropolitan Cattle-Market', *The Times*, 14 June 1855, p. 7.

5. 'The Metropolitan Cattle Market, Copenhagen Fields', *Builder* (2 December 1854), pp. 618–19.

6. 'The Metropolitan Cattle-Market', *The Times*, 14 June 1855, p. 7.

7. No specific breeds were represented, in order to avoid complaints from farmers who noticed their own breed had not been represented. 'The New Metropolitan Cattle Market', *Farmer's Magazine*, 26 (1854), pp. 468–80.

8. E. Walford, 'The New Cattle Market', *Old and New London* (Cassell & Company: London, 1892), p. 374.

9. 'The New Metropolitan Cattle Market', *Farmer's Magazine*, new series, 26 (1854), p. 470.

10. Walford, 'The New Cattle Market', p. 375.

11. *Farmer's Magazine* (1854), p. 478.

12. R. Chambers and W. Chambers, *Chambers' Edinburgh Journal*, 16:420 (1852), pp. 90–3; 'The New Metropolitan Cattle Market', pp. 468–80, 469; T. Standage, *The Victorian Internet: The Remarkable Story of the Telegraph and the Nineteenth Century's On-line Pioneers* (New York, NY: Berkley Books, 1999), p. 56.

13. Thornbury, *Old and New London*, p. 374; *Farmer's Magazine* (1854), pp. 469–70.

14. Minutes of the London Gas Light Company, LMA. Papers read at the Royal Institute of British Architects, Session 1862–3, London: RIBA, 1863, 136. Also, N. Arnott, *On the Smokeless Fire-place, Chimney-valves, and Other Means, Old and New, of Obtaining Healthful Warmth and Ventilation: And Other Means, Old and New, of Obtaining Healthful Warmth and Ventilation*, 1855.

15. the *Farmer's Magazine* (1854), pp. 469–70.

16. Initial plans also included the 'experimental' idea of including a meat market with the live cattle market. The implementation of this idea came in 1868 with the opening of the new Smithfield dead market, the Metropolitan Meat and Poultry Market.

17. Concerns remained about the public slaughterhouses who employed men who are 'a rough lot' and not inclined to the quality work of the private butchers. 'The Metropoli-

tan Cattle-Market', *The Times*, 14 June 1855, 7. The slaughterhouses incorporated many of the ideas in the Parisian system that was designed by Napoleon.

18. 'The Metropolitan Cattle-Market', *The Times*, 14 June 1855, p. 7; 'The Metropolitan Cattle-Market', *Illustrated London News*, 16 June 1855, p. 602.

19. 'Metropolitan Cattle Market, Copenhagen Fields, June 13, 1855', *London Gazette*, 19 June 1855, p. 2349. 'The Metropolitan Cattle-Market', *The Times*, 14 June 1855, p. 7. 'The New Metropolitan Cattle Market', p. 474. During the construction of the market, the first stone covered a Parian vase (Parian Ware, an artificial substitute for marble made from unglazed porcelain was developed in England in 1842) containing 'current coins of the realm', another gesture that indicated the Market's relationship to the Empire.) 'The New Metropolitan Cattle Market', *Builder*, 12:582, 1 April 1854.

20. I. Maclachlan, 'A Bloody Offal Nuisance: The Persistence of Private Slaughter-Houses in Nineteenth-Century London', *Urban History*, 34, No. 2 (2007), p. 228.

21. 'Metropolitan Meat Market', *The London Gazette*, 24 November, 1857, p. 4028.

22. 'The Metropolitan Meat and Poultry Market', *The Engineer*, 23 August, 1867, p. 152, 11 October, 1867, p. 316; W. Thornbury, 'The Metropolitan Meat Market', pp. 491–6.

WORKS CITED

Archival Sources

'Minutes of the Markets Improvement Committee, October 18, 1849–13 February 1851'.

Robson's London directory, street key, classification of trades, and Royal Court guide and peerage: particularizing the residences of 70,000 establishments in London and its environs, and fifteen thousand of the nobility and gentry, also an extensive conveyance list, alphabetical list of public carriers, together with the street guide (London: Robson, 1842).

A Country Meat Salesman, An Important Improvement in the Supply of London Wholesale Meat Markets, by the Total Abolition of Smithfield Live Stock Trade and London Slaughter-houses (London 1832).

Gamgee, J. S., 'The Cattle Plague and Diseased Meat, A Second Letter to Sir George Grey' (London, 1857).

Pittman, W., *On London Improvements, On the Necessity for Making More Markets,* MS 496 (Guildhall, 1826).

A Brief Statement of the Facts Respecting the Existing Nuisance of Smithfield Market (London: 1834).

Removal of Smithfield Market, Case of the Purchasers of Cattle who Petition against the Bill, April 1809 (London: Street and Woolfe, 1809).

Appendix to Committee of City Lands Report (2 March 1809).

Report 1, By Royal commission on historical manuscripts, 6 (1872).

Statement to Shew the Practicability of enlarging Smithfield market and that No necessity exists for removing it (London, 1810). Guildhall c45.1, T-1810.

On the Necessity of the Removal of Smithfield Market, and the Advantages the Principal Opposers of that Measure Would Obtain by Such Removal, 2. CLA/016/AD/01/005 (1810).

Smithfield Market, Substance of the Bill now before Parliament, for enlarging and improving the Market-Place with Observations thereon; also the Objections to the proposed Measure, and Answers thereto (London 1813).

'An Account of the Expenses in prosecuting the Petition to Parliament against the Islington Market Bill' (London: Guildhall, Chamber of London, 1847).

'An Appeal to the British Public, Or, the Abuses of Smithfield Market and the Advantages of a New Central Cattle Market Fairly Considered' (London: E. Wilson , *c.* 1850).

'Islington Cattle Market' (1836). *B'side 30.18.*

Islington Market Bill Evidence, 5 (30 March 1835).

Papers read at the Royal Institute of British Architects, Session 1862–3 (London: Royal Institute of British Architects, 1863).

Statutes and Parliamentary Papers

Hansard, Parliamentary Debates, House of Commons and House of Lords: http://hansard.
millbanksystems.com [accessed 10 June 2009].

Select Committee Reports:

    1828, 1847, 1849, 1851

Royal Commission Reports: 1850

    11 & 12 Vict. C 107.

    10 & 11 Vic. C 34.

    6 & 7 William IV, c 68.

Metropolitan Buildings Act, 7th and 8th, Vict. Cap. 84, with Notes, London, 1844.

*Petition in Parliament 3 Richard, II, 12th Rich. 11 c 13m and Rot. Parliament 16 Rich 11,
'Early State of the Law for the Protection of Public Health'.*

Second Report from the Select Committee on the State of Smithfield Market, Ordered by the
House of Commons, 19 July 1828.

Printed Sources

By the King, *A Proclamation for keeping of markets to supply the City of London with Provisions,
and also for prevention of Alarms and Tumults* (London: J. Bill and C. Barker, Printers to
the King, 1666).

A History of British Livestock Husbandry, 1700–1900 (London: Routledge, 2006).

'Common Sense: Richard Martin 'Humanity Dick' (1754–1834)', *History Today*, 54:6
(2004), p. 60.

The Publications of the Pipe Roll Society (Lincoln: Ruddock: 1954).

*The Proposed Central Live & Dead Meat Market for the Metropolis: The Opinions of, and
Extracts from, the Public Journals* (London: E. Wilson, 1851).

Working Man's Friend, and Family Instructor (1850).

Notes and Queries (1849).

Journal of Agriculture (1843).

Tablet (1840).

London Quarterly Review. (1834).

British Farmer's Magazine (1826).

'Blackwood's Edinburgh Magazine', *Blackwood's Edinburgh Magazine* (1817).

The Experienced Butcher: Shewing the Respectability and Usefulness of His Calling, ... the Laws Relating to it, ... (London: Darton [etc.], 1816).

An Abstract of a Plan of Mr. F-G for Reducing the Prices of Butchers Meat and Regulating Smithfield Markets, Laid before the Grace the Duke of Bedford, President of His Majestys Council, and the Right Hon. Sir William Stevenson, Lord Mayor, and the Court of Aldermen and Common Council of the City of London. *London Magazine, Or Gentlemen's Monthly Intelligencer* (1764), p. 661.

A. K. Copus, 'Changing Markets and the Development of Sheep Breeds in Southern England 1750 – 1900', *Agricultural History Review*, 37 (1989), pp. 36–51.

Alexander, D., *Retailing in England during the Industrial Revolution* (London: Athlone Press, 1970).

Allen, M. E., *Cleansing the City: Sanitary Geographies in Victorian London* (Athens, OH: Ohio University Press, 2008).

Allison, K. J., 'Flock Management in the Sixteenth and Seventeenth Centuries', *Economic History Review*, 11:1 (1958), pp. 98–112.

Anderson, B. L., A. J. H. Latham and Liberty Fund. 'The Market in History: Papers Presented at a Symposium Held 9–13 September 1984 at St. George's House, Windsor Castle, Under the Auspices of the Liberty Fund' (Croom Helm, 1986).

Andrade, B., *Trade Truths and Fireside Fancies: Selected from the Miscellaneous Writings of Benjamin Andrade* (London: Printed by W. H. & L. Collingridge, 1873).

Appleby, J., 'Ideology and Theory: The Tension between Political and Economic Liberalism in Seventeenth-Century England', *American Historical Review*, 81:3 (June 1976), pp. 499–515.

Ashton, J., *When William IV Was King* (Detroit, MI: Singing Tree Press, 1968).

Association for Promoting Rational Humanity towards the Animal Creation, *The Voice of Humanity for the Association for Promoting Rational Humanity Towards the Animal Creation* (London: Published by J. Nisbet, Berners Street, 1830).

Auerbach, J. A., *The Great Exhibition of 1851: A Nation on Display* (New Haven, CT: Yale University Press, 1999).

Ball, M., and D. Sunderland, *An Economic History of London, 1800–1914* (London: Routledge, 2001).

Barbon, N., *A Discourse of Trade* (London: Printed by Tho. Milbourn for the author, 1690).

Barker, T. C. and M. Robbins. *A History of London Transport: The Nineteenth Century* (London: Routledge, 2007).

Barnett, D., *London: Hub of the Industrial Revolution; A Revisionary History 1775–1825* (London: Tauris Academic Studies, 1998).

Barton, N., *The Lost Rivers of London: A Study of Their Effects Upon London and Londoners, and the Effects of London and Londoners Upon Them* (London: Historical Publications, 1992).

Baugh, D. A., *British Naval Administration in the Age of Walpole* (Princeton, NJ: Princeton University Press, 1965).

Baylee, J. T., *History of the Sabbath, Or, Day of Holy Rest ...* (London: C.F. Hodgson, 1857).

Besant, W., *London* (New York: Harper & Brothers, 1892).

Billington, S., 'Butchers and Fishmongers: Their Historical Contribution to London's Festivity', *Folklore*, 101:1 (1990), pp. 97–103.

Bohn, H. G., and J. Ray, *A Hand-Book of Proverbs. Comprising an Entire Republication of Ray's Collection of English Proverbs, with His Additions from Foreign Languages, and a Complete Alphabetical Index; in which are Introduced Large Additions, as Well of Proverbs as of Sayings, Sentences, Maxims, and Phrases* (London: H.G. Bohn, 1855).

Bonser, K. J., *The Drovers: Who They Were and How They Went: An Epic of the Countryside* (London: Macmillan, 1970).

Brantz, D., 'Slaughter in the City: The Establishment of Public Abattoirs in Paris and Berlin, 1780–1914' (2003).

Brewer, J., *The Pleasures of the Imagination: English Culture in the Eighteenth Century* (New York: Farrar Straus Giroux, 1997).

Briggs, A., *Victorian Cities* (New York: Harper & Row, 1965).

—, *The Age of Improvement, 1783–1867* (London; New York: Longman, 1979).

—, *The Age of Improvement* (London and New York: Longman, Green, 1999).

Brown, S. E., '"A Just and Profitable Commerce": Moral Economy and the Middle Classes in Eighteenth-Century London', *Journal of British Studies*, 32:4 (October 1993), pp. 305–32.

Bull, L., *History of the Smithfield Club, from 1798 to 1925* (London: Smithfield Club, 1926).

Burn, R., and G. Chetwynd, 'The Justice of the Peace, and Parish Officer' (London: Printed by A. Strahan for T. Cadell and W. Davies, 1820).

Burnett, J., *Plenty and Want: a Social History of Food in England from 1815 to the Present Day* (London: Routledge, 1989).

Bushnan, J. S., *The Moral and Sanitary Aspects of the New Central Cattle Market as Proposed by the Corporation of the City of London, with Plans* (London: W. Orr, 1851).

Cameron, D. K., *The English Fair* (Thrupp: Sutton, 1998).

Campbell, R., *The London Tradesman being an Historical Account of all the Trades, Professions, Arts, both Liberal and Mechanic, Now Practiced in the Cities of London and Westminster, Calculated for the Information of Parents, Instruction of Youth in their Choice of Business; to which is Added an Appendix* (London: Printed by T. Gardner, at Cowleyd's-Head in the Strand, 1970).

—, *The London Tradesman: Being an Historical Account of all the Trades, Professions, Arts, both Liberal and Mechanic, Now Practiced in the Cities of London and Westminster. Calculated for the Instruction of Youth in their Choice of Business* (London: Printed by T. Gardner, 1757).

Campkin, B., and R. Cox, *Dirt: New Geographies of Cleanliness and Contamination* (London and New York: I.B. Tauris, 2007).

Capie, F., and R. Perren, 'The British Market for Meat 1850–1914', *Agricultural History*, 54:4 (October 1980), pp. 502–15,

Carlyle, T., *A Carlyle Reader: Selections from the Writings of Thomas Carlyle* (Cambridge: University Press, 1989).

Chadwick, E., D. Gladstone, and S. E. Finer, *Edwin Chadwick: Nineteenth-Century Social Reform* (London: Routledge and Thoemmes, 1997).

Chadwick, E., and Great Britain Home Office, *Report on the Sanitary Condition of the Labouring Population of Great Britain: A Supplementary Report on the Results of a Special Inquiry into the Practice of Interment in Towns* (London: Printed by Clowes for H.M.S.O., 1843).

Challis, T. M., and F. Byng, *Smithfield and Newgate Markets as they should and might be: An Answer to the Hon. Frederick Byng* (London: J. Ridgway, 1851).

Challis, T. M., and England Central Markets' Association (London: *Free Trade in Food: Letter to the Right Hon. Lord John Russell ... on the Proposed Removal of Smithfield Market* (London: The City of London Central Markets' Association, 1851).

Chambers, J. D., and G. E. Mingay. *The Agricultural Revolution, 1750–1880* (New York: Schocken Books, 1966).

Chambers, R., *The Book of Days: A Miscellany of Popular Antiquities in Connection with the Calendar, Including Anecdote, Biography, and History, Curiosities of Literature and Oddities of Human Life and Character 1* (London: Chambers, 1863).

Chambers, R., and W. Chambers, 'Chambers' Edinburgh Journal', *Chambers' Edinburgh Journal* (1832).

Chambers, W., and R. Chambers, *Chambers' Information for the People: A Popular Encyclopædia* (Philadelphia, PA: G.B. Zieber, 1848).

Chaucer, G., and A. C. Cawley. *Canterbury Tales* (New York: Knopf: Distributed by Random House, 1992).

Chaucer, G., and D. Wright, *The Canterbury Tales* (Oxford; New York: Oxford University Press, 1998).

Chew, K., A. Wilson and Science Museum (Great Britain). *Victorian Science and Engineering Portrayed in the Illustrated London News* (Stroud: Science Museum, Sutton, 1993).

City of London (England) Corporation, J. Carpenter and H. T. Riley. *Liber Albus: The White Book of the City of London* (London: R. Griffin, 1861).

City of London (England) Court of Common Council, *The Lawes of the Market* (London: Printed by W. Iaggard, printer to the honourable city of London, 1620).

Clark, G., *A Farewell to Alms: A Brief Economic History of the World* (Princeton NJ: Princeton University Press, 2007).

Clark, G., M. Huberman, and P. H. Lindert, 'A British Food Puzzle, 1770–1850'. *Economic History Review*, 48:2 (1995), p. 215.

Clark, P., D., M. Palliser and M. J. Daunton, *The Cambridge Urban History of Britain* (Cambridge; New York: Cambridge University Press, 2000).

Cleveland, C. D., *A Compendium of English Literature: Chronologically Arranged from Sir John Mandeville to William Cowper* (Philadelphia, PA: E.C. & J. Biddle, 1857).

Cholera Epidemics in 19th Century Britain, Institute of Biomedical Science, http://www.ibms. org/index.cfm?method=science.history_zone&subpage=history_cholera [accessed 15 June 2009].

Cockayne, E., *Hubbub: Filth, Noise & Stench in England 1600–1770* (New Haven, CT and London: Yale University Press, 2007).

Colman, H., *European Agriculture and Rural Economy from Personal Observation* (Boston: A.D. Phelps, 1846).

Coltman, E., *Cursory Remarks on the Evil Tendency of Unrestrained Cruelty: Particularly on that Practised in Smithfield Market* (London: printed for Harvey and Darton, 1823).

Connecticut Academy of Arts and Sciences, *Transactions of the Connecticut Academy of Arts and Sciences* (1866).

Coxworthy, F., *Pollution of the Atmosphere by the Ventilation of the Sewers: And how it may be Remedied* (London: George Pierce, 1848).

Crafts, N. F. R., *British Economic Growth during the Industrial Revolution* (New York: Clarendon Press, 1985).

Creighton, C., *A History of Epidemics in Britain* (Cambridge University Press, 1894).

Cronon, W., *Nature's Metropolis: Chicago and the Great West* (New York: W.W. Norton, 1991).

Culley, G., *Observations on Live Stock; Containing Hints for Choosing and Improving the Best Breeds of the most Useful Kinds of Domestic Animals* (London: Printed for G. Wilkie and J. Robinson, 1807).

Culley, M., G. Culley, A. Orde and Surtees Society. *Matthew and George Culley: Farming Letters, 1798–1804* (Woodbridge: Published by Boydell Press for the Surtees Society, 2006).

Cunningham, P., *Handbook for London, Past and Present* (London: J. Murray, 1850).

Daunton, M. J., *Progress and Poverty: An Economic and Social History of Britain, 1700–1850* (Oxford and New York: Oxford University Press, 1995).

Daunton, M. J., and M. Hilton, *The Politics of Consumption: Material Culture and Citizenship in Europe and America: Leisure, Consumption and Culture* (Oxford: Berg, 2001).

Davidson, P., *The Violin: Its Construction Theoretically and Practically Treated: Including an Epitome of the Lives of the most Eminent Artists, a Dictionary of Violin Makers and Lists of Violin Sales* (London: F. Pitman, 1881).

Davis, J., *Reforming London: The London Government Problem, 1855–1900* (New York: Clarendon Press, 1988).

Deane, P., 'The Output of the British Woolen Industry in the Eighteenth Century', *Journal of Economic History*, 17:2 (June 1957), pp. 207–23.

—, *New Estimates of Gross National Product for the United Kingdom 1830–1914* (Cambridge: Cambridge University Press, 1971).

Deane, P., and W. A. Cole,, *British Economic Growth, 1688–1959: Trends and Structure* (Cambridge: Cambridge University Press, 1967).

Defoe, D. and P. Rogers, *A Tour through the Whole Island of Great Britain* (Exeter: Webb & Bower, 1989).

Dellheim, C., *The Face of the Past: The Preservation of the Medieval Inheritance in Victorian England* (Cambridge: Cambridge University Press, 2004).

Dennis, R., *Cities in Modernity: Representations and Productions of Metropolitan Space, 1840–1930* (Cambridge and New York: Cambridge University Press, 2008).

Denton, J. B., *Drainage of Lands, and the Sewerage of Towns. A Paper on Model or Relief Mapping, as the Best Index to the Capabilities of a Surface, with a Description of the Mode of Constructing Model Maps* (London: J. Weale, 1849).

Dickens, C., *Oliver Twist* (New York: Hurd and Houghton, 1866).

Dintenfass, M., and D. Wahrman. 'Imagining the Middle Class: The Political Representation of Class in Britain, c. 1780–1840', *Journal of Social History*, 30:2 (1996), p. 553.

Dodd, G., *The Food of London: A Sketch of the Chief Varieties, Sources of Supply, Probable Quantities, Modes of Arrival, Processes of Manufacture, Suspected Adulteration, and Machinery of Distribution, of the Food for a Community of Two Millions and a Half* (London: Longmans, Brown, Green and Longmans, 1856).

Donald, D., '"Beastly Sights": The Treatment of Animals as a Moral Theme in Representations of London c. 1820–1850', *Art History*, 22:4 (1999).

—, *Picturing Animals in Britain, 1750–1850* (New Haven, CT and London: Yale University Press [for] The Paul Mellon Centre for Studies in British Art, 2007).

Douglas, M., *Purity and Danger: An Analysis of Concepts of Pollution and Taboo*, (London: Routledge, 2005).

Driver, F. 'Moral Geographies: Social Science and the Urban Environment in Mid-Nineteenth Century England', *Transactions of the Institute of British Geographers*, new series, 13:1 (1988).

Drummond, J. C., A. Wilbraham and D. Hollingsworth, *The Englishman's Food: A History of Five Centuries of English Diet* (London: Pimlico, 1994).

Drummond, W. H., *The Rights of Animals: And Man's Obligation to Treat them with Humanity* (London: J. Mardon, 1838).

Dyos, H. J., and M. Wolff, *The Victorian City; Images and Realities* (London; Boston: Routledge & Kegan Paul, 1973).

Earle, P., *The Making of the English Middle Class: Business, Society, and Family Life in London, 1660–1730* (London: Methuen, 1989).

Eliot, G., and J. W. Cross, *George Eliot's Life as Related in Her Letters and Journals* (Edinburgh: W. Blackwood and Sons, 1887).

Ellis, H., *Speculi Britannaerpars: An Historical and Choreographical Sedcription of the County of Essex* (London: The Camden Society, 1840).

Epstein, S. R., and M. R. Prak, *Guilds, Innovation, and the European Economy, 1400–1800* (Cambridge and New York: Cambridge University Press, 2008).

Ernle, Lord, *English Farming: Past and Present* (London: Frank Cass & Co., 1961).

Eyre, G., and A. Spottiswoode, *A Collection of the Public General Statutes* (London: Steven Richards, 1844).

Falkus, M. E., 'The Early Development of the British Gas Industry, 1790–1815', *Economic History Review*, 35:2 (May 1982), pp. 217–34.

Farr, W., and N. A. Humphreys, *Vital Statistics: A Memorial Volume of Selections from the Reports and Writings of William Farr, M.D., D.C.L., C.B.* (London: Sanitary Institute, 1885).

Fielding, T., *Select Proverbs of all Nations: Illustrated with Notes and Comments: To which is Added, a Summary of Ancient Pastimes, Holidays and Customs: With an Analysis of the Wisdom of the Ancients, etc* (London: Longman, 1824).

Finberg, H. P. R., and J. Thirsk. *The Agrarian History of England and Wales; General Editor, H.P.R. Finberg* (Cambridge: Cambridge University Press, 1967).

Finer, S. E., *The Life and Times of Sir Edwin Chadwick* (London: Methuen, 1952).

Fisher, F. J., 'The Development of the London Food Market, 1540–1640', *Economic History Review*, 5:2 (April 1935), pp. 46–64.

Fletcher, J., 'The Metropolis: Its Boundaries, Extent, and Divisions for Local Government', *Journal of the Statistical Society of London*, 7 (1844).

—, 'Statistical Account of the Markets of London', *Journal of the Statistical Society of London*, 10:4 (Nov. 1847), pp. 345–60.

Forshaw, A., and T. Bergström, *Smithfield, Past & Present* (London: Heinemann, 1980).

Fowler, A., 'The Literary Gazette', *Literary Gazette* (1834).

Foxell, S., *Mapping London: Making Sense of the City* (London: Black Dog, 2007).

Freeman, S., *Mutton and Oysters: The Victorians and their Food* (London: V. Gollancz, 1989).

Fressoz, J., 'The Gas Lighting Controversy: Technological Risk, Expertise, and Regulation in Nineteenth-Century Paris and London', *Journal of Urban History* (2007).

Friedel, R. D., *A Culture of Improvement: Technology and the Western Millennium* (Cambridge, MA: MIT Press, 2007).

Fussell, G. E., *Farms, Farmers and Society: Systems of Food Production and Population Numbers* (Lawrence, KS: Coronado Press, 1976).

Gant, F. J., *Evil Results of Over-Feeding Cattle: A New Inquiry; Fully Illustrated by Colored Engravings of the Hearts, Lungs, &c. of Diseased Prize Cattle, Lately Exhibited by the Smithfield Cattle Club, 1857* (London: John Churchill, 1858).

Gash, N., *Sir Robert Peel; the Life of Sir Robert Peel after 1830* (Totowa, NJ: Rowman and Littlefield, 1972).

Geddes, P., *Cities in Evolution; an Introduction to the Town Planning Movement and to the Study of Cities* (London: Williams & Norgate, 1915).

Gilbert, E. W., 'Pioneer Maps of Health and Disease in England', *Geographical Journal*, 124:2 (June 1958), pp. 172–83.

Gilbert, P. K., *Cholera and Nation: Doctoring the Social Body in Victorian England* (Albany, NY: State University of New York Press, 2008).

Gilley, S., and W. J. Sheils. *A History of Religion in Britain: Practice and Belief from Pre-Roman Times to the Present* (Oxford and Cambridge, MA: Blackwell, 1994).

Girdler, J. S., *Observations on the Pernicious Consequences of Forestalling, Regrating, and Ingrossing, with a List of the Statutes, &c. which have been Adopted for the Punishment of those Offences; and Proposals for New Laws to Abolish the System of Monopoly: Remarks on the Impolicy of the Consolidation of Small Farms: Thoughts on, and Acts Relative to the Coal Trade; as also on the Sale of Cattle at Smithfield, Contractors, Carcass and Cutting Butchers, Fish and Cheesemongers, Poulterers, &c., with an Account of some Convictions of Regrators; and Reflections on the Act Lately Passed for Incorporating the London Flour, Meal, and Bread Company, with various Notes, Hints, &c* (London: Printed by H. Baldwin and Son, for L.B. Seeley; [etc.], 1800).

Gordon, W. J., *The Horse-World of London* (London: The Religious Tract Society, 1893).

Grantham, R. B., *A Treatise on Public Slaughter-Houses, Considered in Connection with the Sanitary Question. Describing the Practice of Slaughtering in France and England, with an Historical and Statistical Account of the Abattoirs of Paris, and Accompanied by Plans, with the View to the Introduction of Similar Establishments into England* (London: J. Weale, Architectural Library: Henry Renshaw, 1848).

Great Britain Board of Agriculture and John Middleton, *View of the Agriculture of Middlesex; with Observations on the Means of its Improvement, and several Essays on Agriculture in General. Drawn Up for the Consideration of the Board of Agriculture and Internal Improvement* (London: Sherwood, Neely, & Jones, 1813).

Great Britain. Parliament, 'Cobbett's Parliamentary Debates during the ... Session of the ... Parliament of the United Kingdom of Great Britain and Ireland, and of the Kingdom of Great Britain ...', *Cobbett's Parliamentary Debates during the ... Session of the ... Parliament of the United Kingdom of Great Britain and Ireland, and of the Kingdom of Great Britain* (1812).

Great Britain. Parliament. House of Commons. *Committee on Smithfield Market Removal Bill: Minutes of Proceedings, 23rd may, 1851* (London: W. Johnson, 1851).

—, *Second Report from the Select Committee on the State of Smithfield Market ...* (London: 1828).

—, 'Report of the Committee of the Honourable the House of Commons to Whom the Petition of the Retail Butchers in London, Westminster, the Borough of Southwark, and the Places Adjacent Thereto was Referred' [s.n.].

Great Britain Parliament House of Lords, C. Clark and W. Finnelly, 'Reports of Cases Heard and Decided in the House of Lords on Appeals and Writs of Error during the Sessions', *Reports of Cases Heard and Decided in the House of Lords on Appeals and Writs of Error during the Sessions* (1833).

Great Britain Parliament House of Lords and J. E. Thorold Rogers, *A Complete Collection of the Protests of the Lords, with Historical Introductions* (Oxford: Clarendon Press, 1875).

Great Britain Royal Commission on Market Rights and Tolls, *First Report of the Royal Commission on Market Rights and Tolls: Containing the First Report of the Commissioners,*

Together with the Report of Mr. Charles I. Elton, and Mr. B.F.C. Costelloe, on Charters and Records Relating to the History of Fairs and Markets in the United Kingdom (London: Eyre and Spottiswoode, 1889).

Great Britain Smithfield Market Commission, *Report of the Commissioners Appointed to make Inquiries Relating to Smithfield Market and the Markets in the City of London for the Sale of Meat* (London: H.M. Sta. Off., 1850).

Great Britain. J. Daw, and City of London (England). Commissioners of Sewers. *The City of London Sewers Act[s], 1848 ... 1851* (London: printed by Lowndes, 1858).

Gwynn, J., *London and Westminster Improved, Illustrated by Plans to which is prefixed, A Discourse on Publick Magnificence; with Observations on the State of Arts and Artists* (London, 1766)

Haldane, A. R. B., *The Drove Roads of Scotland* (Edinburgh: Edinburgh University Press, 1968).

Harris, J., *Private Lives, Public Spirit : A Social History of Britain, 1870–1914* (Oxford; New York: Oxford University Press, 1993).

Halliday, S., *The Great Stink of London* (Thrupp, Stroud, Gloucestershire: Sutton Publishing, 1999).

Harrison, B., 'Religion and Recreation in Nineteenth Century England', *Past and Present*, no. 38 (December 1967), pp.98-125.

—, 'Animals and the State in Nineteenth-Century England', *English Historical Review*, 88:349 (October 1973), pp. 786–820.

Harrison, J. F. C., *The Early Victorians, 1832–1851* (New York: Praeger, 1971).

Hazlitt, W., *A Reply to the Essay on Population: In a Series of Letters, to which are Added, Extracts from the Essay, with Notes by the Rev. T. R. Malthus* (London: Printed for Longman, Hurst, Rees, and Orme, 1807).

Herbert, W., 'The History of the Twelve Great Livery Companies of London Principally Compiled from their Grants and Records: With an Historical Essay and Accounts of each Company, its Origin, Constitution, Government, Dress, Customs, Halls, and Trust Estates and Charities, Including Notices and Illustrations of Metropolitan Trade and Commerce, as Originally Concentrated in those Societies, and of the Language, Manners, and Expenses of Ancient Times : With Attested Copies and Translations of the Companies' Charters'. (W. Herbert. 1968).

Hertslet, E., *Recollections of the Old Foreign Office* (London: J. Murray, 1901).

Himmelfarb, G., *Victorian Minds* (New York: Knopf, 1968).

—, *The Spirit of the Age: Victorian Essays* (New Haven, CT and London: Yale University Press, 2007)

Hobsbawm, E. J., *Labouring Men; Studies in the History of Labour* (New York: Basic Books, 1965).

—, *Industry and Empire; an Economic History of Britain since 1750* (London: Weidenfeld & Nicolson, 1968).

Hope, V., C. Birch, G. Torry and C. Birch, *The Freedom: The Past and Present of the Livery, Guilds, and City of London* (Buckingham: Barracuda Books, 1982).

Horne, T. H., 'The Complete Grazier, or, Farmer's and Cattle Breeder's and Dealer's Assistant ... Together with an Introductory View of the Different Breeds of Neat Cattle, Sheep, Horses, and Swine, the Present State of the Wool Trade, and the Improvement of British Wool: Also, an Appendix, on Prize Cattle, Farm Accounts, and Other Subjects Connected with Agriculture' (Printed for Baldwin and Cradock, 1805).

Hughson, D., *London; being an Accurate History and Description of the British Metropolis and its Neighbourhood: To Thirty Miles Extent, from an Actual Perambulation* (London: J. Stratford, 1806).

—,*Walks through London Including the Suburbs* (London: 1817).

Hurd, D., *Robert Peel: A Biography* (London: Weidenfeld & Nicolson, 2007).

Inwood, S., *A History of London* (New York: Carroll & Graf Publishers, 1998).

J. Pigot & Co., *Pigot and Co.'s London Alphabetical and Classified Commercial Directory of 1836: Comprising an Alphabetical Arrangement of the Names, Residence and Occupation of 87,000 Merchants, Manufacturers, and Traders of the Metropolis, and Six Miles Round ... Also an Extensive Conveyance Guide ... Lists of all the Streets & Public Buildings in the Metropolis & its Vicinity, the Bankers & Newspapers of the United Kingdom, and a Full Detail of the General and Two-Penny Post Office Regulations: The Work is Accompanied by a Large New Map of England & Wales* (London; Manchester: Published by J. Pigot & Co., and sold by them and the following Booksellers, viz. Simpkin, Marshall and Co. and five others, 1836).

Jack, S. M., 'Clark, the Cambridge Urban History of Britain. Vol. II: 1540–1840', *English Historical Review*, 117:471 (2002), pp. 387–8.

Jackman, W. T., *The Development of Transportation in Modern England. Vol.2* (Cambridge: Cambridge University Press, 1916).

Johnson, P., 'Market Discipline', in P. Mandler (ed.), *Liberty and Authority in Victorian Britain* (Oxford: Oxford University Press, 2006), pp. 212–13.

Johnson, S., *The Ghost Map: The Story of London's Most Terrifying Epidemic – And How It Changed Science, Cities, and the Modern World* (New York: Riverhead Books, 2006).

Johnston, W., *England as it is: Political, Social and Industrial, in the Middle of the Nineteenth Century* (London: J. Murray, 1851).

Jones, E. L. *Agriculture and Economic Growth in England, 1650–1815* (London Methuen, 1967).

Jones, P. E., *The Butchers of London: A History of the Worshipful Company of Butchers of the City of London* (London: Secker & Warburg, 1976).

Jonson, B., and C. Counsell, *Bartholomew Fair* (London: Nick Hern Books, 1997).

Joyce, P., *The Rule of Freedom: Liberalism and the Modern City* (London; New York: Verso, 2003).

Kean, H., *Animal Rights: Political and Social Change in Britain since 1800* (London: Reaktion Books, 1998).

Kellett, J. R. 'The Breakdown of Guild and Corporation Control over the Handicraft and Retail Trade in London', *Economic History Review*, 10:3 (1958), pp. 381–94.

—, *The Impact of Railways on Victorian Cities* (London and Toronto: Routledge & Kegan Paul; University of Toronto Press, 1969).

Kerridge, E., *Trade and Banking in Early Modern England* (Manchester and New York: Manchester University Press, 1988).

Kidder, D. P., *London in Modern Times, Or, Sketches of the English Metropolis during the Seventeenth and Eighteenth Centuries* (New York: Lane & Scott, for the Sunday School Union of the Methodist Episcopal Church, 1851).

King, G., *Natural and Political Observations and Conclusions upon the State and Condition of England, 1696* (London: Printed for J. Stockdale, 1804).

Knight, C., *London* (London: H.G. Bohn, 1851).

Landes, D. S., *The Unbound Prometheus: Technological Change and Industrial Development in Western Europe from 1750 to the Present* (London: Cambridge University Press, 1969).

Langford, P., *A Polite and Commercial People: England 1727–1783* (Oxford and New York: Clarendon Press, 1989).

Lardner, D., *Railway Economy a Treatise on the New Art of Transport, Its Management, Prospects and Relations* (New York: Harper, 1855).

Lee, P. Y. (ed.), *Meat, Modernity, and the Rise of the Slaughterhouse* (Durham, NH: University of New Hampshire Press, 2008).

Lewis, R. A. *Edwin Chadwick and the Public Health Movement, 1832–1854* (London: Longmans, Green, 1952).

Ligoe, A., 'A Copy of a Letter, Written to the Lord Mayor of London, and the Gentlemen of the Committee at Guild-Hall Giving them an Account of the Customary Prices of Cattle, Sheep, &c. ... also the Average Price of Butchers Meat ... Likewise Shewing the various Causes of the Present and Past High Prices of Cattle, Sheep, and Butcher's Meat: Also Describing a Method to Lower the High Prices ...' (Printed by R. Ferguson).

London (England). Local Government and Statistical Department. and London (England). London Government, Special Committee on City Markets Accounts. *Analysis of the Receipts and Expenditure of the City Markets on Capital Account and on Revenue Account, Showing to what Extent the Markets of the City of London have been a Source of Profit Or of Loss to the Corporation during the Thirty-Eight Years 1855 to 1892* ([London: 1894]).

London (England) and W. de Gray Birch, *The Historical Charters and Constitutional Documents of the City of London* (London: Whiting, 1887).

Lubenow, W. C., *The Politics of Government Growth; Early Victorian Attitudes Toward State Intervention, 1833–1848* (Hamden, CT: David & Charles, 1971).

Macaulay, T. B., *Essays: Critical and Miscellaneous* (Philadelphia, PA: A. Hart, 1850).

Mackinnon, W. A., *On the Rise, Progress, and Present State of Public Opinion in Great Britain, and Other Parts of the World* (London: Saunders and Otley, 1828).

MacLachlan, I., 'A Bloody Offal Nuisance: The Persistence of Private Slaughter-Houses in Nineteenth-Century London', *Urban History*, 34:2 (2007), pp. 227–54.

Malcolmson, R. W., and S. Mastoris, *The English Pig: A History* (London; Rio Grande, Ohio: Hambledon Press, 1998).

Mantoux, P., *The Industrial Revolution in the Eighteenth Century: An Outline of the Beginnings of the Modern Factory System in England* (New York: Macmillan, 1961).

Marks, M. A. M. (Hoppus), *The Corn Laws; a Popular History* (London: A.C. Fifield, 1908).

Matthews, D., 'Laissez-Faire and the London Gas Industry in the Nineteenth Century: Another Look', *Economic History Review*, 39:2 (May 1986), pp. 244–63.

Maudslay, A., *Highways and Horses* (Gardners Books, 2007).

Mayhew, H., *London Labour and the London Poor: The Condition and Earnings of those that Will Work, Cannot Work, and Will Not Work* (London: Griffin, 1866).

McKellar, E., *The Birth of Modern London: The Development and Design of the City 1660–1720* (Manchester: Manchester University Press, 1999).

McKendrick, N., J. Brewer and J. H. Plumb, *The Birth of a Consumer Society : The Commercialization of Eighteenth-Century Englan* (Bloomington, IN: Indiana University Press, 1982).

—, *The Birth of a Consumer Society: The Commercialization of Eighteenth-Century England* (Bloomington, IN: Indiana University Press, 1982).

Miller, T., *Picturesque Sketches of London, Past and Present* (London: National Illustrations Library, 1852).

Mingay, G. E., *The Agricultural Revolution: Changes in Agriculture, 1650–1880* (London: A.&C. Black, 1977).

Mitchell, B. R., *British Historical Statistics* (Cambridge: Cambridge University Press, 1988).

Mitchell, J., *Sketches on Agriculture* (London: 1828).

Moffit, L. W., *England on the Eve of the Industrial Revolution: A Study of Economic and Social Conditions from 1740 to 1760 with Special Reference to Lancashire* (London: Frank Cass, 1963).

Moore, F. [pseudo.], and G. Cruikshank, *The Age of Intellect* (London: W. Hone, 1819).

Moore-Colyer, R. J., *The Welsh Cattle Drover: Agriculture and the Welsh Cattle Trade before and during the Nineteenth Century* (Cardiff: University of Wales Press, 1976).

Morley, H., *Memoirs of Bartholomew Fair* (1880; Detroit, MI: Singing Tree Press, 1968).

Mulhall, M. G., *Mulhall's Dictionary of Statistics, by Michael G. Mulhall* (London: G. Routledge and Sons, 1884).

—, *The Progress of the World in Arts, Agriculture, Commerce, Manufactures, Instruction, Railways, and Public Wealth since the Beginning of the Nineteenth Century* (London: E. Stanford, 1880).

—, *The Dictionary of Statistics* (London, 1892).

Mumford, L., *Art and Technics* (New York: Columbia University Press, 1952).

—, *The City in History: Its Origins, its Transformations, and its Prospects* (New York: Harcourt, Brace & World, 1961).

Munday, S., *An Important Improvement in the Supply of London Wholesale Meat Markets, by the … Abolition of Smithfield Live Stock Trade* (London: Causton, 1832).

Nead, L., *Victorian Babylon: People, Streets and Images in Nineteenth-Century London* (New Haven, CT: Yale University Press, 2000).

Nef, J. U., 'The Progress of Technology and the Growth of Large-Scale Industry in Great Britain, 1540–1640', *Economic History Review*, 5:1 (October 1934), pp. 3–24.

Nelson, J., *The History and Antiquities of the Parish of Islington in the County of Middlesex: Including Biographical Sketches of the most Eminent and Remarkable Inhabitants: With some Account of several Objects of Interests in the Adjoining Parishes* (London: the Author, 1823).

Nelson, W., *A Proposal for a New Cattle market for the Supply of London to be erected on the North Bank of the Thames near Blackwall* (London: Waterloo & Sons, 1851).

Nightingale, P., 'Knights and Merchants: Trade, Politics and the Gentry in Late Medieval England', *Past & Present*, 169 (2000), p. 36.

Oswald, J., 'The Cry of Nature, Or, an Appeal to Mercy and to Justice on Behalf of the Persecuted Animals' (Printed for J. Johnson).

Otter, C., 'The Vital City: Public Analysis, Dairies and Slaughterhouses in Nineteenth-Century Britain', *Cultural Geographies*, 13:4 (2006), pp. 517–37.

—, *The Victorian Eye: A Political History of Light and Vision in Britain, 1800–1910* (Chicago, IL: University of Chicago Press, 2008).

Overton, M., *Agricultural Revolution in England: The Transformation of the Agrarian Economy, 1500–1850* (Cambridge and New York: Cambridge University Press, 1996).

Owen, D. E., and R. M. MacLeod, *The Government of Victorian London 1855–1889: The Metropolitan Board of Works, the Vestries and the City Corporation* (Cambridge, MA and London: Belknap Press of Harvard University Press, 1982).

Passingham, W. J., *London's Markets; their Origin and History* (London: S. Low, Marston & Co., 1935).

Pearce, A., *The History of the Butchers' Company* (London: Meat Trades' Journal Co., 1929).

Pearson, C., and Great Britain Parliament House of Commons, *The Substance of a Speech Delivered before the Committee of the House of Commons on Wednesday, June 4, 1834 ... in Supporting the Petition of the Graziers ... in Opposition to the ... Islington Market Bill* (London: printed by W. Tyler, 1834).

—, *The Substance of an Address; Delivered by Charles Pearson, at a Public Meeting, on the 11th, 12th, and 18th of Dec. 1843 ... Containing a Brief History of the Corporation of London as the Asylum of English Freedom in Past Ages, with a Statement of its Public Services in More Modern Times* (London: P. Richardson, 1844).

Pepys, S., *Diary of Samuel Pepys* ed. G Smith (London: Macmillan, 1905).

Perkin, H. J., *The Origins of Modern English Society 1780–1880* (London and Toronto: Routledge & K. Paul; University of Toronto Press, 1969).

Perren, R., 'The Meat and Livestock Trade in Britain, 1850–70', *Economic History Review*, 2nd series, 27:3 (1975).

—, *The Meat Trade in Britain, 1840–1914* (London and Boston, MA: Routledge and Kegan Paul, 1978).

—, *Taste, Trade and Technology: The Development of the International Meat Industry since 1840* (Aldershot, England and Burlington, VT: Ashgate, 2006).

Pevsner, N., *The Buildings of England. 12, 1, London, the Cities of London and Westminster* (Harmondsworth: Penguin, 1957).

Picard, L., *Victorian London: The Life of a City, 1840–1870* (New York: St Martin's Press, 2006).

Pinks, W., *The History of Clerkenwell*, 2nd edn (London: Charles Herbert, 1881).

Plumptre, J., 'The Experienced Butcher' (Printed for Darton, Harvey and Darton).

Poovey, M., *A History of the Modern Fact: Problems of Knowledge in the Sciences of Wealth and Society* (Chicago, IL: University of Chicago Press, 1998).

Porter, D. H., *The Thames Embankment: Environment, Technology, and Society in Victorian London* (Akron, OH: University of Akon Press, 1998).

Porter, T. M., *Trust in Numbers: The Pursuit of Objectivity in Science and Public Life* (Princeton, NJ: Princeton University Press, 1995).

Randall, A., and A. Charlesworth, *Moral Economy and Popular Protest: Crowds, Conflict and Authority* (New York: St. Martin's Press, 2000).

Rappaport, E. D., *Shopping for Pleasure: Women in the Making of London's West End* (Princeton, NJ: Princeton University Press, 2000).

Reach, A. B., 'John Bull and His Bullocks', *Douglas Jerrold's Shilling Magazine*, 5 (1847), p. 121.

Rees, A., *The Cyclopedia; Or, Universal Dictionary of Arts, Sciences, and Literature* (London: Longman, Hurst, Rees, Orme & Browne, 1820).

Rees, H., *The Industries of Britain: A Geography of Manufacture and Power, Together with Farming, Forestry, and Fishing* (London: Harrap, 1970).

The British Isles: A Regional Geography, 2nd edn (London: Harrap, 1972).

Ritvo, H., *The Animal Estate: The English and Other Creatures in the Victorian Age* (Cambridge, MA: Harvard University Press, 1987).

—, *The Platypus and the Mermaid, and Other Figments of the Classifying Imagination* (Cambridge, MA: Harvard University Press, 1997).

Rixson, D., *The History of Meat Trading* (Nottingham: Nottingham University Press, 2000).

Roberts, D., *The Social Conscience of the Early Victorians* (Stanford, CA: Stanford University Press, 2002).

Robey, A., '"All Asmear with Filth and Fat and Blood and Foam". The Social and Architectural Reformation of Smithfield Market during the Nineteenth Century', *Transactions – Ancient Monuments Society*, 42 (1998), pp. 1–12.

Robson, W., *Robson's London Directory, Street Key, Classification of Trades, and Royal Court Guide and Peerage: Particularizing the Residences of 70,000 Establishments in London and its Environs, and Fifteen Thousand of the Nobility and Gentry, also an Extensive Conveyance List, Alphabetical List of Public Carriers, Together with the Street Guide for 1842* (London: Robson, 1842).

Rogers, B., *Beef and Liberty* (London: Chatto & Windus, 2003).

Russell, N., *Like Engend'Ring Like: Heredity and Animal Breeding in Early Modern England* (Cambridge and New York: Cambridge University Press, 1986).

Schivelbusch, W., *The Railway Journey: The Industrialization of Time and Space in the 19th Century* (Berkeley, CA: University of California Press, 1986).

—, *Disenchanted Night: The Industrialization of Light in the Nineteenth Century* (Berkeley, CA: University of California Press, 1988).

Schlesinger, M., and O. von Wenckstern, *Saunterings in and about London* (London: N. Cooke, 1853).

Schmiechen, J., and K. Carls, *The British Market Hall: A Social and Architectural History* (New Haven, CT: Yale University Press, 1999).

Secord, J. A., *Victorian Sensation: The Extraordinary Publication, Reception, and Secret Authorship of Vestiges of the Natural History of Creation* (Chicago, IL: University of Chicago Press, 2000).

Shapin, S., *A Social History of Truth: Civility and Science in Seventeenth-Century England* (Chicago, IL: University of Chicago Press, 1994).

Shapiro, B. J., *A Culture of Fact: England, 1550–1720* (Ithaca, NY: Cornell University Press, 2000).

Shaw, G., and M. T. Wild, 'Retail Patterns in the Victorian City, *Transactions of the Institute of British Geographers,* new series, 4:2, *Victorian City* (1979).

Sheppard, F. H. W., *London, 1808–1870: The Infernal Wen* (Berkeley, 1971).

—, *London: A History* (Oxford; New York: Oxford University Press, 1998).

Simmons, J., *The Victorian Railway* (New York: Thames and Hudson, 1991).

Simmonds, P. L., *The Curiosities of Food* (London: Richard Bentley, 1859).

Skeel, C. A. J., 'The Cattle Trade between Wales and England from the Fifteenth to the Nineteenth Centuries', *Transactions of the Royal Historical Society*, 9 (1926), pp. 135–58.

Sloane, B., and G. Malcolm, *Excavations at the Priory of the Order of the Hospital of St John of Jerusalem, Clerkenwell, London* (London: Museum of London Archaeology Service 2004).

Smith, C., 'The Wholesale and Retail Markets of London, 1660–1840', *Economic History Review*, 55:1 (2002), pp. 31–50.

Smith, J. T., and C. Mackay. *An Antiquarian Ramble in the Streets of London, with Anecdotes of their More Celebrated Residents* (London: R. Bentley, 1846).

Stamp, G., *The Changing Metropolis: Earliest Photographs of London, 1839–1879* (Harmondsworth, Middlesex, England: Viking, 1984).

Steel, C. *Hungry City: How Food Shapes our Lives* (London: Chatto & Windus, 2008).

Stow, J., and J. Strype, *A Survey of the Cities of London and Westminster: Containing the Original, Antiquity, Increase, Modern Estate and Government of those Cities* (London: Printed for A. Churchill, 1720).

Strong, R., *Feast: A History of Grand Eating* (London: Pimlico, 2003).

Tames, R., *Feeding London: A Taste of History* (London: Historical Publications, 2003).

Taylor, A. J., *The Standard of Living in Britain in the Industrial Revolution* (London: Methuen, 1975).

Temple, P., *South and East Clerkenwell* (New Haven, CT: Yale University Press, 2008).

Thirsk, J., *The Agrarian History of England and Wales* (Cambridge: Cambridge University Press, 1985).

Thomas, K., *Man and the Natural World: A History of the Modern Sensibility* (New York: Pantheon Books, 1983).

Thompson, E. P. *The Making of the English Working Class* (New York: Pantheon Books, 1964).

—, 'The Moral Economy of the English Crowd in the Eighteenth Century', *Past & Present*, 50 (February 1971), pp. 76–136.

Thornbury, W., and E. Walford, *Old and New London: A Narrative of its History, its People, and its Places* (London and New York: Cassell, Petter & Galpin, 1880).

—, *London Recollected: Its History, Lore and Legend* (London: Alderman Press, 1985).

Tillson, G. W., *Street Pavements and Paving Materials a Manual of City Pavements; the Methods and Materials of their Construction* (London: Wiley, 1912).

Timbs, J., *Romance of London: Strange Stories, Scenes and Remarkable Persons of the Great Town* (London: R. Bentley, 1865).

Trentmann, F., *Free Trade Nation: Commerce, Consumption, and Civil Society in Modern Britain* (Oxford: Oxford University Press, 2008).

Trow-Smith, R., *English Husbandry* (London: Faber and Faber, 1951).

—, *A History of British Livestock Husbandry, 1700–1900* (London: Routledge & Kegan Paul, 1959).

Turner, M., 'Counting Sheep: Waking Up to New Estimates of Livestock Numbers in England *c* 1800', *Agricultural History Review*, 46:2 (1998), p. 142.

Turner, M. E., J. V. Beckett and B. Afton, *Farm Production in England: 1700–1914* (Oxford: Oxford University Press, 2001).

Turner, M. J., *British Politics in an Age of Reform* (Manchester: Manchester University Press, 1999).

Vaughan, A., *Railwaymen, Politics and Money: The Great Age of Railways in Britain* (London: J. Murray, 1997).

von Thünen, J. H., and P. G. Hall, *Isolated State: An English Edition of Der isolierte Staat* (Oxford: Pergamon Press, 1966).

Wahrman, D., *Imagining the Middle Class: The Political Representation of Class in Britain, c. 1780–1840* (Cambridge; New York: Cambridge University Press, 1995).

Walford, C., 'Early Laws and Customs in Great Britain regarding Food', 8 (1880).

Walton, J. R., *The Diffusion of the Improved Shorthorn Breed of Cattle in Britain during the Eighteenth and Nineteenth Centuries* (1984).

Webb, S., and B. Potter Webb, *English Local Government: S. and B. Webb* (London: Frank Cass, 1963).

Webb, S., and B. Webb, *English Local Government from the Revolution to the Municipal Corporations Act: The Manor and the Borough* (London and New York: Longmans, Green and Co., 1908).

Westerfield, R. B., *Middlemen in English Business, Particularly between 1666 and 1760* (New York: A.M. Kelley, 1968).

Williams, D. E., 'Morals, Markets and the English Crowd in 1766', *Past and Present*, 104 (August 1984), pp. 56–73.

Winter, J. H., *London's Teeming Streets: 1830–1914* (London: Routledge, 1993).

—, *Secure from Rash Assault: Sustaining the Victorian Environment* (Berkeley, CA: University of California Press, 1999).

Wohl, A. S., *Endangered Lives: Public Health in Victorian Britain* (Cambridge, MA: Harvard University Press, 1983).

Wolch, J. R., and J. Emel, *Animal Geographies: Place, Politics, and Identity in the Nature-Culture Borderlands* (London; New York: Verso, 1998).

Wolmar, C., *The Subterranean Railway: How the London Underground Was Built and How It Changed the City Forever* (London: Atlantic Books, 2004).

Wriothesley, C., and W. D. Hamilton. *A Chronicle of England during the Reigns of the Tudors, from A.D. 1485 to 1559* (Westminster: Printed for the Camden Society, 1875).

Wynter, A., *Curiosities of Civilization* 3rd edn (London: R. Hardwicke, 1860).

Yelling, J. A., *Common Field and Enclosure in England, 1450–1850* (London: Macmillan, 1977).

Youatt, W., *Sheep, their Breeds, Management and Diseases* (London: Simpkin, Marshall, 1878).

Young, A., *Tours in England and Wales. Selected from the Annals of Agriculture* (London: P. Lund, Humphries & Co.,Ltd., 1932).

Zwart, P., *Islington; a History and Guide* (London: Sidgwick and Jackson, 1973).

INDEX

For Product Safety Concerns and Information please contact our EU
representative GPSR@taylorandfrancis.com
Taylor & Francis Verlag GmbH, Kaufingerstraße 24, 80331 München, Germany

www.ingramcontent.com/pod-product-compliance
Ingram Content Group UK Ltd.
Pitfield, Milton Keynes, MK11 3LW, UK
UKHW021618240425
457818UK00018B/619

9 781138 661912